The Battle Against Hunger

Advance praise for: *The Battle Against Hunger*

It would be a mistake to see *The Battle Against Hunger* as simply the 40 year story of the rise and decline of free-standing nutrition lending by the World Bank in India. It is that. But it is also much more.

The Battle Against Hunger is a breathtaking ethnography of the complex multi-layered world of international development assistance. From decisions taken in boardrooms in Washington, DC by world figures like Robert McNamara, through the agonizing tangles of international, national and local politics, on to the grinding machinery of the international aid bureaucracy, down to the excruciatingly difficult conditions of men, women and children struggling to live healthy and productive lives in Indian villages, the book captures the big picture as well as the minute details that end up making all the difference.

Sridhar gives us a vivid and nuanced picture of the strange combination of insights, altruism, single-mindedness, idealism, arrogance, factionalism and careerism of the aid bureaucracy, and shows how these forces interact with the worlds of finance, politics, economics, nutrition, health, and ultimately life at the village level.

In a world where nothing turns out as we might have hoped or expected, the ability to learn, to adjust, to adapt, is a core competence. Sridhar reveals in detail how, in the aid bureaucracy, theoretical constructs and fictions become unchallengeable 'realities', which then make it difficult either to get the World Bank to do something new, or to shift direction in the light of experience.

The Battle Against Hunger sheds a strikingly clear light on the Achilles heel of international assistance—systematic inattention to the realities of what is actually happening on the ground.

This book should be read by anyone seriously interested in the future of international assistance.

Stephen Denning, former Director of Knowledge
Management, World Bank
former Division Chief in Population, Health and
Nutrition Department, World Bank
Author of *The Secret Language of Leadership*

The Battle Against Hunger

Choice, Circumstance, and the World Bank

Devi Sridhar

Dear Michael,
with appreciation for all
your support.
      Devi

OXFORD

UNIVERSITY PRESS

OXFORD
UNIVERSITY PRESS

Great Clarendon Street, Oxford OX2 6DP

Oxford University Press is a department of the University of Oxford.
It furthers the University's objective of excellence in research, scholarship,
and education by publishing worldwide in

Oxford New York

Auckland Cape Town Dar es Salaam Hong Kong Karachi
Kuala Lumpur Madrid Melbourne Mexico City Nairobi
New Delhi Shanghai Taipei Toronto

With offices in

Argentina Austria Brazil Chile Czech Republic France Greece
Guatemala Hungary Italy Japan Poland Portugal Singapore
South Korea Switzerland Thailand Turkey Ukraine Vietnam

Oxford is a registered trade mark of Oxford University Press
in the UK and in certain other countries

Published in the United States
by Oxford University Press Inc., New York

British Library Cataloguing in Publication Data

Data available

Library of Congress Cataloging in Publication Data

Data available

Typeset by SPI Publisher Services, Pondicherry, India
Printed in Great Britain
on acid-free paper by
Biddles Ltd., King's Lynn, Norfolk

ISBN 978–0–19–954996–2

10 9 8 7 6 5 4 3 2 1

Dedicated with love to Kasi Sridhar

Contents

Foreword

There is a story about an economist and an anthropologist which goes something like this: The economist asks the anthropologist, 'I see you know everyone in this village closely, but do you know anyone outside this village?' 'But explain to me', replies the anthropologist, 'you know a little bit about everyone in the world, but do you know anyone at all?' Economists and anthropologists do work, typically, with very different types of data. Most economists seem to be at home with data relating to a huge population observed rather thinly, whereas the typical anthropologist tends to concentrate on a small population, very minutely observed.

Devi Sridhar has given us an interesting and important anthropological work on a largely economic subject. This involves some traverse, which she undertakes with much skill. The main focus of this work is on a critical scrutiny of the achievements and shortcomings of one nutritional project of the World Bank—the Tamil Nadu Integrated Nutrition Project in south India. But she uses the results of her investigation to illuminate some general problems of policymaking to remove hunger in India as a whole and perhaps in the world beyond the limits of the country.

How does this traverse work, and why is it plausible and relevant? Part of the explanation lies in the fact that Devi Sridhar casts new light on an old problem—that of 'choice versus circumstance' as a social explanation. Should we, in this case, focus on the 'choice' that families make that weakens their ability to overcome nutritional inadequacy, or concentrate instead on the adverse 'circumstances' that these families face? Choices of families include such decisional variables as seeking work and earning an income, allocating family income between different commodities and between different types of food, deciding whether to undertake weight monitoring especially of children, and so on. The circumstances that affect families include the availability of work and sources of income of the families, their epidemiological surroundings, the prevailing social traditions of male dominance and gender inequality, and so on. Devi

Sridhar's investigation of the results achieved—and not achieved—in the Tamil Nadu Integrated Nutrition Project (TINP) throws considerable light on the relative importance of the two.

The second reason why Sridhar's traverse is of much interest is the nature of the TINP project and the role of the World Bank in setting it up and then using it as a kind of a successful 'model' that could be emulated elsewhere. Sridhar finds an inadequate appreciation in the work of the project—and in the approach on which that work is based—of the importance of circumstance, as opposed to choice, in the afflictions of hungry people. She also shows reasons for being sceptical of some of the claimed achievements of TINP based on behavioural modifications, and also probes the limitation of relying as much as TINP has done on policies aimed at health education, and at growth monitoring and other practices linked more to choice than to circumstance.

The World Bank began as a fairly specialized financial institution, and was initially much preoccupied with problems of 'reconstruction' after the ravages of the Second World War; indeed its old name—still in use—is the International Bank for Reconstruction and Development. Later it turned almost fully to development and became one of the major influences on public policy in developing countries. It has been concerned in a big way with nutritional policy, among other things, in recent years. Not only was TINP influenced, Sridhar argues, by the Bank's approach to nutritional intervention, but TINP's alleged success has, in turn, influenced the Bank's nutritional thinking for other areas of the world. Sridhar acknowledges that there are successes that TINP has had, but shows that the shortcomings are sadly plentiful. And—this is the central theme of her work—she argues that the primary cause of TINP's failings is the presumption that nutritional policy can be largely separated out from other, broader factors that influence nutrition, such as chronic shortage of disposable income and of gainful employment, and very importantly, the prevalence of gender inequality.

It would, of course, be rather amazing if the World Bank had failed altogether to see that these other influences must be *inter alia* influential in the genesis of hunger and deprivation (the Bank has published a huge literature on the subject), but Sridhar's point rather is that whatever recognition that these broader influences get in the making of policy in this Bank-financed nutritional project—and presumably in others like this one—is quite overwhelmed by the implicit conceptual framework that is fairly comprehensively focused on nutritional knowledge and other 'detached' nutritional thoughts that appeal to the Bank's dedicated 'nutritionists'. The results of the interviews she conducted certainly give reason to think that this is indeed a problem of significant importance, and Sridhar brings out its intellectual limitations in causing Bank-led nutritional policy to be far less effective than it could easily have been.

Devi Sridhar's empirical—and largely anthropological—investigation is done with much skill, yielding a critique of the 'narrow-minded nutritionists'—for that is what they are in this account—who are given vast power and plenty of money by the World Bank to do what they know pretty well and who refuse, in effect, to look beyond what they know so very well. Guided by her general concern about conceptual underpinnings of practical policies, Devi Sridhar presents a set of telling interpretative questions, which clearly have a close bearing on removing the incidence and reach of undernourishment. Her main thesis is well derived from her careful empirical study, based on observations as well as interviews, and this brings out a rather serious dissonance that afflicts the effectiveness of the particular nutritional project she examines and the more general approach that lies behind the project.

As it happens, the World Bank also has other departments that deal with gender inequality and purchasing power: indeed the Bank never stops lecturing policymakers—rightly in my judgement—on the need to take them into account in development programmes. Perhaps the source of the lacuna that Devi Sridhar identifies so convincingly lies in the lack of integration within the Bank, with the 'gender guys' working away diligently in one part of 1818 H Street in Washington, DC, even as, quite independently, the dedicated nutritionists do their 'level best' in Tiruvallur district in distant India.

One of the significant constructive effects of the work that Sridhar has done must surely be to draw attention to the case for the World Bank's right hand to figure out—and use—what its left hand is already trying to do. If this is right, then not only the general readers of the book, which includes me, but also the policymakers in the World Bank, have reason to be grateful to Devi Sridhar for the results—and the quality—of her probing investigation. This is certainly a work of significant practical importance as well as much intellectual interest.

Amartya Sen

Acknowledgements

This book would not have been written without the help and support of many individuals. Ngaire Woods has proved an invaluable mentor. Her combination of rigorous academic research, engagement with the policy process, and devotion to voicing the Southern perspective in global debates are an inspiration for younger scholars. David Gellner and David Parkin have been brilliant advisors, and I am hugely thankful for all their effort and time. Amartya Sen and Barbara Harriss-White inspired this research through their path-breaking work on poverty in India which combines economics and anthropology. In addition, Kevin Watkins, Jane Humphries, Christopher Hood, Steve Denning, Michael Lipton, Stanley Ulijaszek, Nick Mascie-Taylor, John Davis, Jim Malcomsen, John Vickers, Laura Rival, Paolo de Renzio, Hayley Lofink, and Danny George have provided insightful critiques of my arguments bringing their particular expertise to strengthen the final book. Discussions and correspondence with Drew Altman, Sudhir Anand, Gerhard Anders, Proochista Ariana, Marcus Banks, Masooda Bano, Alex Betts, Sarmila Bose, Jo Boydon, Anthony Costello, David Craig, Carolyn Deere, Steve Denning, Araballa Duffield, Lia Fernald, Laurie Garrett, Arunabha Ghosh, Michael Goldman, Roger Goodman, Nandini Gooptu, C. Gopalan, Frances Hansford, Ian Harper, Elisabeth Hsu, Andy Hurrell, Alberto Cortez Jimenez, Vijay Joshi, Ravi Kanbur, Hannah Knight, John Komlos, Tim Lankester, Ruth Levine, David Lewis, Steve Lyons, Desmond McNeill, Dave McCoy, David Mosse, Raman Nanda, Bob Parkin, Mike Poltorak, Jochen Prantl, Prema Ramachandran, Alexis Sanderson, Christina Schneider, Donna Shalala, Prakash Shetty, Jeremy Shiffman, Frances Stewart, Anna Taylor, Robert Wade, Andrew Wilson, and Jennifer Welsh have been hugely helpful. I am also very grateful to Dominic Byatt who was a wonderful editor.

I also thank my exceptionally talented colleagues both at All Souls College and at the Global Economic Governance Programme. Both of these institutions supported this research as well as the Rhodes Trust,

Wolfson, University and Pembroke College, the Rajiv Gandhi Foundation, as well as the Department of Politics and International Relations and the Institute of Social and Cultural Anthropology in Oxford.

I also express my gratitude to my informants both in the World Bank and in Tamil Nadu. Although I cannot name them, their candidness and generosity with their time was essential to this research. Aarthi Kandasammy assisted with research in the field. In addition, I thank the All India Women's Conference, especially health workers Sunitha and Savila who inspired me with their tireless dedication to improving the health of India's children. I am also grateful to Shanti Directors, Steven and Carmel, and the health staff of Kamala, Fatimah, Siva, and Ramani. My utmost appreciation goes to the women in Tamil Nadu who took time away from their busy lives to speak with me and answer my many questions.

My family and friends have provided the support for this research. Sonali, Tami, Mella, and Liz have endured me from beginning to end. Sadegh is the star in my life. Words cannot express my gratitude to him, and to Parvin, Mona, and Saber. During my fieldwork in India, my grandparents, G. V. and Lalita Ramakrishna, were extremely encouraging. My grandfather worked for the Indian civil service and his stories of government entertained and educated me. My grandmother who has published four books in the past five years wowed me with her unfailing energy and love of learning. My mother and siblings Divya, Jayanth, Priya and Arun challenge me to work harder and think more about the problems of our world.

My childhood was a constant struggle with my father over being Indian, as I resisted my heritage. Fifteen years later, I have returned to India and only wish I had spent more time listening to his stories and teachings. My father taught me what is important in life, quite simply to make the world a better place. During the time that he was sick with cancer, I saw what it means to suffer and realized how important health is. Hunger is preventable suffering, yet still over 50 per cent of children in India are undernourished. Political and social change need to occur both within development institutions and in developing countries. This book is an attempt at contributing to this change. It is dedicated to my father, Kasi Sridhar.

List of Figures

List of Tables

List of Abbreviations

AIADMK	All India Anna Dravida Munnetra Kazagam (Tamil Nadu)
AIDS	Acquired Immune Deficiency Syndrome
ANOVA	Analysis of Variance Statistical Test
Bank	World Bank
CDC	Centers for Disease Control (US)
DALY	Disability-Adjusted Life Years
DFID	Department for International Development
DMK	Dravida Munnetra Kazagam (Tamil Nadu)
EU	European Union
FAO	Food and Agriculture Organization of the UN
FC	Forward Caste
GDP	Gross Domestic Product
GNP	Gross National Product
GOBI	UNICEF initiative (growth monitoring, oral rehydration, breastfeeding, immunization)
IBRD	International Bank for Reconstruction and Development (part of World Bank group)
ICDS	Integrated Child Development Services
IDA	International Development Association (part of World Bank group)
IFC	International Finance Corporation (part of World Bank group)
IFI	International Financial Institution
IFPRI	International Food Policy Research Institute
IMF	International Monetary Fund
MDG	Millennium Development Goal
MIGA	Multilateral Investment Guarantee Agency (part of World Bank group)
MIT	Massachusetts Institute of Technology

NCHS	National Centre for Health Statistics
NGO	Non-Governmental Organization
NHANES	National Health and Nutrition Examination Surveys
NIN	National Institute of Nutrition (India)
NMS	Mid-day Meal Scheme
OBC	Other Backward Caste
OED	Operations Evaluation Department of the World Bank
PROGRESA	Programa de Educación, Salud y Alimentación in Mexico
SC	Scheduled Caste
ST	Scheduled Tribe
TINP	Tamil Nadu Integrated Nutrition Project
UN	United Nations
UNAIDS	Joint United Nations Programme on HIV/AIDS
UNDP	United Nations Development Programme
UNICEF	United Nations Children's Fund
USAID	United States Agency for International Development
WFP	World Food Programme
WHO	World Health Organization

Glossary

adivasi	tribal member
ammavasai panam	fortnightly saving scheme in women's groups
anganwadi	community nutrition centre
arrack	paddy or wheat country liquor
balwadi	community nutrition centre
cheeyam pal	colustrum
conji	rice water
dal	lentils
Dalit	'untouchables' outside the caste system
dhatu	semen
dirushti	evil eye
jaggery	unrefined sugar made from sugarcane
jati	caste
kallu	alcohol
karu niruthal	sterilization, literally to stop conception
karu thaduppu	family planning
laddoos	small balls of slightly sweetened rice/gram mix
masama irukka	she is pregnant
mathar sangam	women's groups
nai	melted butter (Tamil word for ghee)
nalla chappadu	healthy food
odambu	health
olli	thin
paal	milk
paan	betel leaf chew
pacca udampu	infant's body, literally fresh tender body

panchayat	village council
pasikardu	to be hungry
pongal	porridge of rice and lentils
ragi	finger millet
sambhar	tomato and lentil soup with spices
sathu illaada unavu	undernutrition, literal without any strength from food
sathu maavu	powder used to make laddoos in TINP
suhadharam	hygiene
taipaal	breast milk
tanni	water
tappu	wrong
toddy	palm liquor
valarthiattai	growth chart
varnas	broad caste divisions
veli	pain, ache

1

Hunger: Choice or Circumstance?

In the village of Swaans [in Rajasthan, India], isolated by jolting dirt roads and dry riverbeds, one man Gobrilal lost an eight-year-old son to hunger this fall. He sat recently beneath the shade of a thatched shelter, surrounded by children who were all rib cages and swollen bellies, and recounted two months of agony. On good days they ate once a day, but many days they ate nothing. Gobrilal's son began vomiting, even while asking for food, and died two days later. 'If we had money', his father said, 'we would have bought him [food] so he wouldn't have died.'[1]

We live in an increasingly prosperous world. Yet, the estimated number of undernourished[2] people is on the rise. It has increased to nearly 850 million.[3] In India alone, about 350 million are undernourished while the government hoards wheat surpluses, now at about 52 million tonnes, that would stretch to the moon and back at least twice if all the bags were lined up.[4] A recent report found that the government spends more on storage than on agriculture, rural development, irrigation, and flood control combined.[5] How did a nation that prides itself on its agricultural self-sufficiency and booming economic growth come to have half of its preschool population undernourished? Why have strategies to combat undernutrition failed so badly?

This book takes up these questions and probes the issues surrounding development assistance, hunger, and aid and power. It explores the tension between individual agency, or choice, and the structures within which these choices are made, or circumstance. When I embarked on this project, I wanted to focus on nutrition in India, examine development interventions, and uncover some positive news. Surely, something must have worked. There must be some lessons to be learned from past experiments. My literature search on India and nutrition threw up a strong candidate: one of the World Bank's flagship programmes was constantly referred to as 'successful'. The project was called the Tamil Nadu Integrated Nutrition Project (TINP). Thus, I decided to examine why and how the Bank nutrition initiative had worked so well in south India. However, as I delved into the project, it became apparent that the Bank has used the TINP model as a blueprint to design projects in many different countries. Therefore, I decided to focus on the Bank's nutrition operations in general and on the Bank itself as an organization. I gathered information on the policy process within the Bank: how policy is created, how problems are defined and addressed, and what the actual local effects of projects are.

Given its economic mandate, it might seem surprising that the World Bank is the largest financial contributor to health-related and nutrition projects. Within the World Bank, lending for stand-alone nutrition projects represents a tiny fraction of its total portfolio. However, the World Bank is the single largest donor financing nutrition. Annually, it commits more than US$1 billion towards the Health, Nutrition, and Population sector. Beyond finance, it wields formidable intellectual power. Other than as a lending agency, the Bank performs innumerable complementary functions as an advisory body, an intellectual research institute, and a training centre for developing country civil servants. Its annual World Development Report and staff working papers have established it as an intellectual powerhouse whose research represents the cutting edge of development. Combining intellectual prestige and financial power, the World Bank is the arbiter of development norms and meanings.

In the 1970s, under the presidency of Robert McNamara, undernutrition became a concern of the Bank. The management staff of the Bank struggled with two key questions: (1) was undernutrition a 'development' problem and therefore one the Bank should address, and (2) were there feasible things that could be done about it, particularly with the Bank's assets? The resolution was 'yes' to both questions and, at the urging of McNamara, the Bank's Board decided to finance nutrition projects in four countries that were already principal recipients of Bank aid: Brazil, Indonesia, Columbia, and India.

The Tamil Nadu Integrated Nutrition Project

The project in India, TINP, was jointly funded by the World Bank and the state government and overseen by the Chief Secretary of the state government and senior civil servants. Its objective was to improve the nutritional and health status of preschool children, primarily those 6- to 36-months-old, as well as pregnant and nursing women. The overarching approach of TINP was to promote behavioural change among mothers. A central tenet of TINP and the Bank approach is that undernutrition is the result of inappropriate childcare practices and 'not of income, famine or unpreventable health problems'.[6] TINP is a growth monitoring, food supplementation, and intensive nutrition counselling programme. These services are provided at a community nutrition centre. Further details of TINP are provided in Chapter 2.

It is important to note here that the Tamil Nadu project did not reflect the general activities of the World Bank, because the project was unusual in several ways. First, it was one of the first projects in a new sector in which the Bank did not have much experience. Second, the Health, Nutrition, and Population sector and the TINP approach did not enjoy broad support among the World Bank managers. The proponents of this project were a small group of enthusiasts who felt themselves under siege and having to fight the whole organization to try to obtain a larger programme of lending for free-standing nutrition projects. Even today, there is a relatively small group acting as advocates for nutrition within a wider health sector. Thus, it must be noted that most of the actors in the World Bank that are referred to in this book constitute a narrow group of enthusiasts trying to expand the scope of nutrition lending in the Bank and represent a tiny fraction of the Bank.[7]

In terms of the project's impact, TINP was labelled a success by the World Bank. This followed the 1986 midterm evaluation, which found a reduction in rates of severe undernutrition. The Bank also heralded the project as being extremely cost-effective: the cost per death averted was estimated at US$1,482 per year, which was much less than other mortality prevention projects such as malaria control and polio immunization.[8] Subsequently, the Bank used TINP as a model for effective nutrition programme design and used its framework to create a Bank nutrition 'toolkit' and 'package' that could be exported to any country facing 'an epidemic of malnutrition'.[9] The success of TINP was used as proof that a 'silver bullet' to address undernutrition existed.

After the first phase of TINP (TINP-I) ended in 1989, funding was resumed for a period of eight years for a second phase (TINP-II). The assessment at the end of this phase was less glowing. The official TINP-I terminal evaluation showed a decline in the prevalence of severe undernutrition but an increase in mild and moderate undernutrition. However, the analysis of the TINP data was problematic. Interviews with key Bank officials revealed that there were major shortcomings with the baseline and midterm evaluations. These included inadequate matching of controls in the TINP-I midterm and terminal evaluations, delays in the TINP-I midterm evaluation, and the poor quality of data collection. A World Bank consultant noted that

Part of the controversy about TINP has been due to uncertainties about what the program achieved. These arise because of a variety of flaws in successive evaluations of the program. In the case of some interventions, data to measure impact were not collected, so evaluation was impossible. Some evaluation surveys were much delayed; the worst case was the 'midterm' evaluation survey of TINP II, which eventually took place a year before the end of the project. The reliability of the data collection or processing was questionable in this and some other surveys. Throughout the TINP program, there were issues about the validity or absence of controls, which made it difficult to know whether reductions in malnutrition were due to TINP or other factors.[10]

Other observers raised wider concerns. David Pelletier and Roger Shrimpton noted that the evaluation studies were 'plagued by noncomparability from one survey to the next, by a preoccupation with finding impact rather than investigating process issues for midstream changes, and by superficial analysis compounded by limited facilities and human resources'.[11] Sabu George et al. note that 'the claims of successful growth monitoring...have been based on anecdotal and impressionistic evidence'.[12] In addition, the evaluations tended not to distinguish the effects of TINP from those of other programmes or the background secular trend. The first main evaluation was carried out by the Department of Evaluation and Applied Research of the State Planning Commission. However, this department did not have experience with evaluating nutrition and behavioural change, so the resulting report was quite weak.

To compensate for this, the Bank provided technical assistance in preparing terms of reference and reviewing the evaluation design through a consultant. However, these were not independent evaluations. They were formulated and directed by the Bank. Even with the Bank's assistance, there was poor quality control for data collection. A professor of child health recounted how he had attended a Bank seminar on TINP and found the results presented showing dramatic success impossible in the given timeframe. A Food and Agricultural Organization report notes, 'As the evaluation was not systematic [nor] supported by statistical analyses, all conclusions should be interpreted carefully.'[13]

Transparent evaluation is essential for accountability to borrower governments and project beneficiaries, especially since these investments are loans. However, evaluation and monitoring data on TINP are not publicly available. Although I contacted the Bank for the data-set used in analysis, they did not respond to my request. The Terminal Evaluation report gives the final evaluation outcome (e.g. per cent reduction in grade 4 undernutrition) but does not have data tables attached. It also mentions that the data had been cleaned but with no explanation as to why and how this was done, or whether or not the 'cleaning' influenced the findings.

By 1999, the Bank had loaned over US$750 million to India despite the lack of substantive evidence that the design and implementation of TINP were effective. Two other questions that should have been considered were what was the relative importance of food insecurity as a cause of undernutrition and how effective has TINP been in reducing undernutrition compared to other nutritional schemes and economic growth effects in other parts of Tamil Nadu and in Kerala. One Bank consultant noted that it is quite surprising how the World Bank has avoided a detailed examination of the components of TINP and their implementation. TINP has become a black box into which certain inputs were entered which resulted in a very favourable output.

Why does all this matter? For two obvious reasons. First, it matters for the potential beneficiaries of the nutrition programme in question. Second, it matters because of the way in which TINP has been showcased. Despite the lack of rigorous evaluation, TINP has come to represent the ultimate success story of the World Bank's lending for stand-alone nutrition projects. In almost every Bank conversation or document on growth monitoring, TINP is used as a model of an effective, successful project that can be used as an example for nutrition lending in other countries. For example, a Save the Children UK report notes:

In May 2001, the Ethiopian Government and the World Bank called a meeting in Addis Ababa to discuss the development of the community growth promotion component of FSP [Food Security Project]. The World Bank consultant called the meeting to try to incorporate the views of the technical experts of the federal and regional Government and other organisations into the nutrition programme. The consultant had not visited Ethiopia before (although she had been instrumental in developing similar World Bank funded programmes in India, Bangladesh and Uganda)...The consultant made constant references to India and the success of the Tamil Nadu Integrated Nutrition Project (TINP), but as the vast majority of the participants had never been to India or been involved in a GMP

[Growth Monitoring and Promotion] project, it was extremely difficult for them to accurately assess whether or not such a comparison was fair...As a result of the inexperience of the participants in GMP programmes, the meeting was controlled by the experience of the World Bank consultant and not by the invited participants.[14]

In addition, the nutrition team within the Bank has used the perceived success of TINP to argue that individual nutrition counselling, through tools such as growth monitoring, is the 'cornerstone of an effective and efficient program' and is much more effective than, for example, women's working groups.[15] A Bank staff member explains, 'Tamil Nadu was perceived by the Bank as an experiment: it was closely planned, executed, monitored and evaluated. When it was proved successful, then the model would be presented elsewhere'.

Leaving aside the use of the term 'frozen', the model has been interpreted and deployed on a selective basis. TINP had many components including the creation of women's groups and supplementary feeding. However, the components of growth monitoring and nutrition education have been deemed the successful aspects of the project by the nutrition team. It is these two inputs that have been integrated into nutrition projects across the world.[16] Although other projects based on the design, such as the Bangladesh project, have been judged as having a limited effect,[17] the Bank continually returns to TINP to validate its actions in the field of nutrition in the developing world. Wider concerns have been well under the carpet. As a Bank consultant has noted,

TINP has been a controversial program. Its proponents, in the Bank and outside, have sometimes promoted it as an unalloyed success story and model for other countries, without mentioning that it failed to achieve a number of its planned objectives, and without pointing to aspects of its design and implementation which had serious shortcomings, or which might not be replicable elsewhere.[18]

Save the Children UK's Campaign

In the midst of my study of TINP, Save the Children UK launched a campaign against the World Bank's nutrition blueprint of growth monitoring and health education. They were alerted to the problems with the package by on-the-ground staff in Bangladesh, Uganda, and Ethiopia. Local staff were concerned by the enormous resources injected into these projects which they were convinced had no nutritional impact. The year the campaign was launched, 2003, was crucial since Phase I of the Bank's Bangladesh Integrated Nutrition Project (BINP) was ending and the Government of Bangladesh was deciding whether it should take another loan for Phase II. Save the Children UK wanted the Government of Bangladesh to have accurate data on the Bangladesh project and on what it was and was not achieving. Save the Children UK contacted the World Bank team to request the Bank's data on the Bangladesh project. The Bank did not respond to this request. Save the Children UK obtained its own data and concluded that the project had no effect.

Save the Children UK contacted the Bank with this data. The World Bank called a meeting on the Bangladesh project with Save the Children UK in January 2003 where each presented their viewpoints on the Bank's approach to undernutrition. Save the Children UK's main point was that, 'spending these large quantities of money on an intervention which has a limited evidence base is not appropriate given the fact that so many other basic services are so fundamentally undersourced'. The World Bank's response was,

This is far from perfect. But this is one of the best things we've found yet and we continue to improve upon it. TINP was flawed. We've learned from that...It brings me to ask: What's your agenda?...The risk is that the Bank is just going to drop nutrition. I think we're doing a very conscientious...the Bank is doing conscientious stuff. It is learning from experience. It is trying to improve. I think we're working in a very deliberate and thoughtful and moral way, and I think it is immoral to put this report out in the very political way it's been put out, sending it to the President, making it publicly available...I think it is immoral because the risk is a lot less money to go toward addressing nutrition problems...the nutrition community spends all of its time shooting at each other instead of saying, okay, we're going to move forward together and we're not going to discredit anybody or anything, we're going to get it on the ground.

Prior to this meeting, Save the Children UK had produced a critical report called *Thin on the Ground* which was disseminated to the media, all levels of the Bank (including former Bank President Wolfensohn), and academics. In addition, a peer-reviewed article was published in the journal *Health Policy and Planning* presenting the Bangladesh project data analysis and conclusions.[19] In July, *The Guardian* ran a front-page article in its international section titled, 'World Bank Poverty Drive a Failure: World Bank Projects Aimed at Cutting Malnutrition Among Children in Developing Countries have Completely Failed to Make a Difference, According to Report.'[20]

What were the motivations of Save the Children UK to take on the Bank on this topic? While it is true that NGOs might have a financial interest in generating controversy using mechanisms such as newspaper headlines to gain publicity, this did not seem to be in the case in this instance. The evidence underlying the campaign was solid (appearing in a peer-reviewed publication) and an impartial senior academic Howard White, of the Operations Evaluation Department (OED) of the Bank, agreed with many of their points.[21]

The postscript to this story is that in spite of Save the Children UK's activities, the Government of Bangladesh decided to take the loan for Phase II. The World Bank nutrition team started planning eight new nutrition projects for Sub-Saharan Africa and one for Sri Lanka. During this time, key Bank staff refused to cooperate with Save the Children UK on the design of these, or even discuss which countries they were considering. Then, with the appointment of Paul Wolfowitz as World Bank President in 2005, the Bank became officially even tighter on disclosing information and engaging with external actors.

Studying What Works

For anyone with an interest in undernutrition, or in the persistence of mass hunger in an increasingly prosperous world, the World Bank approach to undernutrition matters at many levels. It matters because of the sheer pervasiveness of the TINP model and the grip it continues to hold on donors. It matters because of the many questions that remain unanswered about its effectiveness. Most immediately, of course, it matters for India. This, after all, is the country with the largest number of undernourished individuals, and the World Bank is the biggest player in nutrition. TINP is the ideal case study to understand what parts of the package work, and do not work. This book uses the case study of TINP to probe issues surrounding development assistance, strategies used to eliminate undernutrition, and ultimately the way in which poverty is conceived. The specific research questions that I look at are how nutrition is understood and addressed by the Bank in the TINP package, the effectiveness of this package on the communities at which they are aimed, and finally the reasons for which the Bank nutrition team has promoted an approach based on TINP.

Methodology

My field of study is not a discrete, local community but a social, political space articulated through relations of power and systems of governance. This research is multi-sited ranging from the World Bank offices to slum and rural areas near Chennai, India. It attempts to trace 'policy connections between different organisational and everyday worlds, on issues where actors in different sites do not know each other or share a moral universe'.[22] Despite this distance (geographical, cultural, linguistic), the activities of those working in development policy in Washington, DC have profound consequences for the 'beneficiaries' thousands of miles away. Three levels of policy have been chosen for this study: the designer and funder of the policies (the World Bank), the front-line implementers (the community workers), and the beneficiaries (women and children in Tamil Nadu).[23]

When I embarked on fieldwork at the top level, the World Bank offices, I initially assumed it would be similar to my research in Tamil Nadu. Perhaps naively, I assumed that I could knock on doors and chat informally with staff over tea. However, the World Bank enjoys a protected and layered boundary from external researchers. The difficulty in accessing the Bank is not unique, but similar to many large public sector organizations both within and outside development which attempt to limit access. Traditional anthropological methods devised for the study of non-Western societies are not easily translated to study an organization.[24]

Thus, the traditional anthropological method of participant observation was not feasible (or permissible) at the Bank. When doing fieldwork in Tamil Nadu, there were no formal barriers that hindered me from spending time in a community, or visiting the local *anganwadi* (community nutrition centre). Although women were extremely busy (e.g. working in the fields, cooking, taking care of their children), I was able to spend time freely in the villages. To spend time in the World Bank required official permission, which was not granted.

There are several reasons that staff are not keen to interact with external researchers. The first is that Bank staff are busy. Every day, there are hundreds of people around the world contacting them for interviews and information. There is a constant influx of questionnaires arriving in the mail. They just do not have time to answer every individual. Adding to this pressure is the fact that every interview is a potential minefield. As recent media and NGO activities have shown, the Bank is constantly criticized for its activities regardless of the validity of the critiques. Staff have a lot to lose and little to gain from talking to outsiders. Most staff felt over-researched already.

It was also extremely difficult to access Bank documents. Over the past decade, the World Bank has publicly announced its goal of further transparency. Despite the rhetoric since 1989 to 'open up' the institution to public scrutiny, not much has changed in practice since then. This is similar to what David Mosse has described as a general feature of development institutions.

[O]rganizations—and especially development organizations which exist in a nexus of information, evaluation and external funding—are, among other things, systems for the production and control of information. Development organizations have highly evolved mechanisms for filtering and regulating flows of information. Indeed it is particularly evident here that information generation and its use is inseparable from specific interests. These interests conspire to decide which versions of reality are legitimate, in that, for example, they give legitimacy to chosen courses of action or existing structures. In short, contrary to the tenets of academic research, in organizational settings information is rarely viewed as a 'public good.'[25]

However, the Bank is also an extremely leaky organization. At the individual level, staff enjoy a remarkable freedom of speech, arguably because the nature of their work is so complex that the top management lacks the knowledge or capacity to impose a coherent viewpoint on the staff, even if they wanted to. Thus, disagreements, in areas such as nutrition, are tackled at lower levels of the organization and may continue for decades flowing freely inside and outside the Bank. In fact, staff often try to use outsiders to influence internal debates. In this context, even my interviews with Bank staff, consultants, and critics could reflect the motivations, whether intentional or subconscious, of the informant to influence the Bank's agenda.

How Institutions Think

Unofficially, I was able to conduct semi-structured interviews with staff, consultants, and associates and obtain internal memos, transcripts, and mission documents. These have been used as primary data for this book. Although I had a rough sense of the direction, I wanted the conversation to go in, I allowed the informant to formulate and pursue issues in his or her own terms. Individuals reveal themselves through what they chose to recount and highlight. People do not remember the past objectively but tailor the version either consciously or unconsciously.[26] In addition, I obtained documents both official (e.g. project appraisal documents, reports) and unofficial (e.g. transcripts from meetings, memos) by collaborating with individuals who believe that this information should be accessible to the public. After speaking to many staff, I have developed enormous respect for them. Individuals working at the Bank are not malicious or ignorant people. The Bank staff believe that they are solving world poverty and curing hunger. They believe that what they are doing is right, just as firmly as many of their critics view the World Bank's actions as wrong.

Several other issues emerged in the course of fieldwork. The first is whether it is possible to aggregate at the institutional level, and also where the institution falls in the spectrum from being a monolithic structure to housing a diverse collection of opinions. Mary Douglas has written on this topic, specifically examining the concepts of cooperation and solidarity and the tension between individual and institution. In her 1986 book *How Institutions Think*, she first argues that institutions do not 'have minds of their own' but rather individuals in this social group share a symbolic universe; this results in group solidarity.[27] She notes that institutions manipulate history and systematically direct individual memory to channel the individual's perceptions into forms compatible with the relations they authorize.[28]

Although Douglas did not apply this framework to the Bank, her ideas of sociological integration and prevailing ideology are relevant to understanding the nutrition enthusiasts within the Bank. Throughout this book, I continually refer to the Bank nutrition team as if it promotes one perspective. However, as I discovered through interviews, within this small section of the Bank, individuals have varying opinions and are sometimes even critical of the Bank's operations.

The second issue concerns the consequences of this research and its implications for future nutrition planning. Nutrition policy is an interesting issue to examine since it is politically difficult to question a project created to help hungry children. The Bank started funding nutrition in 1976. In 2003, almost 30 years later, the first major criticism of the Bank's nutrition work emerged from the on-the-ground staff of Save the Children UK. Perhaps this is because hunger evokes feelings of guilt and vulnerability in individuals such that the existence and operations of a project can go unscrutinized. Dr. Abhay Bang, a community health expert in Maharashtra, remarked,

The picture of a hungry, wasted, miserable child moves you. Media can highlight it. The child is malnourished, but still alive, hence it can be visited, photographed, seen...Moreover, malnutrition is associated with food scarcity, poverty, hunger, starvation—all of which are emotive and politically explosive issues.[29]

Since TINP's approach has been promoted as a success by the Bank nutrition team, examining the design and implementation could have implications for whether governments decide to take this loan and package. One senior Bank staff member made it clear to me:

I hope your motives are not ideological. I don't know exactly what happened with Save [criticism of BINP] but I think it was immoral and verging on criminal. I encourage criticism but not when it is negative in terms of publicity. Kids die because of this...other programmes will not run...I guess the motives were ideological, there is nothing better than to criticize the soft issue of nutrition in the Bank but it is costly in terms of the programme, and loss of time, and the Bangladesh government pulling out. Governments views are heavily influenced— it's hard enough for the Bank to convince them to invest in nutrition!

Other than governments not taking loans for nutrition, there is also the fear that nutrition will close up at the Bank. As will be discussed in Chapter 4, economists have doubts about whether the Bank should be lending for micro-scale nutrition projects, and external criticism adds to their argument that the Bank should be a bank, and not a health development agency. My response to these two arguments is that my agenda is not to be negative. It is rather to understand what works to effectively address hunger.

Ethnography of Power

However, this book is not just about one project, or just about nutrition. It is an ethnography of power as demonstrated by World Bank nutrition policy. It is an attempt to uncover the workings of power through a close look at the structures, discourses, and agencies through which nutrition policy operates. In this process, I follow the source of nutrition policy in the World Bank—its discourses, prescriptions, and programmes—through to those affected by the policies in south India.

Anthropologists have long recognized the need to analyse the ways in which international actors and institutions affect the communities they study. Only very partial attempts have been made. Part of this neglect is a result of the difficulty in adapting traditional anthropological methods to study a large, powerful institution. Using the World Bank nutrition programmes and their impact in the field, I employ a theoretical methodology for the study of the links between international organizations and local communities, tracing the ways in which power creates webs and relations between actors, institutions, and discourses over time and space.[30] This approach examines the network of relationships, incentive structures, power dynamics, and ideological constraints on how institutions work.[31] It pays special attention to the complexity of the policy process, the social life of organizations, the heterogeneity of interests behind policy models, and the voices of the actors themselves.[32] This analytical innovation permits me to derive conclusions that relate not just to the impact on local communities but the way in which policy is developed within the institution itself.

Choice or Circumstance?

Throughout this book, the underlying tension between structure and agency is explored. Agency is defined as the capacity of individuals to make their free choices, while structure is defined as the external factors (e.g. societal, economic, political) that influence the choices that individuals can make. While it has been recognized that both structure and agency must be taken into account, the relative balance is contested. How much are individuals able to determine their life choices? What are the constraints on behaviour? How much should policymakers take underlying social forces into account when designing policy?

In the early 1990s, Mark Nichter and Carl Kendall noted that health problems will not be solved by either technology or a preoccupation with agency. They directed further research towards exploring local structures, social, economic, and symbolic, and understandings of gender, class, household, ethnic, and community dynamics.[33] Drawing on their research, this book employs a political-economic approach to health. This approach emphasizes the importance of political and economic forces in the form of power in shaping health, disease, and illness experience.[34] Local conditions are framed in relation to macrohistorical forces with a special focus on the social relations that underlie health.

William Roseberry outlines three key features of political-economic analysis.[35] First, it is historically and geographically specific, conceiving of local communities as products of social, political, economic, and cultural processes. Second, it brings light to the formation of anthropological

13

subjects at the intersection of local interactions and relationships and the larger processes of the state. Third, it concerns the impact of structures of power that shape and constrain daily life. To this list, I would add a fourth: the political-economic approach examines affliction as an embodiment of social hierarchy, a form of violence that results in differential disease rates and health outcomes. Roseberry calls for attention to the 'unity of structure and agency'; people's actions are bound by physical, socio-cultural, and political-economic structures that constrain their behaviour and choices.

This approach has been utilized by several other key scholars who study the links between poverty and health. Nearly a decade before Nichter and Kendall's paper, Nancy Scheper-Hughes focused on the structural constraints on the agency of mothers in a north-eastern Brazilian rural shantytown.[36] Scheper-Hughes stresses the importance of focusing on structure over agency when examining the childcare practices of women. Through an analysis of the reproductive histories of 72 marginally employed residents, she discusses the economic and cultural context that constrains mother's abilities to raise healthy children. This situation forces mothers to make choices on which child to attend to since she is unable to care for all. The perceived phenomenon of selective neglect of certain children by mothers is actually a consequence of the selective neglect of mothers from employment and wealth accumulation. Scheper-Hughes links the increasing rates of infant and child mortality to the structural adjustment and market liberalization occurring at the country level, the Brazilian 'Economic Miracle'.

Similarly, Paul Farmer focuses on structures of power that are biologically manifested as illness, which he terms 'structural violence'. Structural violence refers to the process whereby structural forces and processes come to be embodied as biological events:

Structural violence is structured and stricturing. It constricts the agency of its victims. It tightens a physical noose around their necks, and this garrotting determines the way in which resources—food, medicine, even affection—are allocated and experienced.[37]

These processes have also been referred to as biologized inequality by Didier Fassin.[38] The term 'structural violence' first gained recognition in 1992 with the publication of Farmer's doctoral thesis, *Aids and Accusations*, which examined notions of risk and blame towards AIDS and tuberculosis patients in Haiti. Much like Scheper-Hughes, Farmer identified historical and economic forces at work affecting the health outcomes of the poor in Port-au-Prince. Current pressures include population growth and economic constraints that result in urban migration, gender inequality, political disruption, and the daily difficulty in accessing medical services. Farmer situates these within the history of colonialism in Haiti and the shattered condition of the country after independence:

[Haiti] had a host of technically unprepared health workers in the presence of a population newly liberated from slavery, living for the most part in primitive huts, no water or latrines, decimated by infectious diseases against which so poorly protected. This is the oppressive legacy from . . . former masters, thirsty for profits and little interested in the living conditions and health of the indigenous populations.[39]

In his reflection on future work, Farmer states five pitfalls that should be avoided in research on health: to conflate structural violence with cultural difference, to minimize the role of poverty and inequality, to exaggerate patient agency, to romanticize 'folk healing', and to persist in insularity and classification of the foreign as unknown and exotic.[40] It is my hope that this book avoids these five pitfalls.

This book frames hunger and undernutrition as societal issues involving the problems of poverty, colonial heritage, land deforestation, and gender inequality. These structures result in the manifestation of hunger in a young child. Undernutrition is viewed as a sign, an indication of a community sickness. As Mary Douglas has noted, a body in health offers a model of organic wholeness, while the body in sickness offers a model of social disharmony, conflict, and disintegration.[41]

However, this approach has been criticized for overstepping the boundaries of academia and over-engaging with the policy world. As Karl Reisman notes,

Though Scheper-Hughes does not put it this way, the struggle she is urging anthropologists to join is a struggle against evil. Once we identify an evil, I think we give up trying to understand the situation as a human reality. Instead we see it as in some sense inhuman, and all we then try to understand is how to best combat it. At this point we leave [anthropology behind] and we enter the political process.[42]

This is a common criticism of Farmer and Scheper-Hughes who advocate on behalf of the poor communities they study in Haiti and Brazil, and even extends to those whose academic research could have policy implications.

The political-economic approach can also be used to examine the production of knowledge. This approach frames knowledge as a product of the social, economic, and political conditions of society.[43] Specifically, biomedical and epidemiological categories have been scrutinized extensively. For example, Alberto Cambrosio and Peter Keating, as well as Bruno Latour, have argued that the social construction of biomedical facts, for instance, their production through different institutional, technical, social, cultural, and political operations, does not mean that these are real or universal truths.[44] Biomedicine should be examined as a political system projecting a certain reality. In this book, the production of knowledge on nutrition is viewed to be explicitly tied to political and historical relations of power, and the systems of values that shape representation.

The depoliticizing nature of development has been further explored by Schaffer in the specific context of the policy process. He suggests that development policy is designed to appear neutral and apolitical.[45] For example, he notes that the linear model presented of the policy process is used by institutions to make it seem as if there was no other alternative, no 'room to manoeuvre'. He also focuses on the selective use of data and statistics to either establish a project as a success or failure. This judgement becomes generally accepted due to the socially perceived objective and neutral nature of quantitative analysis.[46]

Thus, the book takes an approach rooted in the 'unity of structure and agency'. It does not aim to reduce the agency of informants depicting them as Foucauldian subjects caught in a web of power. There is space to manoeuvre the system for skilful entrepreneurs. Many of the Bank informants, as this book will show, are aware of the power structures within which they work. They recognize that there are strong ideological and political constraining factors within the Bank. Despite this, Bank staff show considerable ingenuity in negotiating the system and moulding it to achieve their aims. For example, a staff member might translate a project into economic language in order to get the loan approved. Given that individuals are enmeshed in a network of relationships, incentive structures, power dynamics, and ideological constraints that hamper this agency, this book has taken a structure versus agency approach.

Chapter Outline

The organization of this book reflects the multi-sited nature of this research. Chapter 2 begins with a brief history of nutrition and poverty concerns both in India and in the World Bank. The purpose of these sections is to describe the forces that led to the Bank–India partnership in nutrition, to situate TINP historically, and to introduce the key players. It then turns to TINP to examine its design and objectives, the specifics of the policy process as well as provide further details on evaluation.

Chapters 3 and 4 describe how hunger is understood and addressed by the Bank nutrition team using the case study of TINP. It argues that undernutrition is constructed as a matter of choice. Chapter 5 presents findings on the impact of the Bank framework of women as 'agents of change' on the Bank's nutrition projects and the communities at which they are aimed, using TINP. This chapter is a critical analysis of local understandings of TINP, specifically the tools of growth monitoring of preschool children, supplementary feeding, and health education for mothers. In addition, knowledge and practice of childcare in Tamil Nadu and women's groups are discussed along with reflections on the main obstacles to addressing undernutrition in Tamil Nadu. This chapter examines the relative importance of choice versus circumstance in explaining child hunger.

Chapter 6 explores the wider implications of the analysis of choice and circumstance to hunger-reduction strategies. It first outlines the two viewpoints (choice or circumstance) that are currently being used to design nutrition interventions. It then examines the rationale behind growth monitoring and promotion, the cornerstone of community nutrition schemes, as well as issues with its implementation in three areas: as a communication tool, as an educational strategy, and as a screening device. The second half of the chapter examines possible alternatives by discussing different strategies to reduce rates of undernutrition such as economic growth, improved access to health services, and conditional cash transfer schemes. Given the lack of consensus on TINP's achievements, the question is why this approach to nutrition is continually promoted as a success. The chapter concludes by discussing the pressures in the Bank at disciplinary, institutional, and personal levels that nutrition advocates face which limit their ability to pursue new strategies.

The concluding chapter reflects on the way forward. In particular, it focuses on the theoretical and empirical findings that have emerged from this research. It first discusses the theoretical contribution to intellectual understanding of the policy process through the case study of the World Bank. It then turns to the policy implications in an attempt to shed light on the possibilities as well as obstacles to effectively addressing hunger in India.

Notes

1. Waldman (2002).
2. Throughout this book, the terms hunger and undernutrition are used interchangeably. Hunger carries the subjective emotive feeling of an individual not having enough food and as a result is suffering. Undernutrition is a broader scientific term usually defined through input- or output-based measures. This book uses these terms interchangeably in order to stress the importance of individual experience in the process of undernutrition as hunger/undernutrition is a false academic dichotomy that does not reflect the community experience.
3. FAO (2004).
4. Waldman (2002).
5. Ibid.
6. OED (1995).
7. They will be referred to as the Bank nutrition team.
8. Berg (1987).
9. Ibid. p. 61
10. Heaver (2002), p. 21.
11. Pelletier and Shrimpton (1994), p. 177.
12. George et al. (1993), p. 351.
13. Vijayaraghavan (1997).
14. Save the Children UK (2003), pp. 39–40.
15. Griffiths et al. (1996), p. 23. This aspect will be returned to in Chapter 5.
16. Griffiths et al. (1996), p. 31.
17. Hossain et al. (2005); White (2005).
18. Heaver (2002), p. 1.
19. Hossain et al. (2005).
20. Boseley (2003).
21. White (2005).
22. Shore and Wright (1997), p. 14.
23. Later in this book, in Chapter 5, I describe the methods employed for studying the perspectives of the community workers and women and children in Tamil Nadu.
24. See Sridhar (2008).
25. Mosse (1999), p. 175.
26. Chapman (1999).
27. Douglas (1986), p. 16.
28. Ibid. p. 93.
29. Bavadam (2005), p. 15.
30. Reinhold (1994), p. 477.
31. Mosse and Lewis (2006).
32. Ibid.

33. Nichter and Kendall (1991), p. 200.
34. Morsy (1996); Singer and Baer (1995); Farmer (1999).
35. Roseberry (1988).
36. Scheper-Hughes (1984).
37. Farmer (2004), p. 315.
38. Fassin (1996).
39. Farmer (1999), p. 214.
40. Ibid. p. 250.
41. Douglas (1996).
42. Reisman quoted in Scheper-Hughes (2006), p. 507.
43. Morsy (1996).
44. Cambrosio and Keating (1992); Latour (1993).
45. Schaffer (1984, 1985), see Clay and Schaffer (1984); Wood (1985).
46. See Robertson (1984).

2

The World Bank in India

As noted in the introduction, the World Bank's nutrition project in India, the Tamil Nadu Integrated Nutrition Project (TINP), has been promoted by the nutrition team of the Bank as one of the most successful efforts to address undernutrition in India. This chapter examines the history behind TINP to understand why the Indian government was keen to take the World Bank loan, and on the other side, why the World Bank was keen to lend to India for nutrition. The configuration of forces at a particular time in history led to TINP, which provides useful lessons not only for those concerned with hunger in India but also for those keen to understand why certain health issues are promoted instead of others. But to understand what is happening today, it is important to look at the past. Therefore, this chapter begins with a brief history of nutrition and poverty concerns in India.

India and Nutrition

India's food problems are not new. Before the introduction of the railway, famines were sporadic and infrequent occurring roughly once every 50 years.[1] Famines during this time were caused by a temporary cessation of the food supply in the region, most likely due to environmental factors, but not to be interpreted as an overall shortage of food grains in the country.[2]

After 1860, famine became a national issue as a result of the railways integrating British India into a single unified grain market as well as British colonial rule. Between 1860 and 1909, India had 20 famines, a phenomenon unparalleled in the country's history.[3] Despite the myth that there was not enough food during this time, the Report of the Famine

Commission in 1898 noted that there was always a supply of foodgrains available in the market, but these were only purchasable at excessively high prices. The short supply of food grains was responsible for the sharp rise in prices. This resulted in those with inadequate purchasing power being unable to claim ownership over food.[4] K. C. Dutta was commissioned by the government to enquire into the secular rise in prices after 1860. He concluded that this was due to the failure of cultivation to keep pace with the increase in population.[5] His report showed that output of food crops per capita dropped from 587 to 399 pounds between 1893–94 and 1945–46. Adding to the shortage was the fact that India was exporting food during this entire time.[6] Foodgrain exports increased from 0.65 million tons in 1867–68 to five million tons in 1904–05. The increase in global demand for foodgrain raised national food prices such that poor people living in India were priced out of the market.[7]

In 1933, the British official Sir John Megaw estimated that 40 per cent of the population did not get enough food to eat even in a year with no famines.[8] In this pre-independence time period, B. M. Bhatia estimates that between one-fourth and one-third of the population were undernourished because of the lack of purchasing power.[9] However, he argues that during that time period if employment or income would have risen, the increased demand for food grains would have resulted in a national shortage.

The 1943 Bengal Famine is a landmark in the history of food and famine in India. It is estimated that around 1.5–3 million people died from undernutrition. Entering into the 1940s, the government falsely believed that famine was a relict of the past. Despite declining food production per capita, there were no outward signs of food shortage demonstrated by an absence of famine between 1910 and 1940.[10] Prior to the Bengal famine, the colonial government relied purely on market forces for food distribution. Government involvement or regulation was seen as intrusive and unnecessary. However, after this turning point, India's first food plan was created which is commonly referred to as the 'Grow More Food Campaign'.[11] This was a strategy to increase food grain production through a move from cash crops to food crops and an increase in land productivity through irrigation, better seeds, and fertilizers.

The Bengal Famine also had a profound effect on the collective memory of the Indian population tying undernutrition to insufficient food. The legacy of the Bengal Famine is still evident today: to be politically successful, nutrition projects must include some form of food distribution even if this is not the underlying cause of undernutrition in certain regions.

The year 1947 marked two significant events in Indian history. The first was partition of the Indian union into Pakistan and India. Partition worsened the food situation in India for several reasons.[12] Before partition, the Indian union had 24 per cent of cropped area irrigated. Afterwards, India only had 19 per cent of cropped area irrigated compared to Pakistan's 44 per cent. After partition, India had 82 per cent of the total population of the Indian union but only 65 per cent of the total output in wheat and 68 per cent of the total output in rice. In addition, almost all areas which were then prone to drought became part of India which further destabilized food prices.

The other major event in 1947 was Indian independence from British rule. For the new state, food production was the most pressing economic problem. In addition, the dependency on food grain imports weakened the power of the new government on the world stage. Lord Boyd-Orr remarked after independence in Bombay that, 'so long as a country depended for its food on other countries, it was not independent even though it may be free politically'.[13] One of the goals of the new country was to make the country not only self-sufficient in food production but also to build stocks and become a small net food exporter.[14] This was not only the case at the national level but also for state governments who competed among themselves to become self-sufficient. On 19 March 1949, the national government announced a target of achieving self-sufficiency in grain in three years. This was the premise of India's second food plan.

Despite the government's strategy, the dependence on food imports increased during this time from 2.84 to 4.73 million tons between 1948 and 1951.[15] Most of the food aid came from the USA in a political move to rid itself of food surpluses.[16] These imports lowered the domestic food grain prices and thus served as a disincentive for Indian farmers to produce. After two successive crop disasters in 1965–66 and 1966–67 and indication from the USA that it would not aid India indefinitely, India's third food plan was created with the goal of increasing production dramatically through new technologies; thus came the Indian involvement in the Green Revolution.

The Green Revolution was a global phenomenon in which high-yielding varieties of seeds along with complementary technologies were introduced into developing countries such as India, Indonesia, and the Philippines.[17] It was universally thought in development circles that the introduction of high-yielding varieties of grains, new irrigation technologies, fertilizers, and mechanization would result in increased agricultural production and spur economic growth. The optimism that this approach created culminated in the awarding of the 1970 Nobel Peace Prize to Norman Borlaug, the father of the new agricultural technologies. Ashok Mitra, then secretary of the Planning Commission, stated in 1972 that the Green Revolution was the most important programme India had in the field of nutrition.[18] Undernutrition was defined globally at that time as insufficient food intake which could be addressed by the state producing more food. It can be argued that that the push for increased agricultural productivity was more a concern of national security and international relations for the Indian state than public health.[19] Linking undernutrition, as defined by food availability, to national food security made food production rather than increasing purchasing power the central objective.[20]

In parallel to the implementation of India's third food plan, external actors such as the United States Agency for International Development (USAID) under the Johnson administration, the Ford and Rockefeller Foundations, and the World Bank were concerned by rapid population growth in India in the midst of widespread hunger.[21] Evidence provided by the Food and Agricultural Organization's 1961 Third World Survey and by the Ford Foundation's 1960 report on India's food crisis solidified Malthusian fears that food production would not keep pace with population growth, hence leading to imminent famine.[22] The Green Revolution was thus promoted as the solution to feed the world's rapidly increasing population while also gaining time for family planning to spread. Indian government officials, particularly Prime Minister Indira Gandhi, were responsive to the push for family planning.

By the late 1970s, there was extensive criticism worldwide that the Green Revolution had not delivered on its promise.[23] Although it had dramatically increased food grain yields and reduced the dependency on food imports, this aggregate self-sufficiency masked a substantial extent of individual food insecurity, defined as lack of access to sufficient food at the individual level at all times.[24] Although national food security, which indicates the achievement of self-sufficiency in production, is very important in ensuring an adequate and continuous supply of food, it is a poor indicator of household and individual level food security. As demonstrated in India, self-sufficiency at the aggregate masks inequality both between and within households.

In the early 1980s, food insecurity became linked to insufficient entitlements and lack of purchasing power for the poor primarily as a result of Amartya Sen's groundbreaking work. Sen's (1981) book introduced the idea that starvation is a function of entitlements not food availability.[25] Sen argued that undernutrition was not a consequence of inadequate food supply but was rather the result of an inability to enter into the market and claim ownership over food.[26] Human forces make certain groups vulnerable to the state of not being able to claim ownership of food due to social and economic inequality. Human institutions determine who will have claim to food, who will be chronically vulnerable and who will use hunger against whom. A person's ability to command food depends on entitlement, with this term referring to what he or she owns, what exchange possibilities are offered to him or her, what is given to him or her for free, and what is taken away.[27] Entitlements matter more than availability in the incidence of chronic undernutrition. The entitlements approach led to several state governments in India funding food for work programmes.

To address the problem of mass undernutrition, the Government of India requested the assistance of the World Bank in designing and funding a nutrition project in the state of Tamil Nadu. Tamil Nadu was chosen because the state government had placed food and nutrition first on its social welfare agenda yet the state still ranked exceedingly low in average caloric availability.[28]

Tamil Nadu

Tamil Nadu was particularly suited to undertake the nutrition project due to the instrumentalization of hunger for political purposes by caste-based political parties. For those unfamiliar with India, Tamil Nadu is the southern-most state of India and lies between the Bay of Bengal in the east, the Indian Ocean in the south, and the Western Ghats and the Arabian Sea on the west. In 1639, the East India Company arrived at Madras (now the capital of Tamil Nadu, Chennai) and soon most of south India came under British rule referred to by the British as the 'Madras Presidency'. With India attaining independence in 1947, the Madras presidency continued, compromising Tamil Nadu, Andhra Pradesh, Karnataka, and parts of Kerala. Shortly after, the Government of India divided the territory into language-based states, the 'Madras State' being the Tamil speaking area. In 1967, it was renamed Tamil Nadu, literally the land of Tamils, and is constituted of 30 districts. As per the 2001 census, its population was 62.11 million (Table 2.1). It is estimated that 52.1 per cent

Table 2.1. Select demographic indicators for Tamil Nadu[a]

Indicator	1971	1981	1991	2001
Population (million)	41.2	48.2	55.9	62.1
Decennial growth (%)	22.3	17.5	15.4	11.2
Density of population per sq. km	317	372	429	478
Urban population (%)	30.3	33	34.2	43.9
Sex ratio	978	977	974	986
Percentage of 0–14 year olds	37.8	35	30.9	NA

[a] Government of Tamil Nadu (2003).

of children below 5 years of age are underweight (low weight-for-age) in the rural part of the state.[29]

During the last century, nutrition has been a top priority of the area of Tamil Nadu. One cannot understand the history of nutrition of Tamil Nadu without understanding caste politics in the twentieth century. For those unfamiliar with India, caste, or *jati*, is a Hindu system in which a person's membership in society is mediated through his or her birth in a particular group which is assigned a particular status within a broad hierarchy. This group has a particular accepted occupation and only within it can a person marry and carry on close social relations such as dining.[30] The broad *varnas*, or divisions, are Brahmin, Kshatriya, Vaishya, and Shudra. The Kshatriya and Vaishya are basically absent in south India. Within Tamil Nadu, the social structure is effectively threefold: Brahmin, non-Brahmins (high and low-caste Shudras), and *Dalits* (Adi-Dravidas). *Dalits* (untouchables) are outside the caste system and referred to as a-*varna*, 'without *varna*'. Within the Brahmins and Shudras, there are innumerable subgroups which are castes proper. For example, the Brahmins can be divided into Shri Vaishnavas and Smarthas, the non-Brahmins into Kallas, Vellalars, and Marathas, and the *Dalits* into Pallas and Paraiyas. Within the caste, there is often further differentiation into sub-castes, for example, the Vellalars of a particular region, which are—or were traditionally—the effective unit of endogamy. Differentiation only occurs within a *varna*. For example, in the perspective of non-Brahmins or *Dalits*, all Brahmins are an undifferentiated unit.

There is an important overlap of caste and class in that most landowners and businessmen are Brahmins or high-caste Shudras. There are, at the same time, many Brahmins who are poor, but far fewer proportionately, than among low castes. Shudras are usually in the service, artisan, and cultivating sectors. Within the Shudras, there are hierarchical divisions such as high-caste Vellalars and Naidus and low-caste Kallas. Shudras are in the dominant position in the state and constitute the voting base in Tamil Nadu. *Dalits* usually reside in separate settlements outside the main village and work as labourers or coolies.

A village is divided and subdivided as 'to constitute a segmentary structure in which each segment is differentiated from the other in terms of a number of criteria'.[31] However, the hierarchy of the caste system is fluid and ambiguous. The actual position of a *jati* depends on local factors. In addition, the system permits a certain degree of social mobility, for example, Vellalars often make claims to be Vaishyas.

Caste Politics and Undernutrition

Caste plays a crucial role in state politics. This section briefly recounts the political history of Tamil Nadu and then comments on how politics made nutrition a significant issue.[32] The recent political history of Tamil Nadu can be characterized as having three phases: Congress party domination, the Dravidian populist mobilization, and the subsequent fragmenting of this movement.[33]

From 1936 until post-independence, the Congress party dominated electoral politics in the Madras presidency. The Congress party benefited from the number of opposing parties which made it difficult for any one of them to gain a majority as well as from having a friendly government at the centre that provided supportive funds. However, a Dravidian (Tamil) movement was in existence as early as 1920. Pre-independence, E. V. Ramaswamy, popularly referred to as Periyar ('the great one'), rejected the Congress party and led the Self-Respect movement that had two pillars: anti-brahminism and a demand for quotas.[34] The first pillar was driven by the anger of the Shudras and *Dalits* that Brahmins had control of the government, which can be attributed to the British preference for Brahmins during the colonial period. An 1886 British census revealed that Brahmins were only 3 per cent of the population yet held a majority of the well-paying government jobs:

A feature of administrative recruitment in Madras Presidency was the preponderance of the Brahmins...in 1886 the Brahmins held 42 percent of all posts in the Madras Government carrying, a monthly salary of over Rs. 10. Brahmin domination was even more marked at the higher level of the Unconvented Service:

of the 349 elite posts in the executive and judicial lines in 1886, no less than 202 (or 58 percent) were in Brahmin hands. In certain special departments, Brahmin representation was just as preponderant. In the Registration Department, for example, 217 out of 365 officers were Brahmins.[35]

In 1949, C. N. Annadurai formed the DMK (Dravida Munnetra Kazagam) political party which mobilized electoral support by promoting a regional Tamil nationalism. This was an anti-Brahmin movement that established Dravidian identity as a secular cultural concept and anchor of identity.[36] It sought to eliminate the Aryan influence and Sanskritization through awakening the original ethnic identity of the masses.[37] Brahmins are popularly viewed as non-Tamils. This was based in the mythical history that Brahmins were of the Aryan invasions and constituted a separate race from the Dravidians.[38] The anti-Brahmin movement was against all Brahmins whether rich or poor and regardless of occupation: 'Brahmins as a category... acquired a new identity and a new consciousness of unity'.[39] DMK's slogan was *'Onre kulam, Oruvane theivum'* (there is only but one caste, one God). Although Annadurai initially sought secession from India, by the 1960s these radical demands were dropped and the party focused on more realistic issues. A key topic within the central government was the proposal to make Hindi the national language. The DMK seized on this issue and generated popular support by mobilizing concern over the fate of Tamil.

In addition, while the Congress party was controlled by Brahmins and elites, the DMK mobilized the masses and lower castes (mainly Shudras) by using the medium of film.[40]

Such political communication was intensive, creative and highly effective. The DMK used films for propaganda when cinema houses were just being extended to the rural areas of Madras. It was common for people to walk as much as five miles to see a film, and films were (and still are) seen repeatedly...DMK ideas therefore reached every area of life in Madras through either film, books, pamphlets, speeches, drama, poems, songs, or newspapers.[41]

Although there were opposition parties such as the DMK, the communist party, and caste-based parties in existence, the Congress managed to hold power even through 1962. In 1967, the Congress party was defeated in the assembly elections and has never returned to office in the state. Shortly after the DMK came to power, Madras State was renamed Tamil Nadu. In 1947, the Indian Constitution established a national reservation scheme for Scheduled Castes and Tribes (SC/STs), *Dalits,* and *Adivasis.* With the DMK in power, reverse discrimination was extended to other backward

Table 2.2. DMK's goals as given in 1949[a]

Creating intellectual revolution
Removing domination of brahmins
Arresting the expansion of Northern Imperialism (e.g. nationalization of Hindi)
Removing caste discriminations
Annulling religious segregation
Eradicating economic inequalities
Creating an independent Dravidian society

[a] Palanithurai (1991, p. 15).

castes (OBCs). The term OBC refers to those whose ritual rank and occupational status are above *Dalits* yet who are socially and economically depressed.[42] This was executed through the extension of reservations. For example in 1969, DMK increased the reservations in government to 33 per cent for OBCs (46.1% of the population) and from 16 to 18 per cent for SC/STs (20% of the population).[43] DMK's broad goals are listed in Table 2.2.

In 1972, M. G. Ramachandran challenged the DMK leader Karunanidhi and was subsequently expelled from the party. Ramachandran then formed the AIADMK (All India Anna Dravida Munnetra Kazagam). AIADMK went on to win the 1977, 1980, and 1984 elections through appealing to the extremely poor and destitute. Ramachandran's approach has been termed 'paternalist populism' which refers to governance undertaken for the benefit of the poor through the actions of a benevolent, father-like leader.[44] Prior to his entering politics, Ramachandran worked as a film actor for many years. He combined politics with acting generating huge popularity and gaining visibility through playing roles that cast him as a fighter for the people.[45] Ramachandran immediately launched populist policies. For example, he raised the reservations in government to 50 per cent for OBCs. It is worth noting that the increased reservations can be viewed as a symbolic move since only a minority of OBCs were able to take advantage of them. In addition, *Dalits* are usually poorer than OBCs; thus it can be argued that increasing the reservations for OBCs was an anti-poor policy.

As the story unfolds, the importance of caste politics in Tamil Nadu in promoting nutritional schemes will become increasingly clear. For now, the main point is that since the creation of the DMK, a political climate of redistribution and reverse discrimination was established so that the poor, the low caste, and the vulnerable became the priority of the state. Feeding children and ensuring their health and survival was a manifestation of the benign and protective state. Feeding was also a visible and emotionally powerful symbol. In this situation, it was relatively easy for the state to address nutrition and spend a large percentage of the budget on food and health services.

The Creation of World Bank Project TINP

By the second half of the 1970s, the Government of Tamil Nadu was operating 25 different nutrition programmes at a cost of US$9 million annually, although it was estimated that these reached less than 10 per cent of the population in the state. However, data collected by the Government of India indicated that undernutrition rates were unchanging. To understand why rates were so high, a Tamil Nadu Nutrition Survey was undertaken in 1973 by USAID and sponsored by the central and state governments.[46] The study was both a nutritional status report and an applied research study, and one of the most comprehensive and systematic efforts to construct a systems approach to nutrition (Figure 2.1).[47]

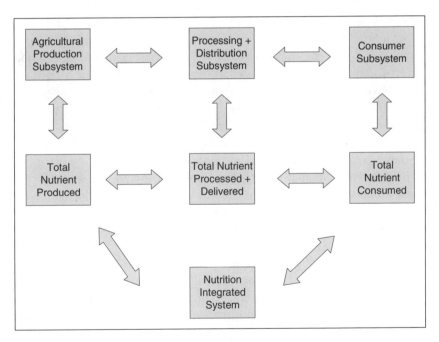

Figure 2.1. Systems approach to nutrition (Venkitaramanan 1973)

The systems approach was viewed as a scientific attempt to bring the business model to nutrition. Nutrition was inserted into a non-causal production model that mapped out the production aspects of nutrition (Agricultural Production Subsystem), the consumption aspects of nutrition (Consumer Subsystem), and the distribution mechanism (Processing and Distribution Subsystem). The industrial 'product' in this situation is 'nutrients' (Total Nutrient Produced, Total Nutrient Processed and Delivered, Total Nutrient Consumed). This type of analysis, drawing on private-sector models, was applied to many development issues, including nutrition.

In the case of Tamil Nadu, the objectives were to analyse and map out the nutrition system, to identify intervention points, to link these to family planning and economic development, and to come up with feasible actions for the government. At the time of the survey, the Government of Tamil Nadu was already running over 25 nutrition programmes in the state and was unable to commit financially to additional nutritional projects especially when the investment seemed to have no impact on rates of undernutrition.

The Government of Tamil Nadu and the Government of India approached the World Bank for funding. In addition, policy specialists bridging USAID and the World Bank presented a strong case to the World Bank for lending in nutrition as part of the Bank's turn towards the development of 'human capital'.[48] The Bank's turn towards poverty-alleviation projects, as will be discussed later in this chapter, coincided with these requests for Bank assistance. After 16 months of intense dialogue between the World Bank and the state government, Tamil Nadu became a policy laboratory in 1980, funded by the World Bank, in which the largest donor-aided nutrition scheme in the world came into being.[49] This was termed the Tamil Nadu Integrated Nutrition Project (TINP).

TINP was also created due to the efforts of a civil servant in Tamil Nadu which demonstrates the profound impact one individual can have in nutrition policy. S. Venkitaramanan was the State's Finance Secretary at the time of the USAID Tamil Nadu nutrition study and became its Chief Secretary during the preparation of TINP.[50] He had previously worked in the central government during the 1966–67 Bihar famine for C. Subramaniyam, then the Minister of Agriculture, and had retained an interest in nutrition and food production. He pushed the state government to make nutrition a priority and undertake the Bank loan for TINP.

The Creation of the State Project: Midday Meal Scheme

Shortly after TINP started, the AIADMK party assumed power in Tamil Nadu. To gain political support, the Chief Minister of Tamil Nadu, Ramachandran, introduced the Chief Minister's Nutritious Meal Scheme on 1 July 1982.

This scheme is an outcome of my experience of extreme starvation at an age when I knew only to cry when I was hungry. But for the munificence of a woman next door who extended a bowl of rice gruel to us and saved us from the cruel hand of death, we would have departed this world long ago. Such merciful womenfolk, having great faith in me, elected me as chief minister of Tamil Nadu. To wipe the tears of these women I have taken up this project ... To picture lakhs and lakhs of poor children who gather to partake of nutritious meals in the thousands of hamlets and villages all over Tamil Nadu, and blessing us in their childish prattle, will be a glorious event.[51]

The concept of midday meal has a long history in Tamil Nadu, having been introduced in the Madras Corporation Area in 1925.[52] Post-independence and until 1982–83 when the midday meal scheme was launched, the state had experimented with a whole range of feeding schemes.

The midday meal scheme offers a school meal originally for children between 5 and 14 years. It was later extended to children from 2 years onwards, to those over 60 years of age, and to destitute widows and people with disabilities.[53] It provides a hot meal consisting of rice, *sambhar* (tomato and lentil soup with spices), different vegetables, and regular supplements. This was a scheme created not just for nutrition but also to increase school enrolment, to create jobs, and to improve social welfare in the state. As an educational tool, it raises the incentives for parents to send their children to school. It also increases the attention span and learning capacity of children who have been shown to perform badly when feeling hungry.[54] As an employment scheme, it attempts to create income-earning opportunities for socially excluded individuals such as those who are low caste, destitute widows, and women. Social welfare may be advanced by breaking down caste and gender boundaries through the sharing of food at school. In terms of this goal, the midday meal scheme has been disappointing as *Dalit* participation has been weak.[55]

Kalpana, a second standard student of a government school located in the dominant caste quarter of Kamalaputhur village in Tamil Nadu, was denied food and chased out of school when she tried to participate with the rest of the students in the government mid-day meal scheme. The reason was that she was a dalit, while her classmates were from dominant castes.[56]

Factors influencing *Dalit* participation include the locality in which mid-day meals are served in terms of village caste geography as well as the inclusion of *Dalit* cooks.

The midday meal scheme was expanded to the national level over 20 years later. On 17 November 2004, the Supreme Court of India ruled that, 'Every child eligible for cooked meal under the midday meal scheme, in all States and Union territories, shall be provided with the said meal immediately, and in any case, not later than January, 2005'.[57] Many states, especially Bihar, Uttar Pradesh, Assam, Jharkand, and Jammu and Kashmir have struggled to comply with this deadline. Even among the states that implemented the midday meal scheme, as of 2004, Tamil Nadu has been the only state to feed all school children for the entire week. Dr. Venkatasubramanian of the central Planning Commission and former Director of Education recounts,

When I submitted a proposal to the Chief Minister...that we could provide meals to every school-going child from Monday to Friday, the Chief Minister had remarked, 'As Director of Education, Mr. Venkatasubramanian has suggested mid-day meals on the working days Monday to Friday for all. But the Director of Education forgets that though schools do not function on Saturdays and Sundays, the stomach functions all the seven days.'[58]

As a result of the Chief Minister's insistence, the midday meal scheme in Tamil Nadu provides food every day of the week, including Saturdays and Sundays. This situation is just one example of the effect that the Chief Minister had on the development of midday meal scheme and generally nutrition in Tamil Nadu.

The midday meal scheme in Tamil Nadu was 20 times larger than that of the World Bank's TINP and was heavily criticized at the time by development professionals and the central Planning Commission as a political ploy and not 'scientifically sound'. For example, when the DMK opposition party came to power, they attempted to woo voters by adding an egg to the meal every two weeks. When the AIADMK came back to power in the 1990s under Chief Minister Jayalakshmi, soya and corn flour were added for meals in school holidays along with sweet *pongal* (porridge of rice and lentils) for the birthdays of certain AIADMK party leaders. The midday meal scheme is quite expensive, costing the state Rs. 3.4 crores in the financial year 1981–82, increasing to Rs. 388 crores in the financial year 1995–96.[59] Salaries are the bulk of the cost since roughly 100,000 individuals are employed as cooks or helpers.

The Central Government Project: Integrated Child Development Services (ICDS)

Along with the midday meal scheme and TINP, the third major nutrition scheme operating in Tamil Nadu is the Integrated Child Development Services (ICDS) programme, which is jointly funded by the central and state governments. It has also been supported by the World Food Programme, CARE, UNICEF, the EU, USAID, and the World Bank. ICDS was created before TINP or the midday meal scheme. In response to the recommendations of a subcommittee of the Planning Commission, a National Policy for Children was adopted by the central government in 1974. ICDS was then created by the Ministry of Social Welfare. The goal was to integrate services for preschool children and pregnant/nursing women all of which had previously been targeted through separate schemes. The programme, which is supposed to run in all Indian states, offers supplementary food (hot meals of lentils, rice, vegetables, grains) for children up to six and pregnant and lactating women. For children between the ages of three and six, it provides preschool education, immunizations (BCG, DPT, OPV,[60] measles), health checkups, and medical referral services. An important distinction regarding education between ICDS and TINP is that TINP exclusively provides nutrition education to mothers while ICDS provides a basic education to children.

ICDS services are delivered at *anganwadis* (community nutrition centres) by an *anganwadi* worker and a helper. *Anganwadi* workers are selected from within village communities and are expected to be women who have completed at least five years of schooling. They are paid an honorarium of US$7.50 to US$10.50 per month (in 2001), depending on education and experience.

ICDS is a highly controversial programme having attracted the criticism of certain World Bank staff, who argue that its impact on nutritional status is limited as is the support of civil servants and prominent academics.[61] Two recent World Bank reports state that ICDS effects are unknown, its quality of services is low, it is poorly targeted and implemented, and that it is a waste of financial resources.[62] When the second phase of TINP ended in 1997, the World Bank hoped that the Government of India would scale it up to the national level. However, both the Government of India

33

and the Government of Tamil Nadu adopted ICDS. In Tamil Nadu, TINP continued but was renamed ICDS.

One senior Bank staff member believes that the reason that the government adopted ICDS over TINP is due to the political appeal of a holistic approach. He noted that Ashok Mitra, who was then Secretary of the Planning Commission and President of the Nutrition Society, advocated the leaky bucket theory. Mitra was a demographer who argued that people were overly concerned with food although nutrition also encompasses water supply, literacy, and feeding habits. Explaining Mitra's theory, the senior staff member said, 'The problem is that if you plug up one hole, there are still going to be leaks so a holistic approach is needed.' ICDS was created to address the many facets of nutrition. He also added another reason for the government preference for ICDS:

You know Gopalan? He's the Indian nutrition guru. Well his nose was out of joint, he wanted to see TINP, [but] through some foul up, whoever answered the phone in the TINP office did not treat him with respect so he never saw the project and resented this. So he talked and wrote against the project in his NFI [Nutrition Foundation of India] newsletter. You can see that nutrition has many political and psychological aspects.

Two other Bank staff members offered their perspectives:

Gopalan was the problem. He believed in a conspiracy theory that vitamin A pills were pushed by Westerners and bad for Indians. Meera [Chatterjee] worked for him and there was competition between the state and central governments, professional jealousy, and bad relations in general. Plus him and [the Mission Director] did not get along—and Gopalan was a formidable opponent to TINP—both ideologically and scientifically... plus ICDS is a political solution. Its goal is not to reduce malnutrition but rather to feed lots of kids and give preschool education- this is what people want. But sometimes what the people want is not best for them. It's gotten better since it's been targeted regionally and geographically but it's still a huge waste of resources. It doesn't help children under three—the children TINP reached. It doesn't focus on growth monitoring which helped strengthen the role of mothers and makes them agents of change. Plus Bank projects have to go through the central government, the small minority of projects are state projects, so TINP was not popular in Delhi since it gave too much control to the state. India is still very top-down despite all the talk of decentralization.

It's really a mystery why ICDS took over TINP—but the government wanted to follow their own model because TINP seemed like a foreign project.

In response to these claims by the World Bank, Professor Gopalan responded:

TINP was a project drawn up by World Bank officials and bureaucrats in Tamil Nadu. The Indian scientific community was totally kept out of the picture. Neither the National Institute of Nutrition nor any of the leading Home Science Institutes were consulted in the formulation or implementation of the programme at any stage. There was also reluctance on the part of World Bank officials acting in collaboration with Tamil Nadu bureaucrats to let any independent individual scientist visit programme sites. Only conducted tours approved by the World Bank were allowed.

TINP was largely a relief programme to ensure child survival; it was not a developmental programme. The emphasis was in identification of the extreme malnourished child and its rehabilitation up to a point. Growth monitoring was the central activity.

ICDS, which was started by the Government of India after prolonged consultations with the Indian scientific community, was very much on ground when TINP was started. ICDS, despite its limitations, is a developmental programme based on sound concepts. I have received the ICDS Programme. There was no question of TINP supplanting ICDS at any stage. Apart from the errors in its basic design, TINP was a far more expensive programme.

TINP, the midday meal scheme, and ICDS are often confused even by those working directly on nutrition in India (Table 2.3). For example, when enquiring about TINP to an advisor to the Planning Commission on health and nutrition, he corrected me and said that I must be confused as Tamil Nadu has had midday meal schemes and ICDS. Outside of Tamil Nadu, not many in government know that that the midday meal scheme and TINP were two separate projects. Although it is recognized in New Delhi that Tamil Nadu has put in place major nutrition efforts, with the recent attention given to the right to food, the focus is on the midday meal scheme. TINP is relatively unknown. This confusion also occurred in conversations with academics in India. When I enquired about the beneficial effects of TINP to a researcher, she remarked that it provided a hot meal to preschool children every day consisting of rice, vegetables, or pulses. TINP only provided supplementary feeding in the form of *laddoos*; so she had mistaken the midday meal scheme for TINP. In addition, the villagers who are targeted by these schemes are unaware that there are three schemes for nutrition. There is general knowledge of school feeding and *anganwadis* but no recognition that these are separate programmes funded by different bodies. The general silence on TINP reveals that not many are aware of this project in India outside of World Bank staff and academic associates, nutrition planners, and a handful of Tamil Nadu civil servants who executed the project.

Table 2.3. Midday meal scheme, ICDS, and TINP

Programme	Started in	Funded by	Activity	Target group
Midday meal scheme	1982	Tamil Nadu government	Provide hot meal to combat hunger	Children 2–14 years, pregnant and lactating women, destitute widows, disabled, and those over 60
ICDS: Integrated child development services	1976	Central government (Tamil Nadu government pays food costs although 55% food provided by CARE and WFP). 3% Bilateral donors, 3.5% UNICEF	Supplementary nutrition (hot meals), immunization, health check-up, and referrals, preschool education	Children 0–6 years. Pregnant and lactating women
TINP: Tamil Nadu Integrated Nutrition Project	1980	World Bank loan 44.3%. Tamil Nadu government 55.7%	Change mothers' behaviour through educational tools of growth monitoring, nutrition education, short-term food supplementation (laddoos)	Children 6–36 months. Pregnant and lactating women

There are also political motives for each of the funding bodies to con-fuse the three nutritional programmes: the Government of Tamil Nadu can generate political support by presenting all three projects as if they are the midday meal scheme; the Bank can promote their design by attributing all nutritional effects to TINP; the Government of India can assert its political control over the state by showing the positive benefits of its creation, ICDS.[63]

The World Bank in India

The reasons for which the midday meal scheme and ICDS were created are evident. But why did the World Bank, which is arguably a bank and not a health development agency, involve itself in nutrition? What were the internal factors that led to the Bank moving into relatively small-scale social sector projects? To understand how the Bank came to play such an important role in hunger reduction in India, it is first important to understand the history, organization, and operations of the Bank.

History of the Bank

The World Bank and International Monetary Fund (IMF) are independent specialized agencies of the UN made up of 184 member countries. They were established at the 1944 Bretton Woods conference and are commonly referred to as International Financial Institutions or the 'Bretton Woods institutions'. The main objective of the two institutions was to ensure global economic stability as well as to invest in the post-war economy. The IMF was established to manage a system of fixed but adjustable exchange rates and lend on a strictly short-term basis to countries facing a short-term balance of payments crisis. The World Bank's role was to invest in the post-war economy by raising capital in money markets and lending it at advantageous rates to war-torn developing countries. The institutions were originally set up to fund European post-war reconstruction. However, last-minute negotiations and lobbying by Latin American delegations at Bretton Woods resulted in the International Bank for Reconstruction and Development (IBRD) obtaining a 'world development bank' mandate.[64] Between 1947 and 1949, the Bank exclusively dealt with the reconstruction of Europe until the Marshall Plan took over this function.[65]

IBRD acquires its funds for operation through two channels. First, it issues AAA-rated bonds, which are guaranteed by the Bank's wealthy nation-state members, to raise funds on private capital markets. Developing country governments that could otherwise not secure access to capital on private markets are able to borrow from the Bank against these IBRD bond issues at market rates. In its first 20 years, the Bank's dominant concern was to assure investors of their bonds' credit worthiness to ensure continued access to Wall Street.[66] This preoccupation resulted in a conservative project portfolio focused on physical infrastructure in relatively credit-worthy developing countries. Second, funds are obtained through state-subscribed capital assessed on the basis of national income. This channel amounts to less than 5 per cent of the Bank's funds.[67]

As politics and the international climate changed during the twentieth century, the World Bank expanded its presence by acquiring three new agencies in addition to the IBRD. In 1956, the International Finance Corporation (IFC) was established to encourage private investment in developing countries through syndications, underwritings, and co-financing. The International Finance Corporation has expanded its presence in countries such as India and Brazil in the past decade.

In 1960, the concessional lending branch of the World Bank group, the International Development Association (IDA), was created, to supply capital to extremely poor countries (below GDP US$800 per capita) at very low interest rates (below 1%). Funds for lending through the IDA come solely from members' capital subscription, thereby protecting IBRD credit ratings. The US contributes 20.86 per cent of IDA fund, followed by Japan at 18.7 per cent, and the UK and France at 7.3 per cent.[68] The creation of the IDA meant that the Bank could lend to less stable countries in riskier areas like agriculture, nutrition, water, and rural development.

Finally, in 1988, the Multilateral Investment Guarantee Agency (MIGA) was established to promote direct foreign investment by providing guarantees in unstable countries with political turmoil or armed conflict. The World Bank has enjoyed a close relationship with the US, from its establishment at Bretton Woods to the current situation both physically (e.g. headquarters in Washington, DC) and politically (e.g. President nominated by the US). It has been stated that the Bretton Woods conference consisted of 'one and a half' parties referring to the USA and the UK.[69] These ties to the original donor countries have influenced its day-to-day operations.

Organization of the Bank

The World Bank consists of a nominated President, an Executive Board, a Board of Governors, and vice-presidential units. The World Bank President is an American traditionally selected by the US. This process has been criticized for not being transparent or following a set of selection guidelines.[70] The President serves an initial five-year term which may be renewed by the Executive Board for five years, or less, with no limit to the number of terms. He is chairman of the Bank's Board of Executive Directors and *ex officio* president of the Bank group: the IBRD, IDA, IFC, MIGA, and the International Centre for Settlement of Investment Disputes.

The Executive Board, the 'political heart' of the Bank, governs the World Bank and all member states are represented on it.[71] It consists of 24 elected and appointed Executive Directors who serve full-time in Washington and make decisions on the day-to-day operations. The representation on the Executive Board is not equal. Only large donor countries such as the US, Japan, Germany, France, the UK, China, Russia, and Saudi Arabia have their own Executive Directors. The other 16 seats are elected for two-year terms by groups of countries (constituencies) represented by just one position. This has been a large source of contention since power is shared unequally. For example, one Executive Director represents 22 African countries.

Although the Executive Board is supposed to work through consensus and discussion, voting power plays a significant role. With this background, it is important to note that not all countries have the same number of votes. Each country has a weighted number of votes depending on its quota. Quotas are established through a cumulative assessment of national income, foreign reserves, international trade, and political calculations. Reviews of these quotas are made every five years and are supposed to serve as a technical assessment. However, as Table 2.4 shows, quote allocations and subsequent voting power are deeply political.

For example, the US is the only member to have individual veto power over major decisions. This is due to the fact that an 85 per cent majority is needed. As the US share has dropped, it has always negotiated an increase in the majority needed so that it retains its veto power. In addition to votes, voice is extremely important. Informally, it has been noted that the US is the most vocal member of the Board as well: 'Representing the largest, most influential member, the US representatives speak on virtually every issue coming before the Board'.[72]

Since 1987, the Bank has been split into major geographical and network vice-presidential units, all based in Washington DC (see Chapter 3 figures).[73] Regional vice-presidencies include Africa, East Asia and the

Table 2.4. International Bank for Reconstruction and Development (IBRD) voting power (%)[a]

USA	16.7
Japan	8.0
Germany	4.6
Russia	2.8
China	2.8
All other countries	62.3

[a] Woods (2002, p. 958).

39

Pacific, Europe and Central Asia, Latin America, Middle East and North Africa, and South Asia. In addition, there are a number of network vice-presidencies such as Human Development, Financial Sector, Private Sector Development, and Infrastructure. Each network has many sub-thematic areas, or sectors, each in charge of its own recruitment and hiring. As a result of the new management structure introduced in 1997, sector staff are also located in regional vice-presidencies and in the Bank's country offices around the world. A sector person in a country office will report to a Sector Manager (in Washington, DC typically) and then to a Sector Director based in the respective regional unit in Washington.

Bank Operations

The Bank has two official functions as a development bank: project lending and policy lending. Project lending refers to when the Bank identifies, designs, and disburses funds for a project with specific objectives and with the government typically executing the plan. Loans are disbursed over a fixed period according to intermediate targets determined over specified project phases. Policy lending refers to lending for budgetary support upon implementation of policy reforms by the government; most recently this has entailed structural adjustment. Bank staff have remarked that policy lending results in less precise evaluation of impact since they have less control over where and how the money is spent. In both project and policy lending, the Bank's Articles of Agreement states explicitly that the Bank shall not be involved politically with member states and only be motivated by technical, economic considerations:

The Bank and its officers shall not interfere in the political affairs of any member; nor shall they be influenced in their decisions by the political character of the member or members concerned. Only economic considerations shall be relevant to their decisions, and these considerations shall be weighed impartially in order to achieve the purposes stated in Article I.[74]

Other functions of the Bank include acting as an advisory body, an intellectual research institute, and a training centre for developing country civil servants. The Bank serves as a training centre for developing country civil servants in three ways.[75] First, many civil servants spend several years employed at the Bank learning about economic structures, policies, and projects in a comparative context.[76] On return to their countries, they often are in prominent economic and political positions. Second, the Bank provides training and sponsors courses to support civil servants through the Economic Development Institute. Third, the Bank finances promising students from developing countries to study in orthodox economics departments such as Harvard, Oxford, and Cambridge.

In addition, Bank research plays a significant role in influencing development knowledge:

A distinguishing feature of the World Bank [is] its role as a conveyor belt of ideas about development policy to the developing countries. It is difficult to overemphasize the part played by the Bank in this regard. Thanks to its far-flung lending operations, the Bank is the single most important external source of ideas and advice to developing-country policymakers. World Bank research and publications . . . are widely distributed around the world.[77]

Changing Objectives

Given the reasons for its creation, the first World Bank loans were to Denmark, France, Luxembourg, and the Netherlands.[78] Unlike other UN agencies, the Bank initially raised funds through donor contributions from wealthier countries and private financial markets. This allowed it to raise money to provide interest-bearing and interest-free loans, credits, grants, and technical assistance to countries that could not afford to borrow money in international markets. The Bank's Articles of Agreement focus on productivity, investment, capital accumulation, growth, and balance of payment. During this time, the Bank focused on loans for infrastructure and utilities.

In the 1960s, with the creation of a new branch of the World Bank, the IDA, the Bank turned its focus to development which was internally and internationally conceived of as economic growth to be achieved through industrialization. The main indicator of development was Gross National Product (GNP) or GNP per capita. Regardless of the country or political circumstances, growth planned by the state was the universal, technical solution to underdevelopment.[79] The Bank's prescription was a mixture of public utility projects, financial stability, encouragement of private investment, as well as small steps into agriculture and education. The IDA financed these projects through interest-free credits to poor countries as opposed to the IBRD which functioned purely as a bank for middle-income countries. Between 1961 and 1965, the IBRD loaned 76.8 per cent of its available funds for electric power and transportation and only 1 per cent for projects in the social sector. Even the 'development-focused' IDA spent a little under 3 per cent of its funding for social services.[80]

The priority on the global agenda given to social sector investment in developing countries was completely changed with the entrance of Robert McNamara as President of the World Bank (1968–81). Prior to his arrival, there was general dismay at the outcome of economic growth strategies in academic and policy circles, reflected in books such as Gunnar Myrdal's highly influential *Asian Drama: An Enquiry into the Poverty of Nations*,[81] and a turn towards a basic needs approach in universities such as Sussex. The basic needs model was a development approach that emphasized short-term interventions for the poor in order to achieve a subsistence level of consumption of basic needs such as water, food, shelter, sanitation, health care, and education.[82] However, these concerns were not globally influential or internationalized. Robert McNamara brought poverty concerns with him and institutionalized them at the Bank. As Martha Finnemore notes, 'Ideas need to be institutionalised for maximum effect', or for any effect.[83]

McNamara arrived at the Bank in 1968 after serving for seven years as Secretary of Defence under Presidents Kennedy and Johnson.[84] He brought to the Bank an agenda outlining the moral imperative of foreign aid both for humanitarian and national security purposes. McNamara formally addressed world poverty in his Nairobi Speech to the Board of Governors on 24 September 1973 where he spoke of improving living conditions, expanding education lending, and focusing on basic nutritional requirements. There he outlined a two-pronged approach to development. The first was to scale up Bank lending and to increase Bank staff at least fivefold. In fiscal year 1968, the Bank's new commitments were US$953.5 million. By 1981, total cumulative lending reached US$92.2 billion.[85]

McNamara's second strategy was to further the Bank's control on the way aid was used by borrower countries. Specifically, he wanted to have greater Bank influence on project design.[86] This would be achieved through the institution being framed as a technical assistance agency that would show countries the 'western way of doing things' through providing advice, furnishing consultants, and giving training.[87]

However, as he reconfigured the Bank's direction, McNamara faced an organizational constraint in that poverty-oriented projects required more staff, more work, and more attention to detail. They were expensive both in terms of time and money. Since McNamara's presidency, the Bank has been torn between being a bank and being a development agency, between spending effectively and moving money fast. The bank was set up to be a financial institution which valued investments that showed a measurable and direct monetary return. Yet, McNamara worked to redefine the bank as a credible development agency. Despite the move to poverty-alleviation projects, he still increased pressure on staff to move loan money for projects to meet the year's financial goals. 'The new style...entailed lending for small projects based on less information, using less well-developed techniques, and involving more costs and benefits that were difficult or impossible to quantify using standard economic tool analysis.'[88]

The Bank's staff, many of whom were economists by training, regarded themselves as technicians providing rigorous scientific analysis of development. They had difficulty applying their technical econometric models to the issues of health and social welfare. Other complications with the change were McNamara's desire for quantification of targets and outputs as well as for short-term results. The fast-paced progression of projects also did not give staff adequate time to address local concerns such as kinship, caste, and local governance structures. Blueprint approaches were preferred to projects designed for the specific needs of local communities. These uncomfortable tensions in the Bank still remain today as will be discussed in Chapter 6.

McNamara's largest support was for population-control projects,[89] which probably emanated from his experience in US foreign policy in the 1960s. McNamara believed that population increase was 'the greatest single obstacle to economic and social advancement of most of the societies in most of the developing world'.[90] Both at the time and in retrospect, the Bank's population projects have been universally judged as failures, primarily attributed to the Bank extending itself into a new, uncharted realm and taking on a highly political national issue which did not have the support of borrower governments or their citizens.[91]

McNamara then turned his attention to nutrition, driven by his attendance at a conference at the Massachusetts Institute of Technology (MIT) in 1971 organized by a prominent nutritionist, Alan Berg, and by the priority given to nutritional planning by USAID and the Rockefeller Foundation. He recruited Berg, who was then working at the Brookings Institute, to join the Bank as an in-house nutrition expert, as well as hired biochemist James Lee to be the Bank's scientific advisor. In January

1972, the Bank established a nutrition unit, and the first loan for nutrition was made in 1976 to the Government of Brazil for US$19 million. In October 1979, the Bank merged the nutrition unit with the population projects department into the Population, Health, and Nutrition Department and allowed it to give stand-alone health loans. Bank officials reported that this merger would make it easier to address family planning projects.[92] While the new department gave nutrition an institutional base, it was considered relatively less important than population or health.

To publicize its new role as a development agency, the Bank focused its 1980 World Development Report on the importance of investing in the social sector since improved health and nutrition would accelerate economic growth. This shift towards address health and nutritional issues was firmly established by the 1993 World Development Report *Investing in Health* which was the first annual report to be devoted entirely to health. The 1993 World Development Report launched a new Bank framework for applying economic principles to health through the use of cost-effectiveness and introduced other cost–benefit analyses. These 'tools' for health were developed with assistance from the World Health Organization which is a partner of the Bank on Health, Nutrition, and Population projects.

McNamara's 13 years as President ended on 30 June 1981. Even though he turned the Bank towards poverty-alleviation projects, Robert Ayres notes that McNamara's approach was not 'super-radical'.[93] Despite the change in portfolio lending from roads and dams to social sector investment, both were routes to the same place, economic growth. In addition, Bank loans were often in the geopolitical and geo-strategic interest of the US, countries accepting loans from the Bank often faced pressure to contract with American companies, and within the Bank, macroeconomic policy remained primary with poverty alleviation as a subsidiary goal.[94]

In addition, McNamara overly depended on technocratic solutions based on neo-liberal macroeconomic ideology, such as structural adjustment, which were developed in Washington, DC then exported across the world regardless of historical, political, social, or environmental circumstances.[95] Ayres argues that McNamara thought it possible to develop 'basically similar projects to reach basically similar poverty groups and solve basically similar problems, wherever they existed'.[96] In addition, it has been noted that McNamara had a particular interest in the use of quantitative data of all kinds in project design and evaluation and often pushed Bank staff to supplement project documents with them. Ayres notes, '[McNamara] was much given to quantification, to the reduction of complex social realities to figures and numbers of target groups, beneficiaries, incremental output, improvements in productivity, changes in incomes, and so forth.'[97] This preoccupation with quantitative analysis continues in the Bank today.

Yet, McNamara was more inclined towards poverty alleviation than his successor Alden 'Tom' Clausen, who established his position on poverty immediately, stating in 1982: 'The World Bank will remain a bank. It is not a Robin Hood . . . nor the United Way of the Development Community. It is a hard-headed, unsentimental institution that takes a very pragmatic and non-political view of what it is trying to do.'[98]

The Selection of Tamil Nadu

I return now to the early 1970s when undernutrition became a concern of the Bank. The management staff of the Bank struggled with two key questions: was undernutrition a 'development' problem and therefore one the Bank should address. If so, were there feasible things that could be done about it, particularly with the Bank's assets? The resolution was yes. At the urging of McNamara, the Bank's Board of Executive Directors decided to finance the implementation and evaluation of projects in countries with a large proportion of the population undernourished.[99] The Bank's strategy on nutrition was to draw attention of government officials to the problem, to assist governments in planning, to further the development of rigorous project analysis, and to provide enough resources to make significant interventions possible. Between 1977 and 1980, the Bank started pilot projects in four countries that were already principal recipients of Bank aid. These were Brazil, Columbia, India, and Indonesia.

India was selected because at that time it was the World Bank's largest borrower and the recipient of the largest sum of interest-free credits from the IDA. Shyam Kamath notes that India has been the World Bank's 'star patient' and almost the *raison d'étre* of its growth.[100] Edward Mason and Robert Asher, the Bank's semi-official historians, write,

No country has been studied more by the World Bank than India . . . India has influenced the Bank as much as the Bank has India . . . This applies particularly to the Bank's conception of development process—the role of government in the process [and] the need for grants, soft loans, and program assistance.[101]

Within India, the state of Tamil Nadu was chosen for two reasons. First, in 1977, the Government of India had requested assistance in reducing undernutrition particularly in this state due to the findings of the Tamil Nadu Nutrition Survey. This survey showed that over 50 per cent of preschool children had low weight-for-age despite the existence of 25 nutrition projects in Tamil Nadu. Second, as described earlier, due to the political and electoral importance of food and nutrition, the Government of Tamil Nadu had shown itself committed to social development.

Due to a particular configuration of forces at a particular time in history for the World Bank and India, the Tamil Nadu Integrated Nutrition Project was created. TINP was designed as a six-year project starting in August 1980 and costing US$84.1 million. It was to be jointly funded by the World Bank (US$37.2 million) and the Government of Tamil Nadu (US$46.3) and overseen by the Chief Secretary of the state government and senior civil servants. A Project Coordination Office was created to coordinate, monitor, and budget among the Directorates of Social Welfare and Health and the Department of Evaluation.

A central tenet of TINP and the Bank approach is that undernutrition is the result of inappropriate childcare practices, and 'not of income, famine, or unpreventable health problems'.[102] The overarching objective of TINP is behavioural change of mothers. TINP consists of five components: (1) child growth monitoring, (2) short-term supplementary feeding to children under 3 and (3) to pregnant or lactating mothers, (4) nutrition education for mothers, and (5) monitoring/evaluation. In 1980, this was the first large-scale use of growth monitoring in a community nutrition project. TINP's services are provided at a community nutrition centre at the village level.

Growth monitoring refers to the monthly weighing of all children 6–36 months old so that mothers whose child's growth is faltering can be targeted for intensive nutrition counselling. Growth monitoring is used as an educational tool to provide mothers with 'an objective feedback about how they [are] caring for their children'.[103]

Supplementary feeding is used as medicine for relatively brief periods for children experiencing growth faltering as well as for pregnant and lactating women. Only children who are severely malnourished or those whose growth fails to increase adequately over three consecutive monthly weighings are eligible for the supplementary feeding programme. The feeding programme lasts 90 days after which children are removed from the programme if their growth is on track again. The World Bank nutrition team emphasizes that this is a supplement not a meal. It is insufficient to meet children's daily caloric requirements. Rather, it should be used as an educational tool to show mothers that very small amounts of additional food 'affordable in almost everyone's household budget' are sufficient to keep a child well-nourished.[104] The feeding programme offers the supplement in the form of *laddoos*, which are small balls of slightly sweetened rice/gram mix. This is made from a mix (*sathu maavu*) combined with water. One hundred grams (g) of *sathu maavu* contains 439 kcal and 8.3 g of protein. This 100 g consists of 35 g of wheat and maize flour, 9 g of malted *ragi* (finger millet) flour, 15 g of Bengal gramflour, 25 g jaggery, 15 g of vegetable oil, and 1 g of a vitamin pre-mix, calcium carbonate and ferrous sulphate. In addition to the supplement, Vitamin A prophylaxis (200,000 IU mega-dose every six months) is administered to all children along with deworming treatment (piperazine citrate, three times a year).

These services are provided by *anganwadi* workers and one ayah at a community nutrition centre or *anganwadi*. Health-service support is provided by the multipurpose health worker who operates from a health sub-centre. Although not carefully observed in practice, selection criteria for *anganwadi* workers include residence in the village, an elementary school education, acceptability to the community, and communication skills. Whenever possible, *anganwadi* workers are chosen from women who are both poor and who have healthy children to serve as examples to other women in the community. They are trained for two months and are paid a small monthly honorarium of 90 Rs. for their six hours of work a day. TINP services are supposed to be provided in the early mornings and in the late afternoons. Each village usually has one centre. Each worker is responsible for roughly a population of 1,500.

Anganwadi workers are supervised by a community nutrition supervisor who is responsible for 10 centres. Supervisors are supported by a community nutrition instructress, one per block. This instructress is supervised by a 'Taluk Project Nutrition Officer' who is responsible for all *anganwadis* in their *taluk*.[105] This individual in turn is supported at the district-level by a 'District-Project Nutrition Officer'.

Initially, TINP covered the rural areas of those districts with the worst nutritional status as determined by the census, less than half the state and a population of about nine million. The TINP-I implementation manual written by Jim Greene and others consists of 136 pages on the design of each component in detail as well as solutions for what could go wrong.

This manual is considered by Bank nutrition staff to be the best, as well as the most detailed, ever prepared for a Bank Health, Nutrition, and Population project.

TINP-I had four specific objectives and targets.[106]

(1) 50 per cent reduction in protein–energy malnutrition from an initial level of about 60 per cent
(2) 25 per cent reduction in infant mortality from about 125 per 1,000
(3) 22 per cent reduction in Vitamin A deficiency in children under 5 from 27 per cent
(4) 35 per cent reduction in nutritional anaemia in pregnant and lactating women from 55 per cent

It is not clear how these targets were identified by the Bank. An additional informal target was that the *anganwadi* workers would reach 80–90 per cent coverage of the target populations.

Was TINP Effective?

One of the key aspects of TINP is the monitoring and evaluations system which *anganwadi* workers report takes about a quarter of their time. Every month over 27 performance indicators are prepared by the TINP Project Coordinating Office using data collected by *anganwadi* workers and collated by their supervisors (Table 2.5).

After assessing the changes in physical growth of children reported by *anganwadi* workers, the project was labelled a success by the World Bank in the 1986 midterm evaluation for reducing rates of severe undernutrition. After TINP-I ended in 1989, funding was resumed for a period of eight years, TINP-II. Since the second phase of the project ended in 1998, TINP has been promoted by the Bank nutrition team as a success in reducing undernutrition. As described in the introduction, the analysis of the TINP data was problematic. Despite the lack of rigorous evaluation, TINP has been portrayed as the ultimate success in the World Bank's lending for nutrition.

Ambiguous about whether TINP may have contributed to a reduction in undernutrition rates, a former Bank nutrition staff member told me that any impact could be attributed to the style of implementation, and not necessarily the project design. He noted that the design of TINP was flexible and often changed in practice based on what was needed in the

Table 2.5. Key monthly indicators prepared by the TINP project coordinating office[a]

1. (a) Number of children 6–36 months/total population
    (b) Number of children 6–36 months newly entered the programme/number of children 6–36 months
2. Number of children 6–36 months weighed/number of children 6–36 months
3. Number of children eligible for feeding/number of children weighed for 6–36 months
4. (a) Number of children 6–24 months in normal and first grade malnutrition/total number 6–24 months weighed
    (b) Number of children 25–36 months in normal and first grade malnutrition/total number 25–36 months weighed
    (c) Number of children 6–36 months in normal and first grade malnutrition/total number 6–36 months weighed
    (d) Number of children 6–24 months in grade 2 malnutrition/total number 6–24 months weighed
    (e) Number of children 25–36 months in grade 2 malnutrition/total number of 25–36 months weighed
    (f) Number of children 6–36 months in grade 2 malnutrition/total number of 6–36 months weighed
    (g) Number of children 6–24 months in grades 3 and 4 malnutrition/total number of 6–24 months weighed
    (h) Number of children 25–36 months in grades 3 and 4 malnutrition/total number of 25–36 months weighed
    (i) Number of children 6–36 months in grade 3 and 4 malnutrition/total number of 6–36 months weighed
5. Number of children receiving food supplementation/number of children 6–36 months
6. Number of children receiving supplement in current month/number of children eligible for supplement in previous month
7. Number of children entering feeding for the first time/total number of children weighed
8. Number of children under feeding for >3 months/total number of children under feeding
9. Number of children under feeding for >6 months/total number of children under feeding
10. Number of children graduated in 90 days/number of children fed in last 3 months
11. Number of children graduated in 120 days/number of children fed in last 4 months
12. Number of children graduated in 150 days/number of children fed in last 5 months
13. Number of children graduated in 180 days/number of children fed in last 6 months
14. Number of children graduated/total number of children in feeding minus number of children underfeeding in first and second month
15. Number of cases of first relapse/number of cases graduated during last 6 months
16. Number of cases of second relapse/number of cases graduated during last 6 months
17. Number of total cases of relapse/number of cases graduated during last 6 months
18. Number of children absent for 5 days or more/number of children receiving food supplement
19. Number of pregnant women entering feeding in third trimester/number of pregnant women in third trimester
20. Number of pregnant and nursing women receiving supplement/number of pregnant women in third trimester and nursing women in first four months
21. Number of women absent for 5 days or more/number of women receiving food supplement
22. Number of children <3 years old given Vitamin A/number of children <3 years
23. Number of children <3 years old dewormed/number of children <3 years
24. Number of diarrhoea cases treated by CNW/number of children affected by diarrhoea
25. Number of children affected by diarrhoea/number of children 6–36 months
26. Number of diarrhoea cases referred to MPHW/number of cases treated by CNW
27. Number of dropout cases/number of children under feeding during the quarter

[a] Shekar (1991).

field. Since TINP has been replicated in other countries, this lesson has been lost and similar projects in other countries have been viewed as failures. Reflecting on the Bangladesh project, a former Bank staff member noted that 'too much time was spent on the design, not enough on implementation'. 'A key part of implementation,' he continued, 'is a serious commitment on the part of the government.' However, he noted that since the Bank likes to move money fast, 'projects were often sold to borrower governments' using huge loans. A senior Bank staff member also mentioned this to me, noting that his thinking has changed in the past 40 years as he has realized how important the political environment is: 'I am more realistic about the political ramifications; with changes of administration or even an individual, everything can be changed.'

The Evaluation of TINP

The quantitative evaluation of large projects is extremely complex. While statistics can suggest possible explanations, it can only rarely show causal relationships. Deciding which data-set to use, the acceptable level of significance, how data is cleaned or rounded, and the choice of variables collected all influence the results of statistical analysis.

Part of the distortion in evaluation occurs at the level of collection. About a quarter of a health workers' time is devoted to data collection which is aggregated at the district level every month. Every month this data is analysed by computer, and poor-performing centres are selected for special attention by supervisors. Community workers are often rewarded for children gaining weight or improving in health through promotions to supervisory level. The purpose of data collection may not be to reflect the nutritional status of the children but rather to serve as a message about a health worker's competence to his or her supervisors.

Evidence of this is present in the rounding up of birth weights as well as estimations of age, which for preschool children may be inaccurate. In addition, nutrition workers report that they are not adequately trained in mathematics and so find the computation of indicators time-consuming and tedious. Finally, each worker is responsible for over 1,500 children. When measuring and recording data for many children across a day, errors can happen quite easily. Anecdotally, it has also been noted that workers might invent numbers in order to meet data targets (e.g. number of children weighed that day). The problems at both levels, data collection and data analysis, result in considerable uncertainty in evaluations of TINP.

Qualitative interviewing is a useful method to address some short-comings of quantitative analysis. However, some economists, especially those based in the World Bank, perceive qualitative interviewing as not being methodologically rigorous. The following conversation with a Bank economist serves an example of this:

D.S.: I just wanted to mention that I have been spending quite a lot of time talking to women and alcohol is always mentioned—it seems like so many men drink and spend the household income on this. Could the Bank design in anyway incorporate this?

W.B.: Well we don't know that's a problem. It hasn't been documented in a quantitatively rigorous way. It's mostly stories you hear now and then.

D.S.: Well it just seems strange that no one has addressed this. I've spoken with over 70 women and I'd say over half report it as a problem.

W.B.: Well, you'd need more like 7000 to make a real case for that.

To address the quantitative focus of economists in the Bank, Chapters 5 and 6 combine ethnography and participant observation with an analysis of data collected during fieldwork in Tamil Nadu. These chapters attempt to tease out the effective and ineffective aspects of the TINP model.

As this chapter has described, the India–World Bank partnership in nutrition occurred at a particular point in history due to the coming together of various forces. Given that India has the largest number of undernourished individuals, and the World Bank is the biggest player in health, this would indicate that the project created, TINP, would be one of the best attempts to tackle child undernutrition. Before examining what happened at the community level, the next two chapters examine how hunger is understood and addressed by the World Bank.

Notes

1. Bhatia (1970), p. 1.
2. See Dyson (2004) for discussion of pre-colonial and colonial population and food trends.
3. Bhatia (1970), p. 2.
4. Sen (1981).
5. Bhatia (1970), p. 3.
6. Dutta, cited in Bhatia (1970), p. 3.
7. Ibid. p. 4.
8. Sinha (1961).

9. Bhatia (1970), p. 17.
10. ibid. p. 20.
11. Ibid. p. 20.
12. Bhatia (1970), p. 22.
13. Ibid. p. 38.
14. Ibid. p. 38.
15. Poleman (1973).
16. Ibid.
17. Sridhar (2005).
18. Mitra (1973), p. 358.
19. Arnold (1988), p. 96.
20. Purchasing power is a politically sensitive issue since it ties directly into issues of land redistribution, inequality, and agricultural subsidies.
21. Corbridge (1997).
22. Poleman (1973).
23. Sridhar (2005).
24. Das (2002) and Srinivasan (2000).
25. Sen (1981).
26. Ibid. p. 5.
27. Ibid. p. 154.
28. Harriss-White (2004), p. 51.
29. Government of Tamil Nadu (2003).
30. This paragraph relies on Béteille (1996), ch. 3.
31. Béteille (1996), p. 60.
32. This politicization of caste by means of Tamil nationalism, through such parties as the DMK and AIADMK, has significantly impacted the history and role of the state in India. The political role of caste has been explored by Sivathambi (1995), Saraswathi (1995), Palanithurai (1991), and Sastri (1964). The anthropology of the state of Tamil Nadu has been discussed by Fuller and Benei (2001), Wood (1984), and Frankel and Rao (1989). Tamil nationalism has depoliticized distinctions between Shudra *jatis* by solidifying distinctions between *varnas*.
33. Wyatt (2004).
34. Sivathambi (1995), p. 20.
35. Pandian (1996).
36. Brass (1994), p. 131.
37. Sastri (1964), p. 30.
38. See Dumont (1971) for a critique of Aryan and Dravidian distinctions.
39. Béteille (1996), p. 77.
40. Dickey (1993).
41. Barnett (1976), p. 83.
42. This indicates that OBCs were the main source of DMK support.

43. Brass (1994), p. 249.
44. Subramanian (1999), p. 75.
45. Harriss (1991), p. 10. In addition, he had a number of fan clubs that became a source of political support and a voting base. Dickey (1993).
46. Cantor Associates et al. (1974).
47. Balachander (1989).
48. Narayanan (1996).
49. Harriss-White (2004).
50. Heaver (2002), p. 17.
51. Ramachandran quoted in Harriss (1986), p. 16.
52. Swaminathan et al. (2004).
53. Harriss-White (2004), pp. 52–3.
54. Drèze and Goyal (2003).
55. See Thorat and Lee (2005).
56. Ibid.
57. Zaidi (2005).
58. Venkatasubramanian (2004).
59. Harriss-White (2004).
60. DPT is the Diphtheria, Pertussis, and Tetanus vaccine, BCG is the Bacillus of Calmette and Guerin (TB Vaccine), and OPV is the Oral Polio Vaccine.
61. Young (1996) states that a recent review of nearly 30 nutritional impact studies confirms that the ICDS programme has had a positive impact on children under 6.
62. Das Gupta et al. (2005) and Measham and Chatterjee (1999).
63. There are tense relations between the central and state government. See Brass (1994), ch. 2.
64. Kapur et al. (1997), pp. 59–60.
65. Lumsdaine (1993), p. 215.
66. Kapur et al. (1997), p. 9.
67. Woods (2002), p. 963.
68. Ibid.
69. Woods (2002), p. 953.
70. Woods (2000).
71. All the information in the following two paragraphs comes from Woods (2002).
72. US Treasury (1998) cited in Woods (2002), p. 959.
73. World Bank (2000).
74. World Bank Articles of Agreement IV, Section 10.
75. Krueger (1998).
76. The Bank currently has a staff of over 10,000. Roughly half remain as lifelong staff while the other half return to their country of origin especially to Ministries of Finance.

77. Gavin and Rodrik (1995), p. 332.
78. Ayres (1983), p. 1.
79. The idea that growth was the solution to underdevelopment was universally shared. However, there was disagreement on how far the state should be involved. This caused tension in the 1970s between the World Bank mission in India and Indira Gandhi. A former Bank Executive Director noted that Indira resented the Bank's presence in India.
80. Ayres (1983), p. 3.
81. Myrdal (1968).
82. Frances Stewart was one of the first advocates of this approach. Stewart (1985).
83. Finnemore (1997), p. 204.
84. Schechter (1988).
85. Ayres (1983), p. 6.
86. It has been noted that given McNamara's goal to increase lending dramatically, and the slow pace at which projects were being proposed and prepared by recipient governments the Bank started to get involved in preparation to speed things up.
87. Ibid. p. 115.
88. Finnemore (1997), p. 213.
89. Ayres (1983), p. 24.
90. McNamara (1977).
91. Crane and Finkle (1981).
92. Ibid.
93. Ayres (1983), p. 233.
94. Ibid. p. 234.
95. Ibid. p. 43.
96. Ibid. p. 251.
97. Ayres (1983), p. 90.
98. Clausen (1982), p. 23.
99. Berg (1987), p. 4.
100. Kamath (1992).
101. Mason and Asher (1973), pp. 675, 681–2.
102. OED (1995), p. 1.
103. Ibid.
104. Heaver (2002), p. 9.
105. A taluk is a sub-division of a district and is divided into blocks.
106. OED (1995), p. 4.

3

Understanding Hunger

In each social system, human suffering is explained in a way that reinforces the controls.

Mary Douglas[1]

This chapter examines how hunger is understood by the nutrition team of the World Bank. In particular, it focuses on the biomedical influence on the Bank's approach to undernutrition in TINP. For those unfamiliar with the system, it starts by outlining certain tenets of biomedicine, before examining the role of biomedicine in the World Bank. Within biomedicine, hunger is conceptualized as a disease, and this representation affects the particular policies prescribed. As this chapter will demonstrate, how hunger is conceptualized crucially affects the way in which strategies to address it are designed.

Tenets of Biomedicine

Biomedicine has different strands and can vary according to medical institution, country, and even individual. However, it can also be viewed as a single hegemonic system with certain fundamental presuppositions worldwide. Based on his research at Harvard Medical School, Byron Good notes that medical students are trained in five biomedical tenets.[2] First, diseases and physiological processes are 'external categories' of universal reference. Second, diseases are fundamentally, even exclusively, biological. Third, biomedicine focuses on the visual, thus physicians must 'think anatomically'. Fourth, physicians must focus on the individual. Fifth, medicine is the most technically efficient health instrument. Bryan Turner adds a sixth tenet of Cartesian dualism: biomedicine divides the individual into the mind and the body with the causal mechanism being located in the latter half.[3]

Expanding on the second and third tenets, Arthur Kleinman describes biomedicine as a 'radically materialist' pursuit of the biological mechanism of disease.[4] In the biomedical framework, disease is an 'it', an independent diagnostic entity resulting from an alteration in biological structure and functioning. Using the example of pain, Kleinman notes that chronic pain is not legitimized in our society because biomedicine cannot correlate it with physiological lesions or biochemical/mechanical processes. Although pain is real to the sufferer, it cannot be objectively verified by biomedicine or visibly located.[5] Since chronic pain is tied up in personal perception and social influence, this phenomenon challenges biomedical knowledge that there is objective truth apart from subjective experience. The biomedical reliance on the visual can be correlated with the rise of technology, such as electrocardiography, in the twentieth century.[6] Illness thus became a physical event to be detected by tools placed physically on the body and the patient's illness narrative and subjective experience diminished in importance to the physical. Biomedicine has become the technical quest for symptoms. Extending this to medical professionals, it has been argued that doctors have lost human touch because of the excessive reliance on technical fixes over the awareness of the patient as a person.[7]

Concentrating only on the fourth tenet, Margaret Lock and Deborah Gordon emphasize that the biomedical models of disease causation, by focusing attention on the neutral terrain of the physical body, serve to depoliticize the medical encounter.[8] Biomedicine serves a functional role in society by extracting the individual from a social and cultural context. This medicalization, Turner notes, functions as an institutional form of social control for the management of deviance and disorder in social groups.[9] Medical professionals, mainly doctors, have legitimate domination of the categorization of normality and deviance.

The Bank and the Biomedical Approach

Within the Bank's Health, Nutrition, and Population sector, biomedicine holds a prominent position. This is evident in the medical background of Health, Nutrition, and Population staff and the close partnership of the sector with the WHO. The Bank's *Nutrition Toolkit*, which aims 'to

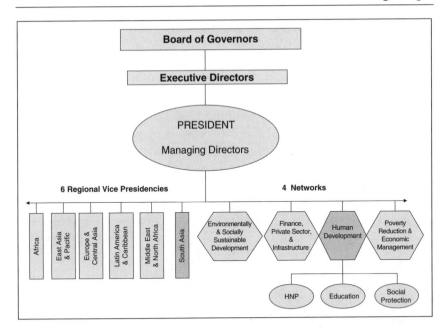

Figure 3.1. Bank organization, 1997 (World Bank human development network 1997)

help World Bank staff design and supervise effective and feasible nutrition projects', is also based on biomedical tenets and will be discussed in the next section.[10] The Bank's Health, Nutrition, and Population sector is located in the Human Development Network and runs parallel to the regional vice presidencies (Figure 3.1). All of the networks are located both within the main Bank office in Washington, DC and also within each of the regional vice presidencies. Within the South Asia region, there are eight country units, each containing six sector units and three service units (Figure 3.2). The India country office is entirely organized into sector and service units (Figure 3.3).

Despite being the largest financier of nutrition initiatives in the world, the Bank has very few staff working on this topic. The main architects and promoters of nutrition during the TINP-era (1980s–1990s) were Alan Berg (US), James Greene (US), and Anthony Measham (UK). In the past few years, a handful of other Bank staff have been directly involved. As of 2004, the Health, Nutrition, and Population sector's nutrition budget was cut, resulting in only one position for nutrition.[11]

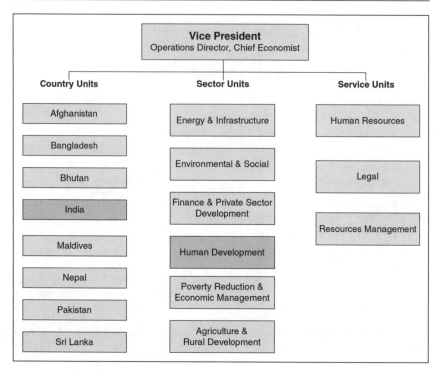

Figure 3.2. Regional management, 1997

Source: (World Bank 2005*b*)

Since 1987, the Health, Nutrition, and Population sector has been located in the Human Development Vice-Presidency. As of 2006, 86 individuals were employed in the South Asia Human Development Sector. Out of that, 25 were based in New Delhi while 40 were based in Washington, DC. The network was primarily composed of economists (20), programme/research assistants (24), consultants (12), and public health specialists (9). There was one social scientist in the network who worked mainly on resettlement issues. As of September 2005, there was no anthropologist located in the New Delhi Health, Nutrition, and Population office.

As demonstrated by the Bank's organization and composition, economists are highly influential in project design and process in all sectors. For example, it has been noted that in the creation of the environmental division, the Bank merely instituted 'a recycling programme' that turned economists into environmental specialists.[12] Although the Bank has been more cautious in the Health, Nutrition, and Population sector to include

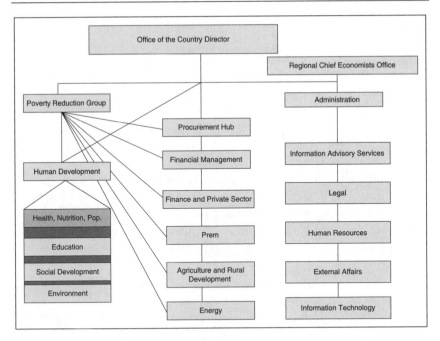

Figure 3.3. India country office organization, 1997 (PREM: poverty reduction and economic management)

Source: (World Bank 2005*b*)

medical professionals, economic principles still form the basis of research and project design. Almost all the public health specialists have obtained a medical degree (D.M. or M.D.) and often also have a masters in public health (M.P.H.). Leadership of the New Delhi Health, Nutrition, and Population sector is usually undertaken by an economist or a medical doctor. In addition, there is a close working relationship and arguably a 'revolving-door' between the World Health Organization (WHO) and the World Bank.

For those unfamiliar with the institution, the WHO was created as a UN agency in 1948 with the objective to aid all peoples in the attainment of health, defined at that time as the absence of disease.[13] It represents itself as a technical agency which takes an empirical and functional position to health.[14] Its recognized strength lies in its biomedical knowledge, its scientific knowledge base, its surveillance and normative regulations, and its data collection.[15] Although the definition of health has been expanded to 'a state of complete physical, mental, and social well-being',[16] the terms health care and medical care are still used interchangeably thus representing the ideology that medicine is the key to health.[17]

The World Bank and the WHO are close partners in the Health, Nutrition, and Population sector. Two forms of official collaboration have been agreed upon. The first is country-level collaboration in which WHO technical expertise is employed to improve the design, supervision, and evaluation of Bank-supported projects. The second is global collaboration in which the WHO and the Bank join together to advance international understandings of Health, Nutrition, and Population issues.[18]

The relationship between the WHO and the Bank has been an uncomfortable one.[19] As Edward Mason and Robert Ascher note, the Bank has a tendency to 'become a partner of various agencies without enabling those agencies to feel that they are full and equal partners of the Bank'.[20] As Callisto Madavo, the Bank's Vice President for Africa, points out,

We have also been a relatively arrogant institution; we thought we knew it all. We would go to countries with our solutions already formulated and it was simply a question of putting them on the table and getting people to buy in. We did not encourage partnerships.[21]

The WHO and the Bank first started collaborating in 1972 when the Bank invited the WHO to provide technical experts for population control project preparation missions. However, the two agencies found it difficult to agree on the role of these experts as well as which agency should provide technical assistance for administration and training.[22] In 1973, a 'memorandum of understanding' was agreed upon in which the Bank undertook to consult the WHO in preparing population projects and to respect the WHO's judgement on health structures and needs. The collaboration on population programmes was followed by partnerships for nutrition and health components of projects.[23]

Adding to the difficulty of the partnership has been the Bank's dominance in the health field, which overlaps with the activities of the WHO. With McNamara's arrival at the Bank, the Bank's involvement in health grew dramatically. In 1980, annual lending in Health, Nutrition, and Population was US$500 million and accounted for 1 per cent of the Bank's total lending. By 1996, lending had reached US$2.4 billion and accounted for 11 per cent of the Bank's total commitments. During this period, WHO's regular budget was roughly US$400 million per year, with another US$400 million provided for in extra budgetary resources (Figure 3.4).

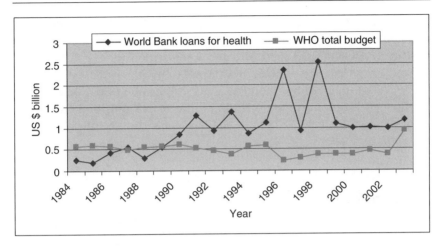

Figure 3.4. World Bank and WHO lending (Hufner 2004; World Bank 2004)

In addition to its financial resources, the Bank has access to senior decision-makers in Ministries of Planning and Finance, while the WHO's influence is confined to the less powerful Ministries of Health. By the beginning of the 1990s, the WHO was seen by many donor governments as weak and overly bureaucratic, which has resulted in reduced funding.[24] As the Bank (and the Bill and Melinda Gates Foundation) replace the WHO as the leading health institutions, the WHO's strength remains its unique technical and biomedical expertise in specific health areas. The resulting partnership with the Bank is one in which the WHO lends technical expertise on topics such as micronutrients and growth standards while the Bank remains the dominant player in the health arena. As one senior economist at the Bank said,

The bank is different from the WHO because WHO is essentially a gentlemen's club for the health people. That's how health ministries look at WHO. It's a clubby atmosphere, and there's no real hard business. The bank is into hard business. When things get tough for a country, we get a little bit brutal, because we say 'look this is gonna be like this, you've gotta do these five things', and WHO can't do that. The bank's relationship is with ministries of finance and planning so it's a very different sort of relationship.[25]

The WHO and the Bank also have informal partnerships in the form of the 'revolving door'. Many of the Bank's Health, Nutrition, and Population staff have worked at the WHO, and vice versa. For example, the current WHO representative to India spent over 16 years at the Bank.

He received his M.D. from the University of Bourdeaux and his M.P.H. in epidemiology from the University of Michigan. He then was a Lead Public Health Specialist at the World Bank from 1987 to 2003.

Due to the close relationship between the two agencies, the expertise of the WHO, namely the biomedical model, has become dominant in the understanding of undernutrition by the Bank's nutrition team. The biomedical influence is evident in the Bank's flagship technical product, the *Nutrition Toolkit*.

Nutrition Toolkit

The *Nutrition Toolkit* is the World Bank's watershed nutrition technical product. It was created by the Washington, DC Health, Nutrition, and Population staff and consultants and aims 'to help World Bank staff design and supervise effective and feasible nutrition projects and project components'.[26] The toolkit currently consists of 12 tools (Table 3.1).

As discussed earlier, one of the tenets of biomedicine is that disease is an autonomous entity that is physically located in the body. Since the body is constructed by biomedicine to be universally the same organic entity, undernutrition in one country is identical to undernutrition in any other country.

These assumptions are evident in the creation of a toolkit that can be used in any developing country to 'fix' the diseased body. The use of the word 'tool' results in a metaphor of a mechanic fixing a car or a machine.

Table 3.1. World Bank *Nutrition Toolkit*[a]

1. Project design	Incorporating nutrition into project design
2. Basic facts	Nuts and bolts of nutrition
3. Economic analysis	Economic analysis of nutrition projects
4. Growth promotion	Promoting the growth of children: what works
5. Food supplementation	Food supplementation for women and young children
6. Food stamps	Food stamps and related nutritional safety nets
7. Early childhood development	Nutrition in early childhood development programs
8. Monitoring and evaluation	Tools to measure performance of nutrition programs
9. Nutrition communication	Using communication to improve nutrition
10. School nutrition	Nutrition for school-age children
11. Food and nutrition policy	Food and nutrition policy
12. Management and supervision	Strategy for project success

[a] Tools 7, 11, and 12 are not available yet. They are still being planned and have yet to be piloted.

In the case of undernutrition, it is Western, advanced biomedicine healing the body and technical, scientific knowledge educating the traditional mind. 'Tool' also represents the excessive reliance on objective and neutral technology, which can be imported into any country. 'Tool' can also refer to a method of surveillance and regulation by the state to eliminate disease and deviance.

The strength of the *Nutrition Toolkit*, as perceived by the Bank, is that it can be used in any regional or country office. Within the Bank, staff rotate quickly with usual terms lasting 2–3 years, so that within a period of 10 years, a staff member could have worked in over 3 countries. For example, for the past few years, Michael Roberts has been the main person in charge of the Bank's work in nutrition in South Asia. However, his doctoral research and work at the World Bank for many years was on Latin America. When I enquired what caused his switch from Latin America to South Asia, he noted that it is expected in the Bank that staff gain experience working in many different parts of the world. For the past few years, he has been visiting India roughly five times a year for a week or so. His time in India is split between the New Delhi Bank office and the Government of India Ministries.

If needed, a local expert provides input to ensure that projects will work in the local circumstances. The past decade has seen this idea packaged as 'participatory rural appraisal' (PRA), which the Bank defines as 'participatory approaches and methods that emphasize local knowledge and enable local people to make their own appraisal, analysis, and plans'.[27] It should be noted that for many Bank staff members and many in the development community, the term 'participation' means partnership with client governments, not the project beneficiaries.

Measuring Hunger

How is hunger measured by the Bank? Drawing on biomedicine, which essentializes the body as an invariant organic entity[28], hunger and malnutrition are defined as problems of the body. To determine whether a child is hungry, two types of analysis are performed in relation to the body: input-based analysis and output-based analysis. In input-based analysis, dietary intake is used for nutritional assessment. The perceived nutritional need of an individual is based on the population constructs:

Recommended Dietary Allowances (RDA), Recommended Dietary Intake (RDI), Reference Nutrient Intake, or Estimated Average Requirement (EAR). These are defined as 'the nutrient recommendations by age and gender for meeting the needs of almost all healthy individuals in a population group'.[29] These constructs indicate the probability that an individual or household is adequately nourished. The Food and Agricultural Organisation provides reference approximations of per capita requirements. In 1946, this assessment involved national averages, but it has now moved to the average intake per person in a household.[30]

Although these measures can be useful, it is important to distinguish between energy requirements and the self-described nutritional need of an individual. Energy requirements are physiologically determined and include a number of value judgements discussed by Simon Maxwell.[31] Energy requirements are a population construct determined by actual measurements of energy expenditure from a sample of individuals belonging to a specific group based on age, gender, and other factors.[32] These measurements are used to construct a normal distribution with the median reflecting the average requirement for energy for a certain group, referred to as the Estimated Average Requirement. Thus, 50 per cent of individuals in the population belonging to this group will have requirements above, and 50 per cent will fall below the Estimated Average Requirement for energy. While the Estimated Average Requirement has become more specific by including work load through the construct Physical Activity Load (PAL), there are still several sources of discrepancies, such as the selection of physiological criteria used to define nutrient adequacy, the selective use of race/ethnicity, and the exclusion of lifestyle (e.g. vegan) and genetic factors. Other criticisms of Estimated Average Requirement include that it does not allow for illness or stresses in life, or possible interactions that involve nutrients and dietary components because these interactions and their subsequent effect on requirements cannot be adequately quantified.[33]

As the construct EAR demonstrates, measuring intake has three main shortcomings. The first difficulty is that in most cases it does not provide an accurate qualitative or quantitative measure of the adequacy of the diet. For example, the major dietary item, for example, cassava, could be lacking an important nutrient or the diet could be adequate in calories but highly deficient in protein. This difficulty is not present in South Asia where undernutrition is more a problem of lack of energy, not inadequate protein intake.[34] A diet sufficient in energy intake will almost always satisfy the protein requirement. However, micronutrient deficiencies in iron and vitamin A, which can lead to anaemia and blindness, respectively, are prevalent.

The second difficulty is that if dietary surveys are carried out at the household level, individuals are not reliable in their reporting of their own food intake or food intake of other members of the household. Social desirability, the tendency to respond in such a way as to avoid criticism, and social approval, the tendency to seek praise, are two sources of bias that occur in these assessments.[35]

In my research, men and women of the same household often reported different food consumption. For example, Radha is a young woman who works as a domestic cleaner during the day. Her husband, Prakasthan, has a mobile shopping cart with which he transports vegetables from the market to the rural outskirts of the city. When I asked her if he drinks alcohol, she said that he did not. However, when I asked him, he responded that he drinks about twice a day, in the afternoon and in the evening. When I returned to her home to continue this conversation on diet, she noted that she was ashamed of his drinking and does not want the neighbours to think badly of her. In addition, there is the issue of who speaks on behalf of the family. In many homes that I visited, if the household head (often a man) was present, he was the only one who would talk to me. The husbands might present themselves in a favourable light, or might exaggerate destitution to obtain favours. Once they realized that I was not working for the government, many of them would lose interest.

The third difficulty with input-based analysis arises when average intake is calculated at the household level, and the caloric intake of children is indirectly derived through the application of coefficients based on the assumption that intrafamilial distribution of food conforms to actual physiological need.[36] In South Asia, distribution is rooted in economic, social, and cultural patterns which dictate allocation according to variables such as gender, age, and birth order, and not necessarily physiological need.[37]

As a result of the problematic nature of input-based analysis, the World Bank has primarily relied on output-based analysis, based on comparing measurements of anthropometric indicators with a specified reference in order to assess nutritional status.[38] Anthropometry as an epidemiological tool relies on biomedical and biological anthropological notions of the body and growth. The next section will explore the influence of biomedicine on the World Bank approach to nutrition in the area of anthropometry.

Anthropometry

Anthropometry is primarily used for the assessment of nutritional status in children.[39] Anthropometry is defined as the study and technique of human body measurement and has become the most commonly used method for nutritional status assessment. However, the use of anthropometry to examine growth and nutrition is relatively quite recent. Its first recorded use was in a growth study of newborns in 1753 by J. Roederer. Throughout the nineteenth century, there was a steady increase in anthropometric studies. During this period, standardization of measurement was the main concern.[40] By the twentieth century, Sherwood Washburn (1911–2000) had moved anthropometry towards the functional approach which focused on differences in size in certain organs and parts of the body. During this time, anthropometry was viewed as 'essential, inborn, and racial' and environmental factors were overlooked.[41] A number of studies in the twentieth century have linked anthropometry to mortality and morbidity.[42]

It is now argued that for child nutritional status, body size is likely the best physical indicator of his or her health and well-being.[43] It is worth noting the potential sources of variation for an anthropometric phenotype measured at a given age,[44] especially nutrition–infection interactions (Figure 3.5). In energy deficiency nutritional stunting, the faltering of weight is followed by the faltering in height.[45] Nutritional stunting occurs for several reasons. First, insufficient energy, either due to insufficient utilization of calories or insufficient intake, is available for maximal growth. Second, with limited energy utilization or intake, growth rates decrease to allow for increased physical activity with the development of locomotor function and exploratory behaviour. Third, along with energy deficiency, there is most likely protein deficiency or micronutrient deficiencies in zinc, calcium, or one of the essential vitamins which stunt growth.

There are various ways of evaluating child nutritional status using the measures of height, weight, and age (Table 3.2).[46] The World Bank and most international health organizations define child undernutrition as the extent to which a child falls short of standards for the indicator weight-for-age.[47]

The first measure of child nutritional status is height-for-age. It has been proposed that this index signifies chronic undernutrition.[48] A child whose height is less than two standard deviations below the mean height-for-age

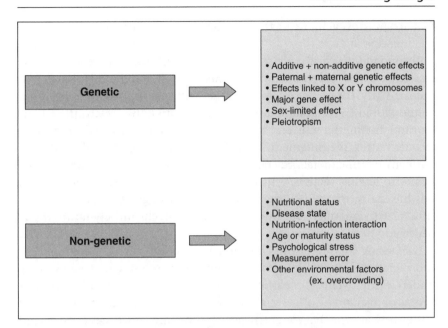

Figure 3.5. Factors influencing anthropometric phenotype (Ulijaszek 1997)

value is referred to as stunted.[49] Height-for-age is particularly useful when serial measurements are made, as in clinics for children under 5 years of age. However, this measurement is rarely used in health centres in developing countries for preschool children since it is less sensitive to acute dietary deprivation and a deficit in length takes time to develop. In addition, height is expensive to measure because of the dearth of cheap, accurate, rugged apparatus available commercially.[50] Finally, accuracy

Table 3.2. Usefulness of weight and height measures relative to reference data[a] (1 indicates best indicator, 4 indicates least useful indicator)

	Weight-for-age	Height-for-age	Weight-for-height
Usefulness in populations where age is unknown or inaccurate	4	4	1
Usefulness in identifying wasted children	3	4	1
Usefulness in identifying stunted children	2	1	4
Sensitivity to weight change over short time frame	2	4	1

[a] Ulijaszek (1997) and Gorstein et al. (1994).

67

may be hard to achieve in the measurement of young children if they are uncooperative.[51]

The second measure is weight-for-height. This index has been proposed to signify acute undernutrition.[52] A child whose weight is less than two standard deviations below the mean weight-for-height is referred to as being wasted.[53] In situations where age is unknown, such as in parts of rural India, the use of this indicator is particularly advantageous. However, this measurement is problematic because it is aligned with the controversial 'small but healthy' hypothesis which will be discussed in the following section.[54] In brief, nutritional stunting occurs in both height and weight which means that a child might be smaller overall, thus healthy by weight-for-height standards, yet chronically nutritionally deprived.

The third measure is weight-for-age. A child whose weight is less than 75 per cent of the median weight-for-age is referred to as being underweight.[55] This is a particularly useful indicator for children under 1 year of age and also in situations where length measurements are not performed accurately. Weight measurements are much easier to record due to the simplicity of using a scale as well as the availability of weighing slings and other devices.[56] As mentioned previously, this indicator is now used by the World Bank and the WHO to determine the extent of under-nutrition in communities. The median weight-for-age value is obtained using international references such as the National Centre for Health Statistics (NCHS 1977). Once a 'standard' or reference value is obtained, a scale, such as that of Gomez, is used as an interpretative instrument. The Gomez scale divides undernutrition into three grades that of mild (90–75%), moderate (75–60%), and severe (below 60%) depending on the child's weight-for-age compared to the standard. However, many, including C. Gopalan, have criticized the use of the scale, because it cannot accurately assess the acuteness of nutritional deprivation since age is not considered.[57] For example, an infant achieving 60 per cent of his or her weight-for-age is likely to be more nutritionally deficient than a 5-year old achieving the same percentage because the younger child would have suffered more intense nutritional deprivation over a shorter period. However, the Gomez scale would classify both children in the same way. A solution offered by Waterlow to account for age examines undernutrition as a deviation in terms of standard deviation units, or z-scores (Table 3.3). Thus, almost universally, underweight refers to a child whose weight-for-age is below two standard deviations of the median, whatever the median is determined to be.

Table 3.3. Classification of malnutrition by prevalence of low weight-for-age[a]

Degree of malnutrition	Prevalence of underweight (% of children younger than 60 months, below −2 z-scores)
Low	<10
Medium	10–19
High	20–29
Very high	>30

[a] WHO Expert Committee (1995), cited in Elder and Kiess (2004), p. 18.

The World Bank integrates anthropometry into the design of nutrition projects such as TINP. A Bank report lists the advantages of anthropometry as being non-invasive and relatively economical to obtain, objective, and comprehensible to communities at large.[58] In addition, the practice of anthropometry produces data that can be graded numerically. Finally, anthropometric measurements can identify individuals in a population who are 'at risk' through the process of growth monitoring.

The Bank report also lists the disadvantages of anthropometry. These include the significant potential for measurement inaccuracies, the need for precise age data in children for the use of indicators, limited diagnostic relevance, and finally the ongoing debate over the selection of appropriate reference data and cut-off points to determine conditions of 'abnormality'.[59]

There are several issues that emerge from the use of anthropometry. One aspect is the subjective experience of hunger and the cross-cultural definitions of hunger. It could be argued that anthropometry implies a view of the body that is simply a physical entity to be measured, weighed, and analysed. In several languages, to explain that one is hungry, phrases are used which can be translated as 'becoming hungry'. Hunger is an embodied process. Second, anthropometry does not provide a direct indicator of micronutrient deficiencies since vitamin and mineral deficiencies do not necessarily make an individual look underweight. Although the child might be suffering through symptoms such as a general sense of malaise or inability to function efficiently, he or she may not be determined as being undernourished from anthropometric measurements.

In addition, anthropometry is often portrayed, by the Bank and others, as objective and technical, especially since numbers are considered apolitical. However, two facets of anthropometry, measurement and inter-pretation, are particularly subjective. Furthermore, the act of measurement can be viewed as a political act since it is a manifestation of the power of the health professional over the body of the patient. Resistance to this power can come in the form of women refusing to have their children weighed or choosing not to attend the community health centres. For example, a community worker noted that many villagers refused to allow their children's weight to be measured. This was a result of many of them fearing that measuring weight and pronouncing a child healthy would attract the evil eye.[60] The villagers asked the worker, 'Why do you weigh the children?' The villagers could not understand why weighing was so important. When the workers go out into the community to do home visits, they reported that people often refused to cooperate with them. In other situations, weighing is seen as an obstacle to be overcome before the child is seen by a nurse or physician at a health centre or hospital.[61]

Interpreting Measurements of Undernutrition

One could argue that the setting of growth standards or references is the most important part of anthropometry. A reference population is one used as a yardstick for internal comparison of a group or population.[62] John Waterlow has identified seven minimal criteria for an anthropometric reference (Table 3.4).

There has been much discussion, and controversy, in nutritional anthropology on whether there should be a fixed standard or variability within the standard due to adaptation and other evolutionary mechanisms.[63] This difference arises from two contradictory theories on

Table 3.4. Minimal criteria for anthropometric reference[a]

1. Population should be well-nourished
2. Each age/sex group of the sample should contain at least 200 individuals
3. Sample should be cross-sectional
4. Sampling procedures should be optimal
5. Sampling procedures should be defined and reproducible
6. Measurements should include all variables used in nutritional evaluation
7. Raw data and smoothing procedures should be available

[a] Waterlow et al. (1977).

human nutrition. The fixed anthropometric standard relies upon the theory that a person's long-term nutritional requirements are predetermined and that the variation in requirements often observed across similar people is explained largely by differences in their innate physiological characteristics. The variability within the standard arises from the theory that, within a wide range, a reduced nutrient intake triggers an auto-regulatory mechanism which permits the individual to adapt to the reduction in a costless manner.[64] The second theory has been largely discounted in the 1990s but has emerged again as the 'Indian paradox' in the twenty-first century.

Prior to 1985, the first theory on fixed physiological requirements was traditionally advocated by the Food and Agricultural Organisation (FAO), and used by the World Bank and the WHO. In 1973, the FAO set the 'reference man' nutritional requirements at 3,000 kcal/day with 2,600 kcal/day allocated to maintenance and 400 kcal/day allocated to 'moderate activity'.[65] The reference man is an adult male aged 20–39 years, weighing 65 kg and living in an environment of 10 °C. The FAO varied the requirements for different populations based on variance in innate physiology and in environmental conditions. In comparison to the nutritional requirements of 3,000 kcal/day for the reference man, the FAO set the 'Indian man' nutritional requirement at 2,800 kcal/day. The lower value was based on the understanding that an Indian man, on average, weighed less and lived in an ambient climate of 25 °C. However, the FAO nutritional assessment did not take into account extremely strenuous labour which, if included, would increase the requirements of the Indian reference man.[66] For many years, the FAO has used fixed nutritional requirements which vary among populations.

However, in 1985, the FAO, the WHO, and the United Nations University convened to take account of the capacity of man to adapt to different nutritional and environmental conditions.[67] They created new energy requirement tables reflecting the wide range in both body size and patterns of physical activity among individuals as well as the additional energy needs for compensatory growth in malnourished children and for recovery from infection. Although they recognized that requirement estimates relate more closely to individuals than to populations, they did not support the adaptation hypothesis discussed in the following paragraph. Rather they created energy tables on what is considered desirable to achieve, roughly based on actual measurements of individual requirements.[68]

The adaptation hypothesis was advocated by P. V. Sukhatme and David Seckler in the 1980s. Sukhatme argued that an individual's requirement for any day or period is not fixed, but dynamic, adapting itself to intake over a fixed range from 60 to 140 per cent of the average dietary allowance.[69] This hypothesis, originally proposed by him, is commonly referred to as 'small but healthy'. It states that when faced with nutritional constraint, the child's body initiates a process of adaptation by reducing its growth. This stunting allows the child to better cope with the nutritional constraints since small body size leads to lower energy requirements. Controversy has surrounded this argument. Most contentious was Sukhatme's claim that adaptation resulting in the modification of nutritional requirements occurs without detriment to child well-being. Within this framework, he lowered the reference 'Indian man' nutritional requirements to 2,300 kcal/day, 500 kcal/day less than that of the FAO.[70]

Like Sukhatme, Seckler also advocated the 'small but healthy hypothesis'. He outlined two theories on growth reflective of the aforementioned theories on nutritional requirements.[71] The first is the 'Deprivation Theory of Growth' where it is assumed that every individual is born with a given, genetically determined, potential growth curve. According to this, the ideal standard against which to compare communities is the growth curve of well-nourished children.[72] Any growth significantly below this curve indicates undernutrition and/or ill health. The assumptions are that there is no difference in the genetic potential of different populations and that anything less than achievement of full genetic potential signifies inadequate nutrition. Seckler discounts this theory in favour of his second theory of growth, the 'Homeostatic Theory'.[73]

The 'Homeostatic Theory of Growth' assumes that there is a range of adaptive growth in response to environmental influences. To support this theory, Seckler made three claims. First, that the regulation of the rate of growth is likely an important defence mechanism against functional impairments due to caloric deficiency, quite similar to Sukhatme's claim of small body size without detriment to well-being. Second, he believed that international standards, such as the NCHS (1977), yield gross overestimates of the incidence of undernutrition in nations such as India by overestimating energy and growth requirements. Third, indigenous standards should be used so that undernutrition is defined as the minimum size below which functional impairments are likely to occur. Seckler continued this argument, adding that the majority of individuals in the developing world have a body size adapted to local conditions, so he believed they should not be considered undernourished. He stated that Indians have a small body size due to their environmental circumstances and that from an ecological viewpoint, smallness has advantages.[74] Using these three claims as validation, Seckler concluded that 80–90 per cent of those conventionally defined as underweight are in fact 'small but healthy' people.

This argument has been specifically applied to female size in the cultural context of preferential feeding of males. Female smallness is interpreted to reflect generations of selection for females who can eat and survive on less than males.[75] Seckler also emphasized that females, due to their smaller size vis-à-vis males, have lower energy needs. Based on this assumption, he argued that female members of a typical Indian household appear to be slightly better off than the males using a revised lower energy requirement estimate.[76] However, putting in doubt Seckler's argument is the fact that this deprivation results in reduced longevity and quality of life thus bringing into doubt the gender adaptation hypothesis.[77] Female child malnutrition is arguably the main factor behind excessive female child mortality rates, especially in the under 5 age group.[78]

Due to its contentious nature, Sukhatme and Seckler's 'small but healthy' hypothesis evoked a torrent of criticism. Indeed, opponents have provided strong evidence to discount their claims. Sven Wilson states that even though genetic influences are important determinants of individual variation in height, differences in average height across populations are almost entirely the product of environmental influences, not genetics.[79] Studies conducted in northern India, such as those of S. Ghosh and N. Banik, and Sri Lanka and Nepal indicate that preschool children from elite subgroups are anthropometrically similar to the NCHS (1977) reference population and are both heavier and taller than less-advantaged children.[80] R. S. Osmani states that although adaptation is designed to avoid some adverse consequences, such as mortality, it does not follow that it has no adverse effects of its own.[81] The 'small but healthy' hypothesis did not take into account consequences of adaptation such as increased morbidity or lower probability or survival, both widespread in Indian populations.[82] The increased morbidity is in part due to the greater susceptibility to infection as a result of being in a nutritionally fragile state.[83]

The most powerful critique of the 'small but healthy' hypothesis is provided by C. Gopalan, President of the Nutrition Foundation of India, who states that to accept Seckler's views is to 'acquiesce in the preservation of the status-quo in poverty, ill-health, undernutrition and socio-economic deprivation'.[84] Gopalan offers evidence of a study carried out by the National Institute of Nutrition in 1973 that found that in an undernourished community, an additional provision of 310 kcal could bring about significant improvements in nutritional status and a reduction in protein–energy malnutrition. He argues that in nearly all nations, both developed and developing, those of high socio-economic status are larger than their counterparts with low socio-economic status.[85] Although Seckler and Sukhatme defend their modified definition of underweight on the basis of only focusing on the neediest individuals, Gopalan argues that if standards are used to determine the magnitude of the problem, it is perverse to tailor them so that the suffering is reduced to 'manageable' proportions.

Although the 'small but healthy' hypothesis has been rejected, the debate has evolved to discussing the 'Indian paradox' presented by David Pelletier.[86] The Indian paradox refers to the enigma that South Asian countries have high rates of low weight-for-age, yet mortality is lower than expected. Pelletier et al. put forth the hypothesis that the effect of body size on mortality varies according to the cause. Child size is determined by birth weight, gestational age, food, health, and care. The authors divide the determinants of low birth weight causes into low and high risk. The high-risk causes of low birth weight result in increased child mortality. These include the body mass index (BMI) of the mother, the mother's nutrition and health during pregnancy, and smoking. The lower risk causes of low birth weight include maternal height and birth weight, infant sex, and genetics. Despite India having the highest rates of low birth weight infants, the authors argue that this is a result of low-risk maternal causes, primarily from low maternal stature and low maternal birth weight.[87] Thus, in South Asia, lower risk causes of low birth weight result in a weaker relation between child smallness and child mortality.

The above discussion indicates the politics of nutritional assessment. The decision to choose a specific standard in order to determine the extent of malnutrition or to determine cut-off points for different grades of malnutrition is a pragmatic and often political act.

Anthropometry as a Screening Mechanism

A key component of the World Bank's efforts in the nutrition sector has been growth monitoring. It is commonly viewed by the nutrition team at the Bank that this is the 'key to success' for nutrition programmes.[88]

Growth monitoring refers to weighing a child and graphing the weight on a chart (weight-for-age) such as the 'Road to Health' chart. The child's growth over a period of months is compared to the WHO growth standard, the NCHS (1977) growth curves. A former nutritionist at the Bank noted,

I think the value of growth monitoring is that it tells us whether or not a child is growing well, and it seems to me that whether a child is growing well is fundamental for trying to understand whether the child is eating well, whether there may be some disease, whether there's some other issues. So it begins a discussion between the mother and the worker around the well-being of this child.

At the individual level, anthropometry is used to assess nutritional well-being and to screen for those in need of nutrition intervention programmes. The Bank's rationale for stressing the importance of growth monitoring is that the chart makes visible to mothers the health status of their child. Visible changes in weight across periods of months and years can be used to 'reinforce positive practices, motivate changes in harmful ones, reward and sustain new behaviours, and target nutrition and health advice and serves at the individual, community and program levels'.[89] Once a child is diagnosed as being 'at risk', the main Bank intervention is to promote behavioural change through nutrition education for mothers.

Conceptualizing Hunger

Before examining the policy prescriptions to address hunger, it is important to understand how hunger is conceptualized by the nutrition team of the Bank. As the previous sections have argued, undernutrition is viewed as a problem of the body. But to probe even further, what particular problem of the body is undernutrition? The World Bank has adopted the framework 'malnutrition as disease'. The Bank continually refers to 'curing undernutrition'. For example, James Lovelace, former Director of the Human Development Network, asks 'Will rights cure malnutrition?' In addition, a key paper notes 'Malnutrition is more prevalent than most infectious diseases'[90] thus drawing a comparison between malnutrition and infectious disease.

The Bank nutrition team's conceptualization of malnutrition as a disease enters into policy prescriptions. The Bank's recommended nutrition package notes that the disease must first be identified through growth monitoring of children, which is perceived as a visible, objectively verifiable method of determining if the child is unhealthy.[91] The Bank *Nutrition Toolkit* notes, 'The purpose of growth promotion is to make hidden malnutrition *visible*.'[92] Once the child has been diagnosed, the traditional 'cures' are supplementary feeding (for a short period until growth, the indicator of the disease, is perceived as adequate) and nutrition education on diet for mothers. In regards to the first cure, a World Bank consultant notes, 'The World Bank finances food...only under exceptional circumstances when *food is used like medicine*.'[93] In addition, a malnourished child is seen as an indication of the mother's lack of knowledge on proper diet. Thus, another Bank 'cure' is nutrition education to mothers. The document notes,

The new generation of nutrition communicators' efforts focus on changing key nutritional behaviours incrementally through face-to-face dialogue with mothers and through mass and traditional communications media...[A] modern message might say 'try to give your child two snacks of mango in addition to meals.'[94]

The Bank's India nutrition project, TINP, can be regarded as the manifestation of this particular approach. A World Bank nutrition consultant remarks, 'TINP can be characterized as an educational/medical model, in which malnutrition is seen as a disease; once education and more food have been used to prevent or cure it, the child graduates from the programme.'[95] Thus, the Bank nutrition and TINP model rely heavily on the conceptualization of hunger as a disease to formulate an intervention. This approach locates both the event, undernutrition, and the cause, mother's behaviour, at the level of the individual.

Explaining Hunger

As noted above, the Bank nutrition team identifies poor caring practices of the mother as the underlying cause of malnutrition.[96] This section explores how the Bank nutrition team explains undernutrition specifically by examining the focus on women, and the continual blame put on harmful 'traditional knowledge, attitudes and practices' (referred to as KAP). The work of the Bank in this area relies on the research of the Manoff Group, a consultancy who works closely with the Bank Health, Nutrition, and Population sector on behavioural change aspects of nutrition projects.[97] The Manoff Group created the *Nutrition Toolkit* in conjunction with the Bank. The company's specialization is incorporating health education into nutrition project design. As their website states, 'Manoff projects focus on *behaviour change* at all levels.' This is achieved through educating women about healthy practices.

The Bank nutrition team's emphasis on behavioural change results from the perspective that 'mild and moderate malnutrition can be eliminated or controlled through simple changes in dietary and food hygiene practices that are amenable to change through well-planned and executed behaviour-change strategies'.[98] This framework makes several assumptions. The first is that inappropriate caring practices are a major cause of malnutrition. The second is that inappropriate caring practices are due to carers' knowledge, attitudes, and practices. The third is that households have the capacity to change their behaviour. The fourth assumption is that women are the household decision-makers.

The Bank nutrition team argues that health education must occur at the individual level through nutritional negotiation between a community worker and a mother. Women's participation in group discussion is considered to be not as effective as noted in the Bank *Nutrition Toolkit*.[99] The information to guide nutrition project design is given in Table 3.5. Sample conversations are presented to show how health education can overcome certain barriers (Table 3.6). This information is given as a universal guide to nutrition project design, part of the Bank's *Nutrition Toolkit*. The purpose of this training tool is to aid future Bank staff and borrower government civil servants during the process of nutritional planning.

Three propositions regarding the Bank nutrition team's explanation of hunger are supported by these tables. First, undernutrition is viewed as being caused at the level of the individual, namely the mother, through an 'ignorant mind'. Second, health education is geared only towards women and women are exclusively defined as mothers, such that the target becomes a 'feminised ignorant mind'. Third, the emphasis on traditional beliefs as an obstacle to beneficial Western education further constructs the mind as 'feminised, ignorant and backward' (Table 3.7).

Table 3.6 demonstrates a hypothetical nutrition negotiation between a community health worker and mother taken from the Bank *Nutrition Toolkit*. When the mother states that she is 'too busy' to feed her child, instead of discussing structural factors that constrain a woman's time, the nutrition worker attributes it to her lack of patience. Women not only face a double bind of having to do both public and domestic labour but also face another burden in that they are blamed for not having certain attributes, such as knowledge or patience, to care properly for their

Table 3.5. Typical barriers to selected nutrition behaviours (Toolkit 9: Nutrition communication[a])

Behaviours	Some typical barriers
Exclusive breastfeeding for six months	Mothers' lack of confidence in their ability to produce sufficient quantity and quality of their breast milk to meet baby's needs Traditional beliefs (need for prelacteals, breast milk can pass on illness, etc.) Mothers' belief that they are not producing sufficient milk, often because of their own poor diet
Initiate within one hour of birth	Traditional beliefs on danger of feeding, colostrums, or that 'milk has not come in' Traditional practice of feeding prelacteals
Feed 3 or 4 meals of 150–200 calories each daily. Practice good food hygiene	Lack of information on baby's needs and feasible ways of meeting them Limited or no belief/understanding of germ theory
Feed child and eat some source of Vitamin A in each meal	Some sources may be expensive, not considered appropriate or digestible by young children Availability, particularly seasonally Lack of information on baby's needs and feasible ways of meeting them Monotony, lack of motivation/ideas for new food preparations or combinations
Feed or add calorie or nutrient-dense foods such as oil, mashed nuts or seeds, fruit, vegetables, and animal products	Traditional beliefs about foods that are difficult for baby to digest, etc. Requires some extra time and work Lack of information on baby's needs and feasible ways of meeting them

[a] Adapted from Favin and Griffiths (1999), p. 36.

children. The authors of this text state that this is purely a mother's perception of being too busy and tired rather than real 'busyness'.[100] There are other implicit assumptions in this conversation: the first is that the mother is the only caregiver, the second is that she has the power to take decisions. The role of grandparents, such as mothers-in-law, and of men is neglected.

In addition, in Table 3.6, the mother attributes her lack of knowledge to the traditional belief that rice and beans are too heavy. The problem is located in the category 'culture and behaviour' which promotes harmful practices to the child. The Bank report categorizes this as an attitudinal barrier which it claims is the most important obstacle to overcome in every country, noting that traditional knowledge is 'a sure-fire prescription for protein-energy malnutrition'. Similarly, Table 3.7 demonstrates

Table 3.6. A World Bank hypothetical nutrition negotiation[a] (Toolkit 4: Promoting the growth of children)

Staff: Cory, what do you see in your child's growth line on the chart?

Mother: My Joshi is not doing well. The line is straight.

Staff: Why do you think Joshi hasn't gained weight this past month?

Mother: He eats too little. It is difficult to feed him.

Staff: What is difficult? Has he been sick?

Mother: No. He is fussy. I am too busy.

Staff: I know it takes patience.

Later in the conversation

Staff: It is good that you are still breastfeeding so much. But you can see that Joshi needs more food. You are feeding only twice, not three times. What do you think? Could you feed him in the late afternoon for example?

Mother: Yes, he could have the rice and beans we eat, but *I am afraid it will be too 'heavy' for him.*

Staff: No, at his age, it would be fine.

[a] Griffiths, Dicken, and Favin (1996), p. 47, emphasis added.

the Bank nutrition team's emphasis on women's ignorance attributing it to traditional beliefs, in this case the decision to feed her child gruel and to take her baby to the faith healer.

It is important to keep in mind that this is a hypothetical conversation written by Bank nutrition staff and consultants in Washington, DC. The fact that these examples are not geographically located or from actual ethnographic data further reinforces the point that this is a representation of malnutrition by the Bank, not a depiction of reality. The Bank nutrition team are projecting a version of reality in which scientific knowledge is opposed to ignorance and superstition. The behavioural explanation is privileged. This is not unique but often a pervasive feature of public health policy.

Table 3.7. World Bank example of how to target advice[a]

Cora is the mother of an 8-month-old girl who often has diarrhoea. Cora is not worried about the baby's feeding because she gives her traditional gruel that her own mother fed her. She does not add milk and does not listen to that advice because that is only for city women who are not following the traditional ways. She decides not to come back to the clinic, but to take her baby to the faith healer for charms to prevent diarrhoea.

[a] Berg (1973), p. 25.

Nutrition as Choice?

I return to the question posed at the beginning of this chapter. How is nutrition understood by the Bank nutrition team? During the period when TINP was being designed, undernutrition was defined as 'the pathological condition brought about by inadequacy of one or more of the essential nutrients that the body cannot make but that are necessary for survival, for growth and reproduction, and for the capacity to work, learn and function in society'.[101] Although the concept of nutrition has evolved, remnants of the previous scientific association linger. One nutrition specialist who works closely with the World Bank in New Delhi said,

> I am a nutritionist. I have been trained in biochemistry and physiology. I look at malfunctions in the body, in biochemistry, not at social stuff. I deal with the immediate causes of malnutrition, not the root social problems. That is why you're an anthropologist and I am a nutritionist. You do the social, I do the science.

Undernutrition is framed as a disease located within the body with an organic basis in biochemistry and physiology. The Bank nutrition blueprint and *Nutrition Toolkit* also conceive of the body as an organic, universal entity that experiences the 'disease' of malnutrition in the same way regardless of social, cultural, and environmental factors. Thus, a 'cure' that works in one country, such as India, is viewed to work the same way in a completely different place, such as Brazil.

There are many levels at which malnutrition can be addressed. The particular understanding of undernutrition advocated by the Bank nutrition team examines one of the immediate causes, poor caring practices, and attributes hunger to them. Hunger is conceived to be a matter of choice, attributable to the deviant behaviour of mothers who need to be educated on how to properly raise their children.

Notes

1. Douglas (1996), p. 110.
2. Good (1994), p. 70.
3. Turner (1987), p. 9, see Luhrmann (2000).
4. Kleinman (1988), p. 5.
5. Scarry (1987).
6. Reiser (1993).
7. Eisenberg and Kleinman (1980).

8. Lock (1988) and Gordon (1988).

9. Turner (1987, 1992).

10. http://www.worldbank.org/nutritiontoolkit.

11. Heaver (2006), p. 34.

12. Caufield (1996), p. 181.

13. http://www.who.int.

14. Navarro (1984).

15. Lee et al. (1996).

16. http://www.who.int.

17. Ibid.

18. World Bank Human Development Network (1997).

19. See Abbasi (1999a, 1999c) and Mason and Asher (1973), p. 750.

20. Mason and Asher (1973), p. 750.

21. Quoted in Abbasi (1999c), p. 866, see Abbasi (1999b).

22. Ibid.

23. Buse and Gwin (1998).

24. Godlee (1997).

25. Quoted in Abbasi (1999c), p. 868.

26. http://www.worldbank.org/nutritiontoolkit.

27. http://www.worldbank.org/wbi/sourcebook/sba104.htm, see Mosse (2003) for critique of participatory rural appraisal.

28. Csordas (1994).

29. Quote from Gibson (2005), p. 200, Elder and Kiess (2004), p. xi.

30. Srinivasan (2000).

31. Maxwell (1996), see Pacey and Payne (1985).

32. Gibson (2005), p. 197, for similar discussion on protein requirements, see Bender and Millward (2005).

33. Gibson (2005), p. 197.

34. Ulijaszek and Strickland (1993), p. 27.

35. Gibson (2005), p. 109, see Buzzard and Sievert (1994), Beaton et al. (1997), Briefel et al. (1997), Price et al. (1997), Zhang et al. (2000), Heerstrass et al. (1998), Gregory et al. (1990), and Pryer et al. (1997).

36. Dasgupta and Raj (1990).

37. See Whitehead (1994) and Harriss (1990).

38. Srinivasan (2000) and Wilson (2001).

39. Elder and Kiess (2004), p. 3.

40. Lasker (1994), p. 2.

41. Ibid. p. 4.

42. Chen et al. (1982), Vella et al. (1992), Tomkins et al. (1989), Tomkins (1986), and Martorell and Ho (1984).

43. Ulijaszek (1997).

44. Mascie-Taylor (1991).

45. Ulijaszek and Strickland (1993), p. 127.

46. It should be noted that almost three decades later this paper is still heavily cited and referred to as the landmark paper. Waterlow et al. (1977).
47. Gopalan (1992).
48. Waterlow et al. (1977).
49. Steinhoff et al. (1986).
50. Jelliffe and Jelliffe (1989), p. 303.
51. Gibson (2005), p. 246.
52. Waterlow et al. (1977).
53. Steinhoff et al. (1986).
54. Seckler (1982a, 1982b) and Sukhatme (1982).
55. Waterlow et al. (1977).
56. Gibson (2005), p. 246.
57. Gopalan (1992).
58. Elder and Kiess (2004), p. 4.
59. Ibid.
60. See Gupta (2001).
61. Tomkins (1994).
62. Ulijaszek (1997).
63. Osmani (1992a).
64. Dasgupta and Raj (1990).
65. Ibid.
66. Ibid.
67. FAO/WHO/UNU (1985).
68. Ibid.
69. Sukhatme (1982).
70. Dasgupta and Raj (1990).
71. Seckler (1982a).
72. Osmani (1992b).
73. Seckler (1982a).
74. Seckler (1982b).
75. Messer (1997).
76. Seckler (1982a).
77. Stini (1988).
78. Sen (1990) and Narayanan (1996).
79. Wilson (2001).
80. Ghosh (1981), Banik et al. (1972), and Brink et al. (1976, 1978).
81. Osmani (1992b).
82. Dasgupta and Raj (1990).
83. Kumar and Stewart (1992). For further evidence, see Chen et al. (1982), Ulijaszek and Strickland (1993), p. 120, and Behrman and Deolalikar (1987).
84. Gopalan (1992), p. 160.
85. Where socio-economic status is determined by education, occupation, and income.

86. Pelletier et al. (2001).
87. See study by Enamul Karim and Nick Mascie-Taylor (1997) on the rela-
    tionship between birth weight, sociodemographic variables, and maternal
    anthropometry in urban Dhaka. The authors used logistic regression analysis
    to show that mother's weight at term was the best single predictor of low
    birth weight (31%).
88. Griffiths, Dicken, and Favin (1996), p. 31.
89. Griffiths, Dicken, and Favin (1996), p. 1.
90. World Bank (2005c), p. 1.
91. World Bank (2005c), p. 4.
92. Griffiths, Dicken, and Favin (1996), p. 7.
93. Heaver (2002), p. 6, emphasis added.
94. Griffiths, Dicken, and Favin (1996), p. 4.
95. Heaver (2002), pp. 21–2.
96. World Bank (2006).
97. http://www.manoffgroup.com.
98. Favin and Griffiths (1999), p. 1.
99. Griffiths, Dicken, and Favin (1996), p. 23.
100. Favin and Griffiths (1999), p. 98.
101. Berg (1987), p. 4. The definition of undernutrition has been recently
    expanded to include the three key factors of inadequate food intake, illness.
    and deleterious care practices (Measham and Chatterjee 1999).

4

Addressing Hunger

It's easy to exaggerate the exceptionalism of health. I've been dealing with public health people for twenty years, and they tend to overdo that. What's unusual about health is just that it's a peculiar asset, because you can't sell it, you can't give it away, you can't get many spare parts for it, and while your body is in the hospital, you can't go get a loaner body the way you can when your car is in the shop. The biology never goes away, but the economics has to be there.

Philip Musgrove[1]
Former Health Economist at the World Bank from 1990 to 2002
Chief Architect of the 1993 World Development
Report Investing in Health

How is hunger addressed by the Bank nutrition team? And, how does nutrition fit into the Bank's wider aims and programmes? Complementing the previous chapter's focus on biomedicine, this chapter explores the economic influence, specifically orthodox, neoclassical economics, on the World Bank's approach to hunger. Ngaire Woods notes,

The similar graduate training shared by staff in each organization [World Bank and IMF] gives them a shared, albeit narrow, methodology and particular understanding of the world, its problems, and their solutions...The term profession...is widely used by neoclassical economists. It underscores the extent to which this kind of economics is a discipline, like medicine or law, requiring the command of a specific body of abstract and complex knowledge, which is then brought to bear on a particular case.[2]

The underlying concern addressed throughout this chapter is whether nutrition is different from other areas the Bank works in.

Mainstreaming Nutrition into an Economics-Dominated Organization: 1971–80

As noted in Chapter 2, the Bank began to fund stand-alone nutrition projects under the presidency of Robert McNamara who brought to the Bank an agenda outlining the moral imperative of foreign aid both for humanitarian and national security purposes. This section examines the reasons why the Bank decided to fund nutrition-related projects. The history of why the Bank chose to make loans for nutrition is extremely relevant as it partially explains how the Bank addresses hunger. It then considers how economists have influenced nutrition methodology, for example, through the derivation of a metrics of nutrition. The section concludes by examining how basic economic principles such as market failure and information asymmetry have affected how the Bank nutrition team approaches nutrition.

In 1971, experts from various fields and government officials from several countries gathered at the Massachusetts Institute of Technology (MIT) for the first International Conference on Nutrition, National Development, and Planning. That same year Alan Berg, then working for Food for Peace, published a paper in Foreign Affairs arguing that nutrition planning was crucial for development. This led to the Council for Foreign Relations sponsoring Berg for a year at the Brookings Institution to write a book on nutrition and national development. Published in 1973, Berg's *The Nutrition Factor* is viewed as catalysing the emergence of food and nutrition policy and nutritional planning on the international stage. Berg gave a presentation on his book to the Board of Brookings, which included Bank President McNamara.

McNamara was intrigued by the economic arguments Berg presented regarding the urgency of addressing undernutrition in developing countries. He contracted Berg to write a policy note on nutrition and economic development. This brief was crucial as it convinced the Bank's Board and several senior managers that the Bank should start lending for nutrition. Berg made two arguments to the Bank. The first was that nutrition was a development concern that impacted on productivity. It was not just a medical or social welfare issue. Second, he argued that nutrition needed the involvement of managers. It needed to move away from its association with 'medical, biochemist, welfare' types. The latter issue, the move from the medically oriented approach to the development planners approach positioned nutrition in the domain of economics. Berg argued that there needed to be a switch to 'macronutrition'. By this term, he meant a move from clinical and laboratory approaches to undernutrition to ones of development planning in institutions such as the World Bank. The mainstreaming of nutrition in development brought it into the domain of economists who dominate the development apparatus in the Bank.[3]

The Bank management was hesitant to engage with nutrition because of its complexity, its inter-sectoral nature, and 'the nature of the Bank's system for assessing and rewarding staff'.[4] Health-related projects were viewed as a 'bottomless pit'. However, with McNamara's urging, the Bank's Board of Executive Directors decided to finance the implementation and evaluation of certain largely experimental actions in countries with high priority. The Bank's main objectives were to draw the attention of government officials to the problem, to assist in planning, to further the development of rigorous project analysis, and to provide enough resources to make significant interventions possible.

Berg and others involved in nutrition during the 1970s and 1980s recount how difficult it was to convince the senior economists to lend for nutrition, calling it an 'uphill battle'. As one staff member noted,

Nutrition has always occupied a strange position, I mean, economists think it's too complicated and there are no clear demonstrations of success. They think the evaluations are ineffective and that food subsidies are a bad idea. During the retreat on this, sceptics want to trash the nutrition programmes so we have to fight quite hard for it. Nutrition goes through cycles at the Bank. The biggest problem is the complexity, and task managers and leaders not knowing how to do it, how to get the project approved, how to push through such a complicated thing.

The final section of this chapter returns to the final point concerning the tactics employed by Health, Nutrition, and Population staff to get projects approved by senior economist managers. Similarly, another staff member explained,

The bureaucratic politics of mainstreaming nutrition, what a story. There were very very high objections and resistance on the part of senior economists who were more concerned with transferring money than what you did with it. They wanted a return. So the nutritionists turned arguments against them and created productivity numbers, they wanted numbers so we played that game ... of course you could say that spurious economic analysis such as using unrealistic gains in nutritional status was used to get economists to approve nutrition lending.

An example of this tactic was the presentation of data by Bank staff showing a possible reduction in low birth weight infants from 23 to 4.5 per cent if projects were implemented in India. According to the National Institute of Nutrition of India, these projected figures are unrealistic in the given time frame.[5] Returning to the emphasis on numbers, several nutrition staff would argue that the Bank's main contribution to nutrition was quantifying the economic and social benefits of involvement in this sector.

Econometrics is defined as the application of statistical and mathematical methods in the field of economics to describe the numerical relationships between key economic forces such as capital, interest rates, and labour. In the push to convince Bank managers to fund nutrition in the late 1970s, a new metrics of nutrition was created in which theoretical models were used to draw relationships between nutritional gains, labour, discount rates, and productivity. Using these models, the previously unquantifiable, such as the value of adequate nutritional status, could be numerically expressed and thus enter into calculations. Economists were uncomfortable with the complexity of nutrition and the difficulty in evaluating the economic gains from nutrition projects. To make nutrition comprehensible to senior economists, production functions were employed such as:

$$Q = AL^l K^k \tag{1}$$

In Eq. (1), Q stands for output, A stands for conversion coefficient, L is labour, K is capital, l is the per cent increase in output per 1 per cent increase in labour, and k is the per cent increase in output per 1 per cent increase in capital.[6] Once this was established, a second equation was derived that included food consumption as a proxy for nutritional status:

$$N(df) = N(dy)(dc/dy)(dq/dc) \tag{2}$$

In Eq. (2), $N(df)$ stands for the expected number of low-income individuals who move from 'poor' diet to 'fair' diet, $N(dy)$ is the number of low-income individuals at risk multiplied by the change in real income of each participant, dc is the change in participant food consumption associated with a change in real income, dy is the family income, dq is the estimated proportion of households with 'poor diets', and dc is the current level of food consumption.[7] Once $N(df)$ is estimated, then the change in labour can be estimated and entered into Eq. (1). Using these two equations, a direct mathematical link can be drawn between an increase in food consumption and an increase in output per person, or productivity.

In addition, by using the proxy of food for nutrition in this time period, Berg could gain the attention of economists:

[E]conomic distinction commonly is made between food and nutrition—ranking food 'high', nutrition 'low'; or food 'essential', nutrition 'welfare'. Food has obvious tangibility features that nutrition lacks. Food costs and supplies can be measured, subjected to economic analysis, and entered into the national accounts. Nutrition in contrast often is invisible and dimly understood, and it seldom commands a price, especially among those who need it most.[8]

Berg had difficulty convincing the senior economists that the Bank should make loans for nutrition. For example, his initial policy paper for President McNamara was neglected for many months since there was an oil crisis in 1971 that diverted attention away from nutrition.[9] Since this time, the numerical equations used to describe productivity gains from investment in nutrition have increased in complexity. Economic functions have been continually used to justify Bank involvement in nutrition as well as to increase the likelihood of management approval of nutrition lending.

Concerning nutrition metrics, since this time period, the Bank has emphasized the use of production functions to justify involvement in nutrition. This dialogue is the only one that is permitted and used. This can be viewed as an 'econometrics of suffering', the situation where mathematical analysis of production relationships is used to determine the magnitude of nutritional deprivation and provides justification for spending to alleviate this destitution. Quantification makes hunger real to economists and to planners.

The previous section discussed how the language of nutrition metrics is one defining influence economists have had on nutrition-related projects. This section examines another influence: how the economic principle of information asymmetry led to a particularly favoured intervention by the Bank to improve nutritional status in developing countries. One of the key concerns in economics is the nature and extent of public sector involvement.[10] The Bank tends to favour the private sector as 'public sector institutions have often been found to operate less efficiently than those in the private sector'.[11] The World Bank argues that government involvement can only be justified in specifically defined cases. These include where there are identifiable failures in the market (i.e.

the private sector), which arise in the case of public goods, externalities, and imperfect information, or where income redistribution is considered desirable.[12]

Bank nutritionists have perceived market failure as one of the key reasons why malnutrition rates are extremely high in South Asia.[13] In this framework, government expenditure on nutrition has been justified on the basis that markets have failed.[14] Information, in the form of nutrition education, mass communication, or counselling, has been viewed as an adequate government response to this market failure. Behaviour modification is expected to occur through nutrition education. This approach is still evident today. As a 2006 Bank nutrition report states, 'People do not always know what food or what feeding practices are best for their children or themselves...the need to correct these "information asymmetries" is another argument for government intervention.'[15]

Since the pilot projects of the late 1970s, nutrition education, using the tools of growth monitoring and supplementary feeding, has been the base of certain Bank projects such as TINP. The underlying assumption has been that once individuals and households have the necessary information, behavioural change will occur and malnutrition rates will drop.[16] Proponents of this perspective have used 'positive deviance' (children who grow much better than the median of their community) to argue that even in conditions of deprivation, households can adopt strategies to improve the nutritional status of their children. As a 1996 Bank document notes, 'Improvements in child nutrition so often depend on changing feeding and care-giving behaviours in the home.'[17] Thus, the economic influence on the Bank's approach to nutrition is apparent through the emphasis on nutrition education to correct the information asymmetry as well as the significance given to rate of return on investment.

Health as a Commodity and Health as an Investment: 1980–93

As a result of McNamara's presidency, which ended in 1981, the Bank moved closer towards the role of a development agency. To publicize its new position, the Bank focused its 1980 World Development Report on the importance of investing in the social sector since improved health and nutrition would accelerate economic growth. Human capital theory achieved prominence during this time. This framework justifies nutrition loans on the basis that they are an investment in the future productivity of a nation. Human capital theory employs an instrumental, rather than intrinsic, approach to project beneficiaries. This will now be explained.

In general, health economists have used two alternative models for describing the attainment of 'good health'.[18] The first is health as one of several commodities over which individuals have well-defined preferences, that is, the intrinsic approach. Health can be viewed as a commodity that individuals use their available resources to acquire.[19] The second approach to health is the human capital approach which constructs health as stock, or a future investment in an individual, that is, the instrumental approach.[20] The economic definition of human capital theory is that individuals allocate resources at one point of time in order to bring about certain outcomes at another point of time.[21] In this model, health and good nutritional status are valuable because the body is used as a productive resource. The more health one is able to acquire, the more valuable this will be in the future.

As noted earlier, health as investment was first emphasized by the Bank in the 1980 World Development Report on poverty. Since this time, the Bank nutrition team has predominantly relied on the human capital framework to lobby governments to take loans for nutrition-related projects. Applying the concept of human capital to health, Alan Berg argued in 1981 that nutrition and national economy were linked through investment in human beings (Figure 4.1):

Recently... the concept of capital has been extended to human beings. Development of the new theory was prompted by the discovery that 'increases in national output have been large compared with the increases of land, man-hours and physical reproducible capital.' Investment in human capital is probably the major explanation for this difference.[22]

Berg then described the many economic benefits of investment in child nutrition.[23] The first is that of savings on medical costs through reduced demand for curative medical services (e.g. hospitalization). The second benefit is that of reduced productivity losses caused by the debility of the labour force: 'The failure to meet basic needs for nutrition means higher death rates and a less productive population.'[24] Although conceding that the assumptions were 'heroic', Berg noted that productivity losses could be measured through a comparison of a country's average caloric need to average national caloric consumption. A country's average caloric need

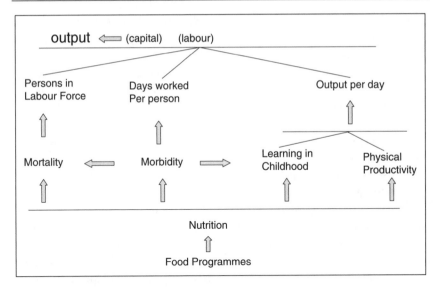

Figure 4.1. Nutrition and human capital (Wilson 1973: p. 138)

could be calculated through the occupational distribution of the labour force. The shortfall in national working capacity could be used to estimate the productivity losses from nutritional deficit.

However, Berg acknowledged the methodological difficulties with estimating productivity losses. First, using an indicator such as physical growth is made complicated because of infection, possible genetic factors as well as the reference used for comparison. Second, using an input-based indicator has problems due to recall, intrahousehold allocation of resources, the special needs of individuals, micronutrient deficiencies as well as food waste. Third, nutritional status is seasonally dependent indicating that it is hard to relate it to human performance at any given time. Finally, the relationship between income and nutritional status has been shown to be weak.

The third benefit of investment in child nutrition is the extension of working years, malnutrition reducing the number of productive working years. Other economic benefits of nutrition investment include a decrease in the incidence of infectious disease, better care for children, and returns on other investments in human capital, such as education. Thus, an economic case was made to 'upgrade the potential productivity of those masses of unskilled, landless, adult workers who have dim prospects of gainful employment'.[25] Nutritional investment and subsequent economic development will 'get the person out of the isolated village and change their fears, beliefs and attitudes'.[26]

Thus, in the human capital framework, initially propagated by the Bank in the early 1980s, child nutritional well-being and health are directly tied to future labour and productivity. This approach is still employed today. For example, in 2005, the World Bank estimated that malnourished children have at least a 10 per cent reduction in lifetime earnings. Thus, investing in child nutrition will have fruitful payoffs in the future when the child becomes an adult member of the workforce.

A 2005 Bank nutrition document, titled 'To Nourish a Nation: Investing in Nutrition with World Bank Assistance' that is used for lobbying governments states, 'The challenges of development require a strong human resource base—a workforce that is physically strong, mentally alert, and healthy. But malnutrition robs a country of these resources.'[27] It continues with the following section titled, 'Children's Growth = Economic Growth' which discusses how 'Children with retarded growth become stunted adults who are less productive...these problems have implications for human achievement and economic development'.[28] It then presents data on how iron deficiency, anaemia, causes, 'a 10–15% reduction in work output in many different occupations. Thus, the productivity of entire populations is needlessly reduced'.[29] Using this framework, the Bank nutrition team estimates that returns on nutrition investment are as high as 84:1.[30]

In the case of countries like India, the World Bank nutrition team estimates that GDP lost to malnutrition is as high as 2–3 per cent. Worldwide, the Bank nutrition team estimates that malnutrition costs at least US\$80 billion per year, and for India, at least US\$10 billion.[31] Thus, health and nutrition have been directly linked to economic growth. The initial productivity arguments that Alan Berg used to convince the Bank's Board to invest in nutrition-related projects are still being employed today.

Using productivity gain estimates and the human capital framework in the 1980s, the Bank nutrition team created 'target groups' of individuals who should be the beneficiaries of nutrition projects.[32] Since their creation for the pilot projects, the composition of target groups has essentially remained the same. These target groups should be viewed as economic constructs. They were defined by the age and gender that would most impact on economic growth in the future. In the creation of target groups, individuals were identified as a beneficiary or an individual 'at risk' based on a single characteristic, such as age or pregnancy status. The beneficiaries were chosen based on their instrumental importance for the economy, rather than for their intrinsic worth as individuals.

World Bank nutrition projects have generally specified three main target groups as beneficiaries: preschool children and pregnant and lactating women.[33] Preschool children have been targeted because it is during the first few years of life that a child's most rapid physical and intellectual growth occurs.[34] Thus, the 'benefits of nutrition and other inputs are...maximised when they are timed accordingly'.[35] A World Bank nutrition paper titled 'Nutrition and Economic Sector work' (2005) states,

Undernutrition's most damaging impact occurs during pregnancy and in the first two years of life, and the effects of this early damage on health, brain development, intelligence, educability, and productivity are largely irreversible. Actions targeted at older ages have little, if any impact...Governments with limited resources are therefore best advised to focus actions on this small 'window of opportunity', between conception and 24 months of age.[36]

The World Bank nutrition team has targeted its projects at preschool children because improving their nutrition and investing in their human capital will have the strongest impact on productivity.

Similarly, during the nine months of pregnancy and six months of lactation, a woman becomes the target of nutrition interventions. The predominant reason for this inclusion is that it is during these stages that a woman is constructed as a mother or future mother. She must ensure the health of a future member of the work force. Her nutritional status is valued instrumentally, not instrincally. If her health was valued solely, then a woman would receive health services and food supplements regardless of pregnancy status. However, this is not the case as non-pregnant, non-lactating women have not been included as beneficiaries in nutrition project design.

Pregnant women have been viewed as instrumentally important to decrease the incidence of low–birth weight infants.[37] The most critical determinant of low–birth weight is maternal malnutrition, specifically protein–energy and iron deficiencies.[38] Well-nourished women gain, on average, 10 kg during pregnancy. Low nutrient intake and high caloric expenditure can compromise the health of the developing baby.

Lactating women have been viewed as instrumentally important to ensure that an infant is healthy during its first six months of life. Physiologically, breast milk is the best food for the child during this period, preventing infection while also developing the immune and digestive system. The main interventions that the Bank offers are nutrition counselling (breastfeeding promotion) and supplementary feeding.[39] Although a moderately undernourished woman can produce an adequate amount of breast milk, a severely malnourished woman may produce 20–30 per cent less breast milk than her well-nourished counterpart.[40] To address this problem, the Bank nutrition projects offer food supplements which replenish a woman's nutrient stores and ensure the child is being breastfed sufficiently.

The second benefit of targeting lactating women is that breastfeeding acts as a contraceptive. Physiologically, infant suckling inhibits ovulation.[41] In addition, cultural factors can result in post-partum avoidance of intercourse. For example, Ayurvedic humeral ideology states that food is progressively transformed from a series of body substances from blood, flesh, and bone to breast milk and semen (*dhatu*).[42] As *dhatu* reserves in the form of semen become depleted through sexual experience, the body attempts to replenish these reserves. This leads to a reduction in the amount of breast milk produced.[43] Other cultural beliefs in India include that a mother's breast milk spoils if she has intercourse while lactating.[44] Thus, family planning could also have been a factor in the creation of the target group of nursing women in the 1980s.

The Tool of Cost-Effectiveness: 1993–2006

The Bank's shift towards addressing health and nutritional issues was firmly established by the 1993 World Development Report *Investing in Health* which was the first annual report to be devoted entirely to health. The report launched a new Bank framework for applying economic principles to health through the use of cost-effectiveness and introduced other cost–benefit analyses. Since the 1993 report, cost-effectiveness in health has become the flagship tool of the Bank to evaluate various nutrition schemes. The report attempted to reconcile the specificity of health with the traditional methods of economics.

The Bank argued that the tool of cost-effectiveness was essential in making the 'right choices among sectors and among designs for any given policy and institutional context'. It was necessary to evaluate the different policy options to 'eradicate' hunger and determine which was the most efficient.[45] While attractive in rhetoric, the identification and measurement of costs and benefits for projects have been difficult for the Bank to operationalize. Prior to the 1993 World Development Report, a 1992 World Bank report on cost-effectiveness and nutrition presents limited information on the cost per death averted of select nutrition interventions then concluded that the existing data on cost-effectiveness is inadequate to properly assess projects. It notes, 'existing studies tend to cite over and over again data from the same few projects.'[46]

Within the Bank, since the turn towards cost-effectiveness, there has been confusion surrounding an exact formula for measurement of costs and benefits. Discussing cost–benefit analysis, a 1994 Bank document states,

Although it would be desirable to have a standard cost–benefit methodology with precise rules for calculation for every situation, this is not the present case ... [A]lthough the conceptual methods for identifying and measuring benefits are well-established, the application of these methods depends crucially on a variety of judgements on both the measurement of benefits and their values.[47]

The basic method for estimating benefits is first to identify the positive effects of an intervention on areas such as mortality, morbidity, work output, and productivity.[48] The benefits of reduced mortality are generally considered to be the value of lost productivity, of morbidity the value of lost productivity plus the savings in health care, and of work output and productivity the additional days of productive work and the additional productivity per day. The key step is the application of monetary values to each of these areas. Table 4.1 adapted from the World Bank *Nutrition Toolkit* illustrates the process.

Since 1993, the World Bank has emphasized the indicator 'cost per death' averted and since 1993 the 'cost per Disability-Adjusted Life Year (DALY)' averted as useful measures of the cost–benefit of a project.[49] World Bank staff members claim that, 'Computing the cost per disability-adjusted life year [DALY] of interventions provides an objective measure.'[50] Table 4.2 provides an example of a typical Bank cost-effectiveness analysis. The source given for the information in the table is 'based on author's assumptions'.

When presenting a tentative loan for approval to senior managers, the focus has been on whether the design of the project is the most efficient and the most cost-effective, to achieve the desired impact. For nutrition, projects have been assessed on the cost per death or the cost per DALY averted. The assumptions by which these numbers were computed are seldom investigated. These analyses are based on theoretical models and quantification which are presentable and understandable to

Table 4.1. Benefit–cost ratio of providing food to malnourished children[a]

Information	Value
Transfer of 50,000 calories to malnourished children leads to a height increase of	1 cm
Cost per 1,000 calories	$0.20
Cost per centimetre of height gain in adults	$10
Average adult height	160 cm
Increase in 1 cm as percentage of average height	0.625%
Elasticity of labour productivity with respect to height	1.38
1 cm increase in height is associated with an increase in wages of	0.86%
Annual current income	$750
Increase in annual wages from an increase in height of 1 cm	$6.45
Discount rate	0.03
Real wage increase	0.02
Productive years	18–55 years
The present value of additional lifetime earnings from an increase in height of 1 cm	$174
Benefit–cost ratio	17.4

[a] Adapted from Phillips and Sanghvi (1996), p. 87.

Table 4.2. Cost per death/DALY averted in iron interventions[a]

Parameter	Iron supplementation of pregnant women	Iron fortification
Target group	Pregnant women	All people
Number	4,000	100,000
Average rate (%)[b]	63	50
Programme effectiveness (%)	75	75
Deaths averted	10	10
Immediate productivity gains (%)	20	20
Programme duration (days)	200	Year round
Programme costs (US$)	8,000	20,000
Discounted wage gains (US$)	221,280[c]	1,682,720[d]
DALY gained	624[e]	4, 520[f]
Wage gains divided by programme cost	27.7	84.1
Cost per DALY (US$)	12.8	4.40
Cost per death averted (US$)	800	2,000

[a] World Bank (1994), p. 66.
[b] Rate of anaemia for iron supplementation of pregnant women; rate of iron deficiency for iron fortification.
[c] Calculated as the product of the number of anaemic participants times disability times wages times effectiveness times employment, plus the product of the number of deaths times wage times employment times productive life expectancy.
[d] Calculated as the product of the number of adult participants times disability times effectiveness times employment times wages, plus the product of the number of deaths times wage times employment times productive life expectancy.
[e] Calculated as the product of the number of deaths times life expectancy, plus the product of disability times number of malnourished participants times effectiveness.
[f] Calculated as the product of the number of adult participants times the rate of anaemia times disability times effectiveness, plus the product of the number of deaths times life expectancy.

the economist managers. An example of this from Table 4.2 is the use of the indicator 'the present value of additional lifetime earnings from an increase in height of 1 cm' in which height has become a form of capital, like land. The body has been commoditized to have a certain economic value. Bank staff acknowledge the lack of rigorousness of these indicators and the implicit value judgements that they are based on. However, those in the Health, Nutrition, and Population sector have been forced to present projects in this manner, they argue, to conform to the Bank mandate as well as the related ideology of the Bank.

Both cost–benefit and cost-effectiveness analyses in nutrition suffer from methodological difficulties in practice. First, the impact of nutrition interventions normally occurs over a long period of time compared to immunization or other short-term health interventions.[51] In addition, most nutrition interventions do not occur in isolation. Nutrition education, growth monitoring, and supplementary feeding often occur in conjunction with health services, food subsidies, and school feeding programmes. This makes it difficult to conduct a proper assessment of the nutritional impact of a project. Third, the use of the indicator 'cost per death averted' is an extreme measure of outcome neglecting the toll of malnutrition on well-being and general health. It does not include a measurement of the quality of life for survivors or the 'dark side of child survival' which refers to excessive morbidity. Other problems with analysis are difficulties with data collection in the field and the use of different standards for measuring malnutrition, which are both part of the general problem of large-scale quantitative analysis in nutrition.

Given these methodological problems some academics have argued that the use of cost-effectiveness in decision-making processes can be essentially useless. Development economist Alice Sindzingre notes that models and econometrics work at such a high level of aggregation and use such broad categories that although they may always be proven true (non-falsifiable), they are still meaningless.[52] Although cost-effectiveness can serve a useful allocative function, the conclusions reached are dependent on the values entered into the equation. For example, suppose that two projects are being evaluated to determine which is more efficient in achieving a death averted. If there is a clear preference for one, it is possible to first determine what the outcome should be then work the equation backwards to determine the value of the variables to achieve the preferred options. Reflecting on this, William Ascher notes 'The staff member can, consciously or unconsciously, convert personal disagreement with policy into technical caveats about the applicability of the policy in specific cases.'[53]

Despite its limitations, cost-effectiveness is still a key determinant of a project's approval by the World Bank. The 1993 World Development Report used the term over 200 times to reiterate the Bank's contribution to health, namely in quantification of costs and benefits. Due to its subjective nature and value-added calculation, the label 'cost-effective' has served as the Bank's ambiguous symbol. It has been purposefully ambiguous such that it could reflect a diversity of interests and approaches. In each particular situation, depending on certain circumstances, cost-effectiveness could assume the form needed to justify involvement and garner support or to indicate a flawed design. In addition, 'Power relations may use this very indeterminacy to select particular descriptions and present them as "the truth" (scientific) because the claim of scientificity (of being the exclusive truth) is a helpful tool for the exercise of power.'[54] Cost-effectiveness has not been employed as a conceptual tool; it has been used as a tactical one.

The Bank nutrition team presents its analysis as technical and objective, and based on sound, economic research. However, the assumptions entering calculations include several value judgements taken by Bank staff, both during McNamara's presidency and today. These have been disguised in models and productivity functions which can be used to justify a particular involvement by the Bank in a nutrition project. As Paul Nelson notes,

Economic doctrine helps the Bank shape discourse about development around technique and science rather than values and politics. The presentation of economic theories as scientific formulations shields them from criticism, permitting the Bank to exert financial leverage to promote not 'its' way but a certifiably 'correct way'.[55]

Ideology and Politics in the Bank: 1971–2006

While the importance of lending for nutrition is constantly in flux at the Bank, the Bank's nutrition team has continued to promote the TINP approach. The final section of this chapter addresses the question, 'Why does nutrition have to be addressed in this way in the World Bank?' In particular, it examines the ideological and political factors that have influenced lending for nutrition.

During the negotiations with economists over nutrition-related lending in the 1970s, nutrition staff had to make tactical concessions which pushed them towards econometric models. And, to ensure the survival of lending for nutrition, Health, Nutrition, and Population staff have continued to translate their case into economic terms: 'the weapon of choice was numbers'.

As the evidence presented in this chapter demonstrates, nutrition has been framed within the Bank as an issue of human capital. In nutrition projects, the worth of project beneficiaries has been based on their contribution to the economy and thus to social welfare. This can be demonstrated by the economist function that puts a monetary value on years lost to mortality through using the individual's expected wages and by the creation of target groups. The target group of preschool children has attracted considerable health investment. This has been justified by the World Bank nutrition team on the grounds that proper nutrition is crucial for both 'physical and mental functioning' in their adult years.[56] A healthy child has been defined as a 'public good' in that 'it' (the child) has welfare effects for society as a whole.[57] Likewise, the target group of pregnant and lactating women has been given importance because of the functional role of mothers in raising children to be productive adults.

The human capital framework for nutrition within the Bank is a general reflection of the dominance of economics in public health development projects, which can be viewed as the 'economic gaze'. The economic gaze refers to the process by which those individuals working within the Bank on public health as well as the beneficiaries of public health projects have been disciplined and regulated through the constraints of economic theory. This has resulted in a situation where staff members design projects in a manner consistent with human capital and other economic principles in order to gain loan approval from senior managers as well as be promoted.

The emergence of economics in public health can be traced to the creation of the World Bank. Within the Bank, the discipline of economics can be viewed as hegemonic, the only way of examining problems, of defining their essential features and suggesting solutions. The strength of economic knowledge is seen to lie in its ability to manage the details of a local issue, reduce the complexity, and extract indicators and specific policy goals.[58] Local knowledge is considered messy, complicated, political, and incomprehensible to the institution. Thus, an economic approach reduces problems, such as nutrition, to their core elements so that the professional expertise can digest them objectively and prescribe solutions.

For the above reasons, the Bank has been described as an 'economic fortress' by its staff[59] where internal operations and activities are dominated by economic paradigms and frameworks. This is true within the Bank's Health, Nutrition, and Population sector, which has often been run by an economist who ensures that potential project loans are designed to be consistent with the Bank's economic framework and legal mandate. This principle is a constraining factor on staff who would like to justify loans or Bank involvement on other, that is, human rights, grounds.

It has been argued that economists are diverse, so classifying them into a single group is misleading. While this critique is acknowledged, within the Bank, there is an overwhelmingly Anglo-Saxon approach to economics.[60] Unlike other United Nations agencies, English is the working language of the Bank.[61] Thus, this requirement favours graduates of institutions that teach in English. As fluency in English is 'tended to be correlated with preferred economic and social status', the Bank's composition primarily is composed of elites.[62] A 1991 study of the high-level staff in the Policy, Research, and External Affairs Departments of the Bank shows that roughly 80 per cent had trained in economics and finance at institutions in the US and UK.[63] Ascher notes that the economists in the Bank behave very much alike, whether they are Indian, Brazilian, English, or Canadian.[64] Thus, ideological divisions within the Bank do not reflect a conflict between North and South as much as between the Chicago School and the Sussex School.

The Bank has also been described by its staff as a 'church protecting an orthodox bureaucracy'. One of these principles, a legacy of McNamara's presidency, is quantification and measurability. As one staff member put it, 'If you can't measure it, then it doesn't exist'. The emphasis on quantitative language has resulted in staff becoming bureaucratic entrepreneurs and attempting to develop packages that can be sold to the economists on the operational teams. Alan Berg used this technique in the 1970s to convince economists that nutrition was an issue of lost productivity and bring a health issue into the realm of capital and economic growth. Bank nutrition staff felt that they could gain the attention of senior economists through presenting 'hard numbers' and models.

As Bank nutrition staff are all too aware, lending specifically for nutrition is an issue within the Bank which has not had a stable or powerful position. Some economists have argued that the Bank should be a bank and not a health development agency and that it suffers from 'mission creep'. They have argued that the Bank is a financial institution. It was created to address solvable problems with measurable returns using lending instruments. One staff member noted that there has been continual resistance on the part of senior economists who have been more concerned with transferring money and delivering lending on time rather the quality of lending.

Despite the push to lend fast, economists have wanted a measurable return. This leads to a further problem that economists have had with nutrition: the effects of nutrition interventions are generally hard to discern, difficult to measure, and long term. In the Bank, Task Managers need to sell a package internally and ensure that it is judged successful by the Operations Evaluation Department. Thus, staff are urged to think 'backwards', to pay attention to assessment. However, nutritional status is a complex outcome of multiple forces thus making short-term returns unrealistic to obtain. Reflecting on this tension, one staff member noted, 'It is much harder for the Task Leader to target and follow the money . . . In countries with weak capacity or failing governments, it is impossible to show results.'

Over the past 35 years, the approval of a project, as well as the career and survival of a staff member, has depended on his or her marketing success in making social problems economic ones. This has been done by creating equations and models out of complex issues. However, economic ideology alone does not explain the Bank's approach to nutrition. The internal politics of the Bank has been just as critical.

The importance given to nutrition lending has constantly been in flux at the Bank. It has never been as prominent in the Bank as it was with Berg. During the 1970s, Alan Berg was highly successful at marketing nutrition using McNamara's support advantageously. This big name gave his projects credibility. One anthropologist within the Bank stated that this was the 'pragmatist' way to get things done, to go through unofficial channels using celebrity names to garner support.

However, nutrition continued to be important during the 1980s with an additional focus put on micronutrients. In the 1990s, the Bank's Health, Nutrition, and Population sector turned its attention towards health systems evidenced by a decline in Bank lending for nutrition.[65] Part of the reason for the loss of interest in nutrition has been the difficulty in showing impact, as discussed earlier.

Nutrition has also had to compete with other social issues for attention. For example, one staff member noted that due to the leadership of the UK in the G8 in 2006, the primary focus has been on debt relief and HIV/AIDS in Africa. However, as a result of the centrality of health

to the Millennium Development Goals and their international importance, nutrition has been able to keep its place at the table. The Acting
Director for Health, Nutrition, and Population in 2006 explained this
trend:

Right now, to illustrate the centrality of this discussion and how meaningful it
is to us and why we're attaching the kind of importance that we are, we will
be having...what we call the Annual Strategic Forum. It's a small gathering of
Mr. Wolfensohn, our Managing Directors, our Vice Presidents from all over the
institution, and a few other Bank staff to try to set out the strategic tone...And
the exclusive topic...is around how the Bank can do its part to contribute to faster
progress on the Millennium Development Goals...And within the Millennium
Goals and the way in which the corporate priorities of the Bank have been defined,
there are several themes where nutrition figures very, very prominently...[These
things] are really preoccupying Mr. Wolfensohn as he entered the middle of his
second term and looks at what kind of legacy he'll leave to the Bank and in
development. It's very clear to us who work closely with him or hear from those
who work closely with him that trying to make the focus of what he does over
the next couple of years and what his institution does very much around not
just measuring the Millennium Goals but trying to do something to change what
happens by 2015.

As the Acting Director's comments reflect, for nutrition to be important
within the Bank, it must be framed in a way that attracts the interest
of the President and senior management. The position of nutrition within
the Bank seems to depend highly on the nutrition spokesperson within
the Bank, his or her charisma, and his or her ability to form personal
connections and manoeuvre the system. As a Bank consultant noted,
raising the profile of nutrition in the Bank requires a Task Manager who
is 'capable of making the economic arguments for investing in nutrition,
and who has networking skills and an entrepreneurial approach'.[66] These
qualities are found in the current Bank nutritionist who has successfully
focused attention on nutrition in 2008 to such a level that it featured on
the World Bank's homepage.

Understanding and Addressing Hunger

As discussed earlier, Bank staff have had difficulty adapting their tools
and frameworks to address social sector issues. Undernutrition poses a
particularly difficult area since it is a highly complex and multifaceted
phenomenon. The biomedical understanding of hunger as a disease and

the economic framing of hunger as an issue of human capital interlace to form the Bank nutrition team's approach to undernutrition. This particular approach can be viewed as reflecting the Bank's imperative to create a problem that its own instruments can address.

The framework that was used in TINP and continues to be used by the nutrition team is based on a combination of biomedical and health economic models. As a Bank Health, Nutrition, and Population Economist in Delhi said, 'We use the medical model but bring in the cost aspects.' In the powerful institution of the Bank, the twin hegemonies of biomedicine and health economics interlace to form an unquestioned approach in development to 'curing' malnutrition that has become 'common sense' in development circles. Biomedicine and economics can be defined as hegemonic since they have achieved

the permeation throughout civil society . . . of an entire system of values, attitudes, beliefs, morality, etc. that is one way or another supportive of the established order and the class interests that dominate it . . . to the extent that this prevailing consciousness is internalised by the broad masses, it becomes part of 'common sense.' Thus, [they] operate in a dualistic manner: as a 'general conception of life' for the masses and as a scholastic programme.[67]

In reading of the secondary literature, even academics are hesitant to question the design of TINP since it has been affirmed as 'physiologically successful' by biomedicine and as 'cost-effective' by health economics. These two frameworks are complementary in the sense that both disciplines are perceived as technical, apolitical, and universal.

The disciplines of biomedicine and economics are quite similarly placed and tend to reinforce each other's power, as shown in Table 4.3. It can be argued that biomedicine is hegemonic in the health sphere, much as economics occupies a privileged place in development policy. It is not surprising that when the World Bank, the most powerful development agency, decides to venture into nutrition, commonly viewed as a public health issue, an interlacing of biomedical and economic framework occurs.

It seems as if the Bank's approach to nutrition goes unquestioned since it has been derived from a 'technically accurate', scientific, that is, biomedical and economic, framework. In addition, both biomedicine and economics are applied universally. Local factors, such as the extent of gender inequality, the use of alcohol, proper access to safe water sources and sanitation, and food symbolism and classification, are ignored.

103

Table 4.3. Biomedical and economic influence on the World Bank

	Biomedicine	Economics
Main actors are	Medical doctors, biochemists	Health economists
Agents self-described as	Technicians	Technocrats
Hegemony in realm of	Health	Development
Institution symbolically associated with and mainly composed of	Men	Men
Does this institution fit Mary Douglas's 'Strong grid, Strong group' model?	Yes, strictly conformist, strongly integrated, and rigid boundaries vis-à-vis outsiders	Yes, strictly conformist, strongly integrated, and rigid boundaries vis-à-vis outsiders
Knowledge considered	Scientific, objective, technical, rational	Scientific, objective, technical, rational
Mission is to help	Patients	Beneficiaries
Addresses	Symptoms	Efficient treatment of symptoms
Nutrition framed as	Disease	Element of human capital
Undernutrition framed as	Medical problem (individual)	Educational problem (individual)
Institutional home	World Health Organisation	World Bank
Constructs	Functional groups	Target groups
Women defined as	Mothers	Mothers
Mothers important for	Children to be healthy	Children to be productive
Reliance on visual	Growth charts, anthropometry	Quantitative analysis, statistics, models
Foucauldian framework	Clinical gaze	Economic gaze

An additional similarity is the focus on the individual over community. As discussed in Chapter 3, the biomedical influence on the understanding of undernutrition results in a focus on 'curing' the individual, while economics' methodological individualism results in the modelling of rational, calculated, self-interested individuals. Both orthodox biomedicine and economics privilege agency over structure.[68]

The Bank frames nutrition using biomedical and economic inputs because it ultimately has to construct a problem that its own instruments can address. The Bank is in the lending business, making time-limited, repayable loans. Any Bank actions have to fit within the overall Bank goal of lending for growth. Thus, loans have to be made for profit-creating projects that have measurable economic returns. To address undernutrition, the Bank has to ensure that it is constructed as a 'curable' problem (a disease) that will have an impact on GDP and economic growth (human capital).

Given the significant role the World Bank plays in the global nutrition community, both as a financier and as a norm setter, it is critical to understand how its nutrition policy is formulated within the institution. My key point is that the nutrition policy is a reflection of the political pressures and institutional constraints operating within the Bank. Technical economic expertise is moulded by the political, institutional, and bureaucratic incentives. The prevailing policy is ultimately shaped by 'economic analysis, institutional constraints, and bureaucratic organisation'.[69] But to return to the initial question, how is undernutrition understood and addressed by the nutrition team of the Bank? As has been argued in both this chapter and Chapter 3, hunger is viewed as a matter of choice to be addressed at the individual level. This underlies the World Bank nutrition team's approach to undernutrition.

Notes

1. Musgrove (2005), pp. W5–334.
2. Woods (2006), p. 54.
3. Mosse (2006) discusses the dominance of economists within the Bank in relation to the activities of anthropologists. Selowsky (1978) argues that it was not until the mid-1970s that economists became interested in malnutrition. Buse and Walt (2000) discuss how one of the challenges facing the Bank in the health sector is the influence of health economists.
4. Quote from Alan Berg (1987). This relates to the difficulty in evaluating nutrition, showing quantified outcomes, and moving money fast.
5. Rajivan (2001), p. 134.
6. Wilson (1973).
7. Ibid.
8. Berg (1973), p. 30.
9. Although a major shock to economists, it was also of grave concern to nutritionists as the price of food increased dramatically.
10. Phillips and Sanghvi (1996), p. 15.
11. Jack (1999), p. 271.
12. Phillips and Sanghvi (1996), p. 15.
13. World Bank (2006), p. 9.
14. Behrman (1995), pp. 32–52, World Bank (2005a).
15. World Bank (2006), p. 9.
16. Berg (1987), p. 6.
17. Griffiths et al. (1996).
18. Jack (1999), p. 55.
19. Davis and McMaster (2004).
20. Jack (1999), p. 50.
21. Davis (2003), p. 55.

22. Berg (1981), p. 17.
23. Berg (1973), p. 18.
24. Berg (1987), p. 95.
25. Berg (1973), p. 22.
26. Wilson (1973).
27. World Bank (2005c), p. 1.
28. Ibid. p. 2.
29. Ibid. p. 2.
30. Ibid. p. 11.
31. Measham and Chatterjee (1999), p. 4.
32. See Cernea (2004), p. 7.
33. See Phillips and Sanghvi (1996), p. 34.
34. World Bank, p. 9.
35. Ibid. (2005c)
36. World Bank (2005a), p. 1.
37. Elder, Kiess, and de Beyer (1996), p. 25.
38. Other determinants include smoking and alcohol use by mother, genetics, congenital abnormalities, or infections, and age of mother.
39. Elder, Kiess, and de Beyer (1996), p. 29.
40. King and Burgess (1993).
41. Delgado et al. (1978), pp. 322–7, Huffman et al. (1978), pp. 1155–7.
42. Semen refers to the substance that both women and men release during intercourse.
43. Nichter and Nichter (1996), p. 16.
44. Ibid. p. 121.
45. World Bank (2005c), p. 8.
46. Horton (1992), p. 24, quote from p. 5.
47. World Bank (1994), p. 62.
48. Ibid. p. 62.
49. For nutrition, other indicators used include 'cost per case of child stunting averted', 'cost per 0.1 kg increase in birth weight', 'cost per child removed from third degree malnutrition', etc. See Levinson et al. (1999), p. 121.
50. de Beyer et al. (2000), pp. 169–76.
51. Horton (1992), p. 3.
52. Sindzingre (2004), pp. 233–49.
53. Ascher (1983), pp. 415–39.
54. Sindzingre (2004), p. 233.
55. Nelson (1995), p. 112.
56. World Bank (2005a).
57. Ibid.
58. Woods (2006).
59. This phrase is from Michael Cernea who was the Bank's first in-house sociologist in 1974. Cernea (2004), p. 9.

60. This paragraph is based on information given in Woods (2000), pp. 823–41.
61. Early in the history of the international financial institutions, the United States ensured there would be no national quotas for hiring and that English would be the working language. Woods (2003).
62. Quote from Woods (2000).
63. Stern and Ferreira (1997) cited in Woods (2000).
64. Ascher (1983), p. 437.
65. Heaver (2006), p. 11.
66. Heaver (2006), p. 18.
67. Gramsci quoted in Martin (1987), p. 23.
68. See Humphries (1998).
69. Woods (2006), p. 56.

5

The View from the Community

To understand how the Bank approach actually works on the ground, I undertook fieldwork in Tamil Nadu focusing on the view from the community level. The particular assumptions of TINP I was interested in testing were that women are the household decision-makers, that 'poor caring practices are the biggest cause of protein–energy malnutrition',[1] that inappropriate caring practices are due to women's ignorance, and finally that households have the ability to change their caring behaviours. Ultimately, I was testing the relative importance of choice in the production of hunger.

There are different ways of approaching the evaluation of a project. One is to compare the impact of the project against the impact of no project. Thus, any beneficial impact, despite inefficiencies or leakages, will result in the project being considered successful. In contrast, another approach is to compare the actual project to what it could achieve given the same level of investment and resources.

This chapter examines the local consequences of the Bank model on project beneficiaries using the case study of TINP. It presents data collected during fieldwork in India on the local effects and understandings of TINP in four different caste communities. Although the four communities are situated in close proximity, they are socially distinct. It first presents background information on each community such as family size, occupation, housing conditions, disease prevalence, household income, and child nutritional status. It then presents the results of statistical analysis on the use of *anganwadis* and understandings of growth monitoring, food supplementation, and intensive nutrition counselling. Since poor caring practices are identified by the Bank as the primary cause of malnutrition, data on the state of knowledge and practices of child-rearing will also be presented. This chapter concludes by attempting to identify which aspects of TINP have been effective at reducing rates of undernutrition as well as outlining obstacles to improving child nutritional status in Tamil Nadu.

Methods

My fieldwork in India was conducted in three villages in Tiruvallur (formerly Chingleput) district in Tamil Nadu. Tiruvallur has a population of 2.7 million with 45.5 per cent of the population residing in rural areas. The district consists of 14 blocks, 6 municipalities, and 19 town panchayats. The main religion is Hinduism, but there are also a number of Christians and Muslims. The villages in which fieldwork was conducted are located in Poondi block near the Andhra Pradesh border. The name Poondi is derived from the Tamil word *poondu* which is a shrub found in the block. Poondi consists of 49 villages with a population of 92,168. Approximately 39 per cent of the block population is classified as SC/ST (scheduled caste/scheduled tribe). The block is mainly agricultural with the major crops being rice, *ragi* (finger millet), groundnut (*verkadalai*), green gram, black gram, and sugar cane.

Although the three villages are called by different names, they are located in generally the same area. There is little interaction among the three outside of agricultural labour agreements. The first village is inhabited by a tribal community who live in thatched huts and government-built houses. As a result of the Tribal Welfare Scheme instituted by the government, the community is provided with a primary school and a women's centre, as well as a safe water pump. The community is relatively insular but due to increasing deforestation has been forced to give up its traditional occupations (men: hunters and trappers, women: gatherers of roots and wild fruits) and enter the labour market as agricultural workers. Increased rates of undernutrition signify the change this community is going through. As more and more of their land is taken away, households must find alternative sources of food; often necessity drives them to enter the labour market.

The second village consists of *Dalits* and OBCs (low-caste Shudras) who are separated by a lake. Although considered one village (called by the same name), these two caste communities have almost no interaction. Due to the activities of the local NGO Shanti[2] which is based in this village, the *Dalit* community has a safe water source provided by the local panchayat as well as free health and educational services. The *Dalits* live in thatched huts and mainly work as agricultural labourers. Across the lake, OBCs live in brick houses with thatched roofs. Livelihoods primarily are agricultural but usually in higher-paid, more stable occupations such as running a tractor or supervising coolies.

The third village consists of members of the Forward Caste (high-caste Telugu Naidus) who live next to a paved road. A few of these houses are surrounded by a gate and were several stories high overlooking the paddy fields. The members of this community are usually landowners. There were rumours among Shanti staff that several of these households had sent their children to the US to study engineering. Unfortunately, I was not able to collect data from the wealthiest households on the street because the gatekeeper would not allow us in. Thus, the sample taken from the FC community is taken from the poorer half of the community, not all FC households.

Data collection consisted of both structured and semi-structured questionnaires with women as well as visits to *anganwadis* and women's groups. Interviews were conducted in Tamil with the assistance of a research assistant who had previous experience in health. Concurrently, I attempted to estimate the scale of undernutrition in these communities through anthropometric measurements of children. Children were weighed using a scale and height was taken with a tape measure. For extremely young children, mothers reported the child's weight and height. I do not have estimates of measurement error. Although anthropometry as a screening device at the individual level is problematic as discussed earlier in this book, at the population level it is a useful method of assessing nutritional status.

The quantitative survey data was coded and analysed with the Statistical Package for the Social Sciences (SPSS Version 12.0.1). The dataset initially contained 95 variables on 300 households and included information such as occupation, caste, household income (husband/wife contribution), household expenditure, food expenditure, alcohol expenditure, children's ages, heights, weights, what is usually eaten, what they would like to eat, illness, where health services are acquired, whether *anganwadis* are used, what services it provides, if educational tools such as growth monitoring/supplementary feeding are understood, women's knowledge and practices of child rearing, and participation in women's groups.

Caveats and Challenges with this Study

A methodological issue that emerged during the structured questionnaires was the choice of women as informants. When responding to questions about household income and expenditure, women often did not know and had to guess. In addition, when asked whether their husbands drink alcohol, many women refused to answer the question (21.2% of the sample). Several also seemed hesitant to criticize *anganwadis* since they received food and other benefits and were afraid that their response could affect future assistance. This seems to be a general problem when undertaking evaluations of projects in which respondents feel that something is better than nothing, and want the project to continue.

In addition, the 300 households that were surveyed were not chosen using a random sampling method and thus cannot be viewed as representative of the communities. For the purposes of exploring the social meanings and symbolism of TINP, a sample of 300 households is large relative to other such analyses. To understand the impact of the project at the local level, it is necessary to examine its role in and integration into village life and concerns. Large-scale quantitative data collection can achieve understanding of the project at a different level. However, the concurrent existence of three different nutrition projects makes it difficult to examine changes in anthropometric outcomes and attribute them to certain 'tools' or inputs (e.g. growth monitoring).

There are also universal challenges with studying undernutrition. Undernutrition can be studied quantitatively using anthropometrics or intake-based measures, but as I described in Chapter 3, these are problematic. Undernutrition can also be measured qualitatively using participant-observation, informal conversations, and interviews. However, given the very personal nature of food, it is difficult to obtain access to mealtimes and persuade individuals to reflect on their feeling towards food. This requires a large degree of trust between researcher and informant. To complement data on individual or household practices concerning nutrition, there should be an inclusion of the wider meaning of foods locally, such as the status, the choice or selection, and symbolic nature of various food items.

Table 5.1. Percentage of informants (*n*) per community

	ST	SC	OBC	FC
Informants (*n*)	63	70	71	96
Total number of households	149	309	261	150
Percentage of households interviewed	42.2	22.6	27.2	64.0

The Communities

The four communities reside in the same area, although they have little social interaction aside from work relationships. Table 5.1 displays the number of informants in each community. It should be noted that the sample size indicated in the various tables in this study is dependent on the question investigated as not all informants responded to every question.

Table 5.2 shows the number of individuals employed in different occupations by caste. The most common occupation of all four groups is agricultural. The most common labour for women is as a coolie, or daily agricultural labourer. Only a small number of women of higher caste work as coolies. Thus, women of lower caste have less stable or permanent work since coolie work is of this nature. In contrast, more women of higher caste work as housewives (*veetukaari*). Housewives primarily work in the domestic arena and undertake activities such as childcare, water collection, and cooking. Almost three times the number of FC women stay at home compared to SC women, which might reflect higher-caste women having less pressure to earn in the public sphere or, as Karin

Table 5.2. Number of individuals employed in different occupations by caste

	ST		SC		OBC		FC	
	Female	Male	Female	Male	Female	Male	Female	Male
N	61	61	70	65	71	68	96	96
Coolie	41	47	45	42	32	38	15	37
Agriculture	0	6	1	14	0	18	0	43
Housewife	18	0	19	0	34	0	76	0
Lower-paid specialized worker	2	1	2	2	3	4	0	1
Higher-paid specialized worker	0	4	3	3	2	4	3	8
Office job	0	1	0	0	0	1	2	5
Unemployed	0	2	0	4	0	3	0	2

Kapadia has suggested, that higher-caste women are more restricted to the household for religious and social reasons.[3] I asked a FC woman why she does not work. She replied, 'My husband doesn't let me work. He says to me, "Don't I earn enough?"' However, the relationships between caste and being a housewife, or working as a coolie, are loose. There are some poor high-caste households where the wife has to work as a coolie, and there are some better-off households in all other three castes where the wife is a housewife.

The number of occupations that men reported to be engaged in was 26, while for women the number was 12, reflecting the observation that men have more opportunities in the public sphere. As with women, a smaller percentage of men of higher caste work as coolies than among men of lower castes. The percentage of men working in agriculture, but in more stable jobs, is greater among the higher castes. FC men are more likely to be landowners and own a tractor. More higher-caste men have non-agricultural occupations such as drivers, or working in a bank, or for the government. These occupations give the highest economic return; the mean income for a driver is 1,002 Rs./week while for the latter two it is on average 2,706 Rs./week.

Figure 5.1 shows the age-specific fertility rate by caste. The total fertility rate is between 2.0 and 2.6 which is lower than the all-India rate of 2.85.[4] Family planning efforts have been successful. No household in any community had more than five children. The number of children in the household increases with women's age. However, there is no significant difference in the number of children in a household by caste and there is no significant interaction between the effect of caste and the effect of a women's age group.

Table 5.3 shows that the proportion of school-age children enrolled in formal education in all communities is over 80 per cent. A distinction should be made between formal and informal education. Women who are unable to send their children to school often find other ways to educate their children. One woman explained, 'I do not send my children to school because it is too expensive, so I pay someone two rupees a month to teach them all the subjects.' Again there is no significant difference in whether children attend formal education according to caste.

The main providers of formal education are government schools, private schools, and a school that the NGO Shanti runs for poor children. There is a significant difference in what type of school children attend according to caste. Private schools are primarily used by FC and OBC households. An explanation for this is that private schools charge high

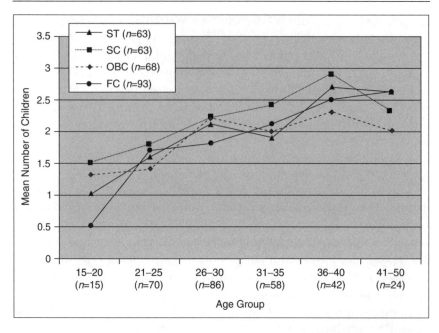

Figure 5.1. Age-specific fertility rate by caste. Two-way ANOVA: caste: $F = 1.4$, $df = 3$, $p = .3$; age group: $F = 10.5$, $df = 5$, $p < .001$; caste–age group interaction: $F = 0.6$, $df = 15$, $p = .8$

fees that lower caste families may not be able to afford. The NGO school primarily serves SC and OBC children. Conversations with the NGO director revealed that the school was of high quality, yet restricted admission to extremely poor households. The ST community is located the farthest from the NGO school and has limited access to the site where it was

Table 5.3. Choice of school by household for school-age children by caste

	N (households)	Attends school (%)	Of those attending school		
			Government (%)	Private (%)	NGO (%)
ST	61	75.4	84.2	10.5	5.3
SC	64	87.5	59.3	5.6	35.2
OBC	65	72.3	56.5	21.7	21.7
FC	78	84.6	84.2	10.5	5.3

School attendance by caste: $\chi^2 = 6.5$, $df = 3$, $p = .09$.
Type of school attended by caste: $\chi^2 = 32.2$, $df = 6$, $p < .001$.

Table 5.4. Women's educational attainment by caste

	N	Completed fifth standard (%)
ST	49	10.2
SC	56	28.6
OBC	47	12.8
FC	65	72.3

$x^2 = 65.0$, $df = 3$, $p < .001$.

located. This is a likely explanation for the low number of ST children attending the NGO school. The ST community has a government school located in their community. Several ST and SC families mentioned that the fees charged for government schools were their main expense.

Table 5.4 shows the proportion of women having attained fifth standard by caste. Significantly fewer ST, SC, and OBC women have completed fifth standard than FC women. Despite the low percentage of women who had completed fifth standard in the ST, SC, and OBC communities, the mass media campaign by the government for education and literacy has been internalized. When I asked several tribal children what they would like to become when they were older, there were responses such as doctor, police-man, and teacher, which indicate that children are aspiring to careers requiring higher levels of education. Despite the wide body of literature discussing discrimination in education towards girls, this phenomenon was not apparent in these four communities. One tribal girl stated she wanted to be Chief Minister (like Jayalalitha) when she was older.

Table 5.5. Type of last illness in family by caste

	N	Illness	
		Infectious (%)	Non-infectious (%)
ST	41	85.4	14.6
SC	47	78.7	21.3
OBC	44	79.5	20.5
FC	62	83.9	16.1

Infectious disease refers to fever, cough, cold, worms, stomach pains, diarrhoea, boils, and tuberculosis.
Non-infectious refers to physical and mental handicaps, organ problems, body pains, and allergies.
$x^2 = 1.0$, $df = 3$, $p = .8$.

Table 5.6. Percentage of women reporting child with serious illness by caste

	N	Serious illness (%)
ST	57	3.2
SC	67	11.9
OBC	69	2.9
FC	92	0

$\chi^2 = 14.3$, $df = 3$, $p < .005$.

Table 5.5 shows the percentage of households reporting their last illness as having been infectious or non-infectious, respectively, according to caste. All four castes report much more infectious than non-infectious disease, there being no significant difference among the castes. Table 5.6 shows the percentage of women reporting that one or more of their children had a serious (life-threatening) illness. There is a significant relationship between serious illness and caste. Possible explanations are that in SC households it is more likely that both parents work and have less time for childcare and for visits to a health centre, and SC households have generally lower incomes compared to FC. While ST households are also on average disadvantaged, the tribal community is insular with high levels of cooperation in childcare compared to SC. This might explain why rates of serious illness are lower in ST households compared to SC. In terms of minor illnesses such as coughs and colds, most households reported disease was relatively infrequent among them. The main explanations given for the generally good health status of the communities were a safe water source which is provided by the local *panchayat* (village council), adequate and free provision of health services at the *anganwadi*, and a free dispensary provided by the NGO.

Household Income

The current official poverty line of the Government of India is 368 Rs. per week. This has been criticized by Indian academics and development practitioners for being deliberately set low in order to reduce the percentage of the poor, for political reasons. The re-adjusted poverty line proposed by Mohan Guruswamy and Ronald Abraham is 840 Rs. per week.[5] The income data was skewed and a log transformation was used to normalize it. Table 5.7 presents the household income distribution by

Table 5.7. Income distribution (rupees/week) by caste

	ST	SC	OBC	FC
N	63	70	71	96
Log mean	2.632	2.762	2.712	2.813
Standard deviation	0.2089	0.2222	0.2389	0.3098
Geometric mean	428.2	577.4	515.6	649.4

$F = 6.8$, $df = 3$, $p < .001$.

caste. The geometric mean household incomes of the ST, SC, OBC, and FC households fall beneath the re-adjusted poverty line. The means that household income of the different groups are significantly different from each other. A Scheffe test reveals that the difference in mean household income in the ST community compared to the other groups is primarily responsible for this statistical significance. Table 5.8 presents the income distribution by caste and by gender. The mean income differs significantly across caste. In both instances, mean FC income is greater than those of the other three castes, as shown in Table 5.9, which gives Scheffe test results.

Household income is highly variable in these communities, variability being higher in FC than in the other three castes. There are likely to be more possibilities for members of higher castes to attain higher incomes through pursuing occupations such as banking or working for the government.

Child Nutritional Status

Figures 5.2 and 5.3 show weights and heights by age of children aged 0–15 years while Tables 5.10 and 5.11 show the proportion of children below the fifth centile of height-for-age, weight-for-age, and weight-for-height. These reveal the scale of the nutritional problem in all four communities.

As Tables 5.10 and 5.11 show, there is no significant variation in nutritional status according to caste or gender (height-for-age: $\chi^2 = 0.8$, $df = 1$, $p = .4$; weight-for-age: $\chi^2 = 0.3$, $df = 1$, $p = .6$; weight-for-height: $\chi^2 = 2.0$, $df = 1$, $p = .2$). For both males and females, there is a trend that higher castes have a smaller percentage of children falling below the fifth centile of the NCHS (1977) reference. For gender, there is no recognizable trend. This runs contrary to research by James Levinson on undernutrition in

Table 5.8. Income distribution (rupees/week) by gender and caste

	ST		SC		OBC		FC	
	Female	Male	Female	Male	Female	Male	Female	Male
N	39	61	47	65	33	66	15	94
Log mean	2.229	2.516	2.303	2.636	2.248	2.637	2.601	2.775
Standard deviation	0.2126	0.2376	0.1915	0.2477	0.1473	0.2662	0.4159	0.2750
Geometric mean	169.4	328.2	201.0	432.5	177.1	433.8	398.9	595.5

Female income distribution by caste: $F = 10.9$, $df = 3$, $p < .001$.
Male income distribution by caste: $F = 12.8$, $df = 3$, $p < .001$.

Table 5.9. Differences in income by caste and gender (Scheffe test)

	Female income			
	ST	SC	OBC	PC
Male income				
ST	—			***
SC		—	*	***
OBC			—	***
FC	*	*	*	—

*Indicates slight significance ($p < .1$).
***Indicates strong significance ($p < .001$).

Punjabi children. Levinson concludes that gender is the most statistically significant determinant of nutritional status.[6]

The difference to my data could reflect two phenomena. The first is that gender differentials are not marked in these communities, which is in agreement with the literature that notes that Tamil Nadu is gender 'neutral' in child rearing and feeding practices. The second is that the weakest, and most nutritionally vulnerable, girls have high mortality rates. Thus, the healthier girl children survive which might be reflected in the data.

Who Uses Anganwadis?

The first aspect of TINP to be examined pertains to the use of *anganwadis*, community nutrition centres which provide three types of nutrition intervention package to households. Each centre provides the NMS (midday meal scheme), ICDS (health services, preschool education), and TINP (growth monitoring, nutrition counselling, supplementary feeding). The specifics of each intervention are described in Chapter 2. Of all the states in India, this arrangement only exists in Tamil Nadu.

Table 5.12 shows that *anganwadi* attendance is high among all groups but is significantly higher in the SC and OBC groups. Members of the FC community associate the *anganwadi* with poor people and are more hesitant to send their children to the mixed-caste environment. In addition, many FC households can afford to send their children to private clinics for health services. Only one FC woman in my survey reported

A. ST

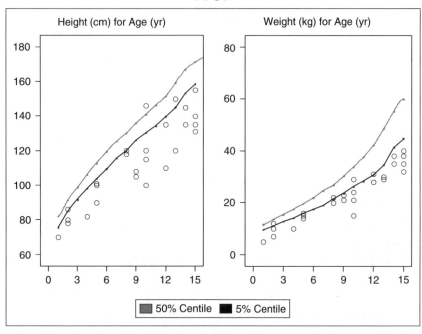

B. SC

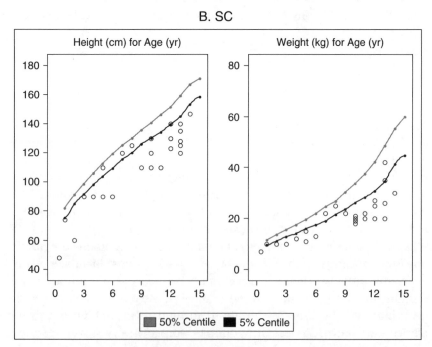

Figure 5.2. Boys' nutritional status (eldest child) relative to NCHS reference

C. OBC

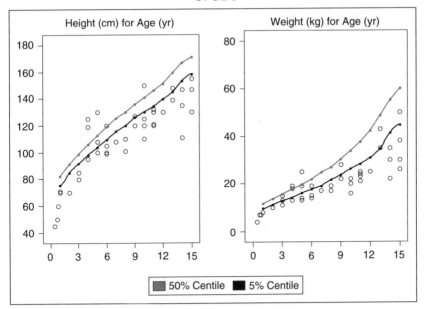

D. FC

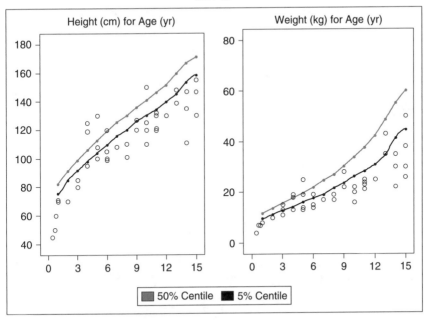

Figure 5.2. (*Continued*)

A. ST

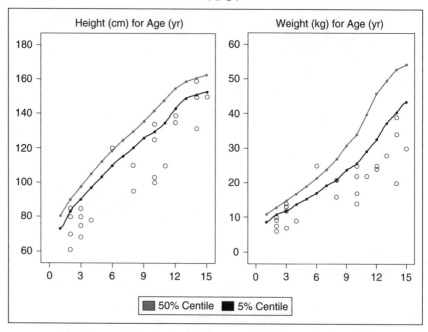

B. SC

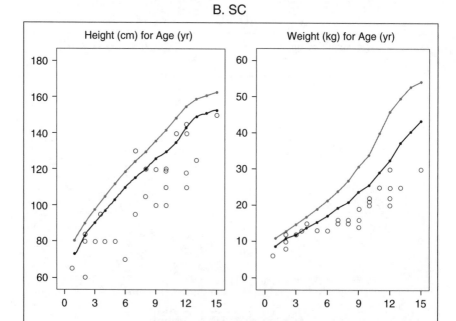

Figure 5.3. Girls' nutritional status (eldest child) relative to NCHS reference

C. OBC

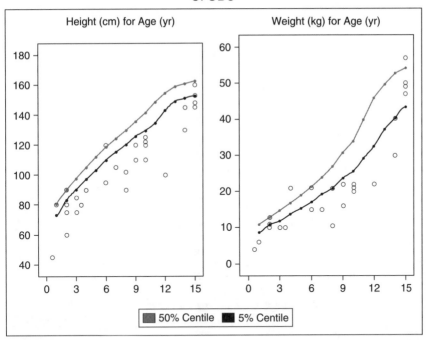

D. FC

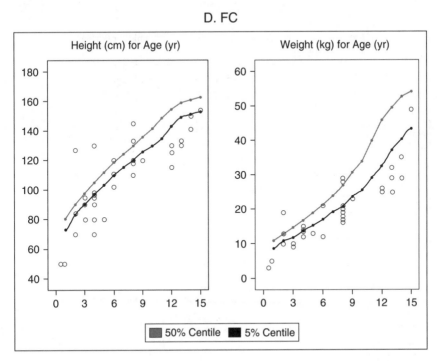

Figure 5.3. (*Continued*)

Table 5.10. Boys' nutritional status (eldest child) relative to NCHS reference

	N	<5th centile (%)	>5th centile (%)
A. Height-for-age			
ST	26	84.6	15.4
SC	22	86.4	13.6
OBC	39	82.1	17.9
FC	40	80.0	20.0
B. Weight-for-age			
ST	26	80.8	10.2
SC	22	72.7	27.3
OBC	39	76.9	23.1
FC	40	72.5	27.5
C. Weight-for-height			
ST	26	23.1	76.9
SC	22	40.9	59.1
OBC	39	17.9	82.1
FC	40	30.0	70.0

Height-for-age: $\chi^2 = 0.5$, $df = 3$, $p = .9$; weight-for-age: $\chi^2 = 0.7$, $df = 3$, $p = .9$; weight-for-height: $\chi^2 = 3.6$, $df = 3$, $p = .3$.

Table 5.11. Girls' nutritional status (eldest child) relative to NCHS reference

	N	<5th centile (%)	>5th centile (%)
A. Height-for-age			
ST	24	83.3	16.7
SC	25	80.0	20.0
OBC	27	85.2	14.8
FC	34	67.6	32.4
B. Weight-for-age			
ST	24	83.3	16.7
SC	25	88.0	12.0
OBC	27	55.6	44.4
FC	34	67.6	32.4
C. Weight-for-height			
ST	24	41.7	58.3
SC	25	48.0	52.0
OBC	27	29.6	70.4
FC	34	29.4	70.6

Height-for-age: $\chi^2 = 3.4$, $df = 3$, $p = .3$; weight-for-age: $\chi^2 = 8.8$, $df = 3$, $p = .03$; weight-for-height: $\chi^2 = 3.0$, $df = 3$, $p = .4$.

Table 5.12. Use and enjoyment of *anganwadi* by caste

	N	Attends *anganwadi* (%)	Fraction enjoying attendance (%)
ST	62	69.4	69.8
SC	66	84.8	73.0
OBC	67	85.1	77.4
FC	92	64.1	57.6

Anganwadi attendance: $\chi^2 = 13.9$, $df = 3$, $p < .005$.
Anganwadi enjoyment: $\chi^2 = 1.4$, $df = 3$, $p = .7$.

that she had never heard of the *anganwadi* before. The ST community is smaller and more isolated than the SC and OBC and due to this intimacy, there are higher levels of co-operation and solidarity (sometimes referred to by economists as social capital). ST women prefer to receive their health messages through kinship networks rather than attend a centre and receive intensive nutrition counselling. As Table 5.12 shows, most women reported enjoying the visits to *anganwadi* especially since they received free food (NMS) and health services (ICDS). Enjoyment was lowest among the FC group. The main reasons given for not liking it were the distance of the centre from their homes and the impracticality and repetitiveness of health advice.

As Table 5.13 shows, most women attend *anganwadi* monthly. Those who are either pregnant or lactating are required to attend daily to receive check-ups, food supplements, and health education. Table 5.14 presents the mean household income according to *anganwadi* attendance and caste. To account for the skewedness of the income data, a log transformation was used on household income. There is no significant difference in mean log household income between those who attend *anganwadi* and

Table 5.13. Frequency of *anganwadi* visits by caste

	N (attending *anganwadi*)	Daily or weekly (%)	Every two weeks or monthly (%)
ST	43	8.1	91.9
SC	56	37.5	62.5
OBC	57	35.0	65.0
FC	59	39.0	61.0

$\chi^2 = 12.6$, $df = 3$, $p = .006$.

Table 5.14. Mean household income (rupees/week) and *anganwadi* attendance by caste

	Yes	No
ST		
Log mean	2.672	2.557
Standard deviation	0.2106	0.1764
Geometric mean	470.0	360.9
SC		
Log mean	2.806	2.757
Standard deviation	0.2975	0.2229
Geometric mean	639.0	571.9
OBC		
Log mean	2.772	2.725
Standard deviation	0.2252	0.4669
Geometric mean	529.1	530.4
FC		
Log mean	2.722	2.834
Standard deviation	0.1835	0.3503
Geometric mean	526.7	682.7

Caste: $F = 7.0$, $df = 3$, $p < .001$; *anganwadi* attendance: $F = 0.4$, $df = 1$, $p = .5$; caste-*anganwadi* attendance interaction: $F = 0.9$, $df = 3$, $p = .9$.

those who do not although the perception exists that *anganwadis* are used primarily by the worse-off.

Growth Monitoring and Promotion

Table 5.15 reports data on the effectiveness of growth monitoring as an educational tool against malnutrition. While most children who attended *anganwadi* were weighed, there is no significant difference in whether a

Table 5.15. Growth monitoring and promotion use and understanding by caste

	ST (%)	SC (%)	OBC (%)	FC (%)
Child weighed	87.2 ($N = 47$)	92.9 ($N = 56$)	96.4 ($N = 56$)	90.2 ($N = 61$)
Seen growth chart at *anganwadi*	11.8 ($N = 51$)	54.4 ($N = 57$)	23.0 ($N = 61$)	25.0 ($N = 62$)
Correctly identify growth chart	11.8 ($N = 51$)	52.6 ($N = 57$)	23.7 ($N = 59$)	38.7 ($N = 62$)
Correctly explain growth chart	2.0 ($N = 51$)	5.3 ($N = 57$)	6.6 ($N = 61$)	8.1 ($N = 62$)

Child weighed: $\chi^2 = 3.2$, $df = 3$, $p = .4$; seen growth chart before: $\chi^2 = 25.5$, $df = 3$, $p < .001$; correctly identify growth chart: $\chi^2 = 23.8$, $df = 3$, $p < .001$; correctly explain growth chart: $\chi^2 = 1.6$, $df = 3$, $p = .7$.

child was weighed according to caste. A high percentage of women in all caste groups could not correctly identify a growth chart. The ability to correctly identify a growth chart and to recognize a growth chart varied significantly according to caste. There is no significant difference in the ability to correctly identify a growth chart according to attendance at *anganwadi* ($\chi^2 = 7.1$, $df = 2$, p = 0.03).

Of SC women, 54.4 per cent (compared to 38.7% of FC) reported that they had seen a growth chart before and 52.6 per cent (compared to 33.9% of FC) tried to explain what it showed. However, only 4.3 per cent of SC women (5.2% of FC) were able to do so correctly. There is no significant difference in the ability to correctly explain a growth chart according to caste. It would be expected that FC women, who come from households with higher incomes and who are more educated than SC (71.8 vs. 28% have completed the fifth standard at school), would be more likely to understand growth monitoring and recognize growth charts. However, this does not hold true in these communities. The correct identification of a growth chart does not vary according to women's educational attainment ($\chi^2 = 3.5$, $df = 1$, p = 0.06).

Supplementary Feeding

Another aspect of TINP is the provision of supplementary food, in the form of a *laddoo*, to children whose growth is faltering. The feeding programme lasts 90 days, after which the child is removed from it. However, eligibility criteria are not always followed at the village level. During my visits to the *anganwadi*, I noticed that all children present received the supplement. Survey data supports this observation (Table 5.16). Whether a child received the supplement did not significantly vary by caste. Feelings

Table 5.16. Supplement received at *anganwadi* by caste

	N	Yes (%)
ST	51	84.3
SC	56	96.4
OBC	61	88.5
FC	61	88.5

$\chi^2 = 4.5$, $df = 3$, p = .2.

Table 5.17. Preferred food at *anganwadi* by caste

	N	'Healthy food' (%)	Supplement (%)
ST	45	88.9	11.1
SC	54	70.4	29.6
OBC	53	94.3	5.7
FC	53	98.1	1.9

$\chi^2 = 22.8$, $df = 3$, $p < .001$.

towards the supplement were mixed. As Table 5.17 shows, only 11.1, 29.6, 5.7, and 1.9 per cent of ST, SC, OBC, and FC women, respectively, reported the supplement as their preferred food to receive at *anganwadi*. All groups preferred to receive what can be classified as 'healthy food' (*nalla chappadu*). The literal translation of this is good food. The term *nalla chappadu* refers to vegetables, rice, *dal* (lentils), and egg, all foods holding a symbolic value beyond their caloric density. There is a significant difference in the expressed food preference among the four caste communities. On average, the SC households prefer the supplement relative to the FC and OBC households.

Intensive Nutrition Counselling

Intensive nutrition counselling is the third main component of TINP. To investigate the relative weight that women give to education, I enquired as to which is the preferred package of services. TINP, NMS, and ICDS have three different strategies to reduce rates of undernutrition: TINP focuses on education, NMS on feeding, and ICDS on health services. As Table 5.18 shows, the highest percentage of women preferred NMS, followed by ICDS, and finally TINP.

Although the preferred package does not vary significantly according to caste, a higher percentage of FC households reported TINP as their preferred package of services. There is the possibility that higher castes are better able to implement the advice given at *anganwadi* and find the health messages useful. Lower castes, who are generally poorer, seem to find the health messages impractical given the time and resource constraints they face. As for NMS, it might seem counterintuitive that more

Table 5.18. Preferred package of services by caste[a]

	N	TINP (%)	NMS (%)	ICDS (%)
ST	45	13.3	44.4	42.2
SC	54	13.0	44.4	42.6
OBC	56	17.9	55.4	26.8
FC	56	23.2	48.2	28.6

[a] TINP category encompasses food supplementation, growth monitoring and health education. NMS category is food. ICDS category is health services and immunizations.
TINP: $\chi^2 = 1.6$, $df = 3$, $p = .7$; NMS: $\chi^2 = 1.3$, $df = 3$, $p = .7$; ICDS: $\chi^2 = 1.0$, $df = 3$, $p = .8$; total: $\chi^2 = 6.4$, $df = 6$, $p = .4$.

women in the OBC community than from SC or ST cited the food package as their preferred, given that the SC and ST communities are poorer. However, qualitative interviews revealed that OBC women are more likely to receive health services from private providers. Thus they have less need for the free health services offered by ICDS. The SC and ST households primarily demand health services from the *anganwadi*. This fits in with the observation that more of these households prefer ICDS health services to food.

Table 5.19 shows what women felt they had learned at *anganwadi*. Women were asked to report what was the primary advice they received through TINP. There is no significant difference in main educational message learned at *anganwadi* according to caste. The results were fairly evenly split between hygiene (*suhadharam*), health (*odambu*), food,[7] and the response 'I don't know'. The high rate of women reporting 'I don't know' indicates that neither educational nor income level had improved understandings of health messages in these communities.

Table 5.19. Main type of knowledge acquired at *anganwadi* by caste

	N	Hygiene (%)	Health (%)	Food (%)	Do not know (%)
ST	63	29.5	29.5	9.1	31.8
SC	53	22.6	35.8	20.8	20.8
OBC	56	23.2	28.6	30.4	17.9
FC	60	40.0	18.3	10.0	31.7

Hygiene: $\chi^2 = 1.3$, $df = 3$, $p = .7$; health: $\chi^2 = 1.3$, $df = 3$, $p = .7$; food: $\chi^2 = 5.4$, $df = 3$, $p = .1$; do not know: $\chi^2 = 1.7$, $df = 3$, $p = .6$; total: $\chi^2 = 19.6$, $df = 9$, $p = .02$.

Knowledge and Practice of Childcare

Table 5.20 shows that there is a high level of knowledge in all four communities on proper caring practices, as defined by the WHO. Over 80 per cent of women in all caste groups had received three ante-natal check-ups as well as iron tablets during pregnancy (*masama irukka*). Over 90 per cent of women in all caste groups reported that it was important to take rest during pregnancy, although fewer actually took it. The structural constraints of lack of time and money were the primary reasons given for this.

As Table 5.20 also shows, most women in all four groups ate more during pregnancy. This dietary change was explained by women in all caste communities as a way either to improve the growth of their baby, to ensure a healthy child, or to maintain the health of the woman. Less cited reasons were to ensure adequate breast milk and to have a good birth. This finding runs contrary to Mark and Mimi Nichter's data collected through interviews with 282 women in coastal Karnataka.[8] The Nichters discovered that the majority of women had a preference for a small baby and that women restricted their food intake during pregnancy. There are several possible explanations for the contrary findings. First, Tamil Nadu may be different to Karnataka in terms of beliefs on the proper infant size at birth. Second, the marketing of transnational companies tying the image of wealth to large size is influencing these communities. Third, health education campaigns by the government and by Shanti which promote large baby size are increasingly accepted by women.

Knowledge concerning the health value of colostrum (*cheeyam pal*) is high (Table 5.20); 100, 95.5, 98.5, and 100 per cent of ST, SC, OBC, and FC women, respectively, were aware of its benefits while 98.4, 93.9, 98.6, and 96.7 per cent had given it to their last child. This is quite remarkable given that some Ayurvedic practitioners recommend colostrum avoidance to the child because it is considered polluting.[9] In Ayurvedic thought, the infant's body is a *pacca udampu* (fresh, tender body) because the body is weak and vulnerable like the tender shoot of a plant. Like a tender shoot, the child needs water and mother's milk and is highly sensitive to fluctuations in the content of the milk. Some Ayurvedic practitioners argue that *cheeyam pal* causes diarrhoea and nausea and is too hard for the *pacca udampu*. Furthermore, colostrum is viewed as deriving from menstrual blood which ceases at conception and which has been stagnating during pregnancy.

Table 5.20. Caring practices by caste

	ST (%)	SC (%)	OBC (%)	FC (%)
Had three ante-natal checkups during last pregnancy	85.2 (N = 60)	98.5 (N = 66)	95.7 (N = 69)	92.3 (N = 91)
Took iron tablets during last pregnancy	87.1 (N = 62)	95.2 (N = 63)	94.1 (N = 68)	92.3 (N = 91)
Knows that rest is important during pregnancy	96.8 (N = 62)	98.5 (N = 67)	98.6 (N = 69)	100.0 (N = 91)
Rested more than usual during last pregnancy	80.6 (N = 62)	72.7 (N = 66)	85.5 (N = 69)	87.0 (N = 92)
Ate more during last pregnancy	91.4 (N = 58)	86.4 (N = 66)	89.9 (N = 69)	95.3 (N = 85)
Knows health benefits of colostrum	100.0 (N = 63)	95.5 (N = 67)	98.5 (N = 69)	100.0 (N = 91)
Gave colostrum to last child	98.4 (N = 61)	93.9 (N = 66)	98.6 (N = 69)	96.7 (N = 92)
Knows health benefits of iodized salt	52.4 (N = 63)	57.1 (N = 70)	54.9 (N = 71)	62.1 (N = 58)
Uses iodized salt	41.9 (N = 62)	54.3 (N = 70)	54.3 (N = 70)	55.2 (N = 96)

Differences according to caste—three ante-natal checkups: $\chi^2 = 11.6$, $df = 3$, $p = .1$; iron tablets: $\chi^2 = 3.4$, $df = 3$, $p = .3$; knowledge about rest: $\chi^2 = 2.8$, $df = 3$, $p = .4$; rested during last pregnancy: $\chi^2 = 6.0$, $df = 3$, $p = .1$; ate more during last pregnancy: $\chi^2 = 3.8$, $df = 3$, $p = .3$; knowledge about colostrum: $\chi^2 = 6.8$, $df = 3$, $p = .08$; colostrum given to last child: $\chi^2 = 2.9$, $df = 3$, $p = .4$; knowledge about iodized salt: $\chi^2 = 0.1$, $df = 3$, $p = .99$; uses iodized salt: $\chi^2 = 6.4$, $df = 3$, $p = .1$

Table 5.21. Duration of breastfeeding of last child by caste

	ST (%) N = 62	SC (%) N = 65	OBC (%) N = 68	FC (%) N = 92
0–12 months	8.1	6.2	7.4	7.6
12–36 months	74.2	84.6	82.4	87.0
>36 months	17.7	9.2	10.3	5.4

$\chi^2 = 6.6$, $df = 6$, $p = .4$.

As Tables 5.21 and 5.22 show, knowledge on breastfeeding (*taipaal*) duration and the timing of introduction of complementary foods were similar to the WHO recommended guidelines (1–3 years breastfeeding, complementary foods introduced after 6 months). Finally, knowledge and usage of iodized salt were not high and did not vary according to caste (Table 5.20). Branded labels of iodized salt were mentioned as being more expensive than regular salt, which is not iodized.

My observations show that, in these communities, inadequate knowledge and ignorance are not the factors implicated in high rates of child undernutrition. Although practices such as eating less during pregnancy have been documented, this is generally not the case in these communities. Cecilia van Hollen made similar observations during her fieldwork in Tamil Nadu in 1995.[10] She argues that cultural conceptions of the body and diet are not responsible for the malnutrition observed because they are used in a flexible way. She observed women consuming taboo foods post-partum and individually constructing rules of avoidance. Such taboo foods included nonvegetarian food (soups made with chicken or fish). Van Hollen concludes that malnutrition is more the result of class and gender discrimination than traditional knowledge leading to detrimental caring practices. This may also be the case in my study.

Table 5.22. Knowledge on complementary foods by caste

	ST (%) N = 61	SC (%) N = 62	OBC (%) N = 68	FC (%) N = 88
0–6 months	13.1	8.1	4.4	4.6
6–12 months	72.1	74.2	86.8	87.4
>12 months	14.8	17.7	8.8	8.0

$\chi^2 = 10.1$, $df = 6$, $p = 0.1$.

Despite the high rates of illiteracy and low rates of fifth standard school completion in these communities, caring knowledge is high in all four caste communities. There is no significant difference in caring practices and knowledge according to caste. The main places where caring practices are learned, other than kinship networks and *anganwadi*, are through women's groups (*mathar sangam*) and television. In each of these communities, almost every household has access to a television. If a family does not own one, they visit a neighbour who does. Women reported that film stars would discuss healthy practices between programmes. The TV, as one health worker stated, 'has replaced sex as the pleasure for the masses' and is extensively employed as a health education medium by the Government of India and the Government of Tamil Nadu.

Drawing Conclusions on the Effectiveness of TINP

Conventionally, the effectiveness of nutrition projects has been defined as increases in child growth or anthropometric status relative to growth reference norms. In this book, I examine effectiveness using a combination of qualitative and quantitative methods.

Growth monitoring is not understood in any of the study communities regardless of income or educational level of the household, indicating a mismatch in the programme at three different levels. TINP's objective is to use growth monitoring as an educational tool. The discourse in Washington, DC, New Delhi, and Chennai revolves around how growth monitoring can make malnutrition 'visible' to the mother. The second understanding is at the level of front-line nutrition workers. They believe that growth monitoring is carried out for data collection purposes only. When I visited the *anganwadi*, the nutrition worker showed me proudly huge orange books of weights, charts, and numbers. Each *anganwadi* maintains 30 registers:

1. Weight
2. Survey/enumeration
3. Beneficiary selection
4. Feeding
5. ANC/PNC
6. Food stock (a)
7. Food stock (b)

8. Food indent
9. Immunization
10. Medicine—volume 1 (Vitamin A)
11. Medicine—volume 2 (deworming)
12. Referral
13. Referral book (printed)
14. Birth and death
15. Women's working group
16. Children's working group
17. Demonstration
18. Educational tools
19. House visits
20. Visitor's notebook
21. Children's attendance at feeding
22. Mother's attendance
23. CNW and Ayah attendance
24. Contingencies/other expense
25. Permanent stock
26. 36-month age completed children's programme
27. Daily diary
28. Weight cards handed over, taken over
29. Stock of papaya plants
30. Monthly reports

In the stand-alone community nutrition projects such as TINP, health workers have the crucial responsibility of generating official statistics for the state and for the World Bank. Nutrition centres seem to become places where record-keeping and data collection become ends in themselves. In growth monitoring and promotion, rather than identifying growth trends to counsel a mother as officially stated, these workers spend a large amount of time filling in the necessary information in books, registers, and forms. Other than growth data, registers must record such things as how many children attended the centre each day, who they were, their caste, their name, their father's name, how much food and fuel was consumed that day, birth dates of each child, as well as the same data for pregnant women.

Every month, the community worker is required to submit 15 reports (Table 5.23). These reports are sent from the community worker to her supervisor to the instructress, to the Taluk Project Nutrition Officer and

Table 5.23. List of nutrition reports submitted each month by community workers[a]

Monthly progress report	Enrolment particulars, grades of malnutrition, numbers eligible, and in receipt of feeding
Percentage chart	Total number of children, numbers weighed, number weighed as percentage of total, numbers and percentages for the 6–12, 13–24, and 25–36-month age groups, numbers and percentages of SC children, and children in various grades of malnutrition, both graduated and relapsed
Information chart	Total population, SC population, total and SC child population, number weighed (total and SC), number selected for feeding (total and SC) and number actually fed, number in various grades and those with inadequate/no weight gain, number graduated and relapsed, number of referrals, and number of antenatal/postnatal women enrolled
Food indent	Indent for food supplies for children in grades 3 and 4 of malnutrition, who have lost or maintained weight, who have inadequate weight gain, who move from grade 3 to 2 and for antenatal and postnatal mothers. This is calculated separately for children for each of the three age groups: 6–12, 13–24, and 25–36 months. Total food indent calculated from number of beneficiaries, grams of food per individual, number of feeding days, and the total food required
Drug position report	Information on supplies of piprazine citrate for deworming and ORS[b] packets.
Health cards particulars	Information on number of health cards exchanged between health subcenter and *anganwadi*
Vitamin A report	Number of children covered in last Vitamin A campaign and number that needs to be covered in next campaign
SC/ST beneficiaries report	Total number of SC/ST beneficiaries in each category (i.e. by age group, and antenatal and postnatal mothers)
Cooking demonstration report	Date on which demonstration is held and expenses incurred
Medical officers meeting report	Date of the meeting, individuals in attendance and issues discussed
In-service training report	Details about training of field workers
Immunization particulars	Immunization information for DPT and polio
Food production particulars	Amount of food produced
Use of communication materials	Use of flip charts, books, etc.
Key-indicator report	Collation of data from above reports

[a] Shekar (1991), pp. 83–4.
[b] Oral rehydration solution for the treatment of diarrhoeal diseases.

finally to the District Project Nutrition Officer. These records are then used by the district, state, and central governments, as well as the World Bank, to justify expenditure on nutrition projects.

When pushed for the reasons why rates of malnutrition were still high among their communities, one nutrition worker explained, 'Compliance is the problem. The uneducated are non-compliant and even when we give them iron or folate tablets, they do not take them because they do not trust government services. All they want is medicine and injections but they do not follow the advice.' She then criticized *anganwadis*: 'They do not give the services to the women they actually need. They give food that is inappropriate, growth charts to illiterate women and the room is just too crowded.' This perspective was shared by several of the staff I interviewed. They are aware of the limitations of their work attributing the shortcomings of the *anganwadi* to factors outside of their control. The third level of understanding is that of the beneficiaries. Mothers come for food and health services and see weighing as an obstacle. Thus, in these communities, growth monitoring is not an effective educational tool.

Supplementary food is supposed to be targeted only to children whose growth is faltering and to pregnant and lactating women. However, both my interviews and observations indicate that all children who attend *anganwadi* receive the supplement. This is not necessarily a negative outcome: the children do enjoy eating the *laddoo*. However, the impact of the supplement on child nutritional status is lessened due to the substitution effect. Although the supplement is not supposed to replace meals, since it is given early in the morning, mothers often went to *anganwadi* to receive it instead of feeding their child *conji* (rice water) or other breakfast foods.

Local foods such as rice, *dal*, eggs, and vegetables are preferred to the supplementary food, eggs holding a particular social value in these communities. Stunting is a biological outcome of inadequate purchasing power to afford protein-rich foods. Supplementation does not solve the underlying problem of poverty. In addition, supplementary feeding reinforces the framing of undernutrition as a disease at the individual level since once the child is 'cured', indicated by adequate growth, then the problem is seen as solved. In these communities, supplementary feeding in TINP does not work as intended, as an educational tool, but rather is viewed by women as a feeding programme. Women do report that the *laddoo* is one of the primary reasons they attend *anganwadi*.

While intensive nutrition counselling is advocated by the Bank as an effective education strategy, the results were variable. A high percentage of women in all communities could not describe what they learned in these sessions. This indicates that either they are not being taught at all, or the messages are impractical and not useful. Observations of *anganwadi* revealed that intensive nutrition counselling sessions were short, since the nutrition worker's time was spent on growth monitoring, data collection, and food preparation. The focus was on data collection, not interpretation or action. In addition, several women disliked the health messages. One stated, 'They told me to eat more during pregnancy. But I did not, there is not enough food, only one man is working. It is more expensive to live.'

Despite the poor quality of teaching at the *anganwadi*, in these communities, knowledge and practices on childcare are similar to those recommended by the World Health Organization. Women receive their health information through women's groups, kinship networks, the media, and Shanti staff. In addition, the inclusion of public health information in the primary school curriculum results in children informing their parents about 'proper' caring practices. For example, when I asked one mother about iodized salt, she answered she did not know what it was. Her 10-year-old child who was listening chastized her mother for not knowing about iodized salt and briefly explained its benefits ('good for health').

Ignorance and poor childcare do not seem to be the main causes of undernutrition in these communities. While education is necessary, it is insufficient in the face of structural constraints on choice and behaviour. In addition, the delivery of health education is as important as the actual health message. Receiving health counselling at *anganwadi* is not as effective in these communities as other mediums such as through women's groups.

Women's Groups

The initial TINP-I design included the formation of women's groups as part of a health worker's responsibilities. However, subsequent Bank projects based on this design have not included women's groups as a main component. I could not find any official monitoring or evaluation data by the Bank on the effect of women's groups on child nutritional status. In an official Bank document, it is argued that women's participation in group discussion is not as effective as individual-level nutrition counselling between a health worker and mother.[11] However, conversations with Bank staff reflected heterogeneity of opinion. A retired Bank staff member noted that the beneficial effects of TINP can be partially explained by the creation of women's groups that 'got women talking'. Another staff member noted that perhaps a women's group provided space to share educational lessons and beneficial caring practices. Health workers reported that the most pragmatic aspect of TINP was the creation of women's groups.

137

Women's groups usually consist of 10–15 women who meet regularly to discuss common problems, undertake collective action, and conduct saving and lending activities.[12] When about 30 per cent of the poor in a village are involved in a group, the groups come together to form a federation. When reflecting on fieldwork in Tamil Nadu, women's groups struck me as extremely important because they are an affordable entry point for education that has a beneficial impact on the health and quality of life for women and children. A discussion about this with Dr. Anthony Costello, a Professor of Child Health at University of London, revealed that he has found significant positive health effects of women's groups in Nepal. His research project in Nepal has shown that birth outcomes in rural populations improved greatly with the formation of women's groups.[13] For example, the maternal mortality rate was 69 per 100,000 in areas which had women's groups, compared with 341 per 100,000 in areas that did not. Costello has since launched self-help groups in two parts of India, in another area of Nepal, and in Malawi.

In addition to the education benefits, an aspect that might account for the positive changes associated with women's groups is that working groups can result in cooperation and collectivity in domestic work and childcare among households. If one mother engages in productive work, another may help her with childcare.[14] During my fieldwork, I noticed that a factor in the households that had healthier children was the proximity of relatives or extended family. For example, Nirmala has three children, two boys and one girl. The boys are aged 7 and 6 years while the girl is 8 years old. Her husband is a tailor and is away most of the day while she sells *udavutti* (scented smoke). Despite both parents being away most of the day, Nirmala's mother-in-law lives with the family and is able to cook during the day and care for the children. Nirmala's extra income allowed them to buy milk, spinach, potatoes, and pumpkin. Her mother-in-law provided the time necessary for cooking and care.

The formation of women's groups is a cost-effective activity that can not only improve women's economic situation through saving and loan schemes but also encourage female solidarity and independence. As one tribal woman stated, 'I learn what to expect of a man. I want to be independent', while another woman added, 'I get confident with other women.' Women form friendships and bonds in these groups which give them stability. Thus, women's groups are effective mechanisms towards female empowerment which could result in negotiations over household expenditure as well as a reduction in domestic violence.

Table 5.24. Reasons given for participation in women's groups by caste

	N	Economic reasons (%)	Female solidarity (%)
ST	45	75.6	24.4
SC	60	68.3	31.7
OBC	64	64.1	35.9
FC	78	65.4	34.6

$\chi^2 = 1.9$, $df = 3$, $p = .6$.

Tiruvallur district has a well-established system of women's groups formed by health workers and the Assistant Director of Shanti. Data was collected on these. 71.4, 87.1, 91.6, and 84.4 per cent of ST, SC, OBC, and FC women participate in women's groups, respectively. 66.7, 74.3, 76.1, and 64.6 per cent of ST, SC, OBC, and FC women, respectively, attended monthly. As shown in Table 5.24, the main reasons given for participation in women's groups can be grouped into the categories economic and social. These provide members with saving and loan schemes (called 'Ammavasai Panam'), which give women greater access to financial resources and increase their ability to make household decisions. In addition, women reported that women's groups addressed issues such as domestic violence, alcohol consumption, and female equality. The provision of a forum for women to voice their concerns and to gather support enabled them to challenge men on issues related to intrahousehold processes.

The Bank nutrition team should be praised for including women's groups in the design of TINP-I in 1980. However, during the last 25 years, this beneficial aspect of TINP has been neglected when rolling out the project. Through both external (increasing purchasing power) and internal (negotiations with men) pathways, women's groups have an instrumental effect on child nutritional status and an intrinsic effect on women's status.

Obstacles to Addressing Undernutrition

There are several factors that make it extremely difficult to address undernutrition in these communities. The three factors that I would argue play

Table 5.25. Major household expenditure by caste

	ST (%) N = 61	SC (%) N = 67	OBC (%) N = 71	FC (%) N = 96
Food	75.4	67.2	73.2	41.7
Medical fees	21.3	11.9	7.0	33.3
Child education	3.3	20.0	19.7	25.0

$\chi^2 = 37.1$, $df = 6$, $p < .001$.

the largest role are inadequate purchasing power, gender inequality, and alcohol consumption by males.

Destitution can be viewed as a major underlying factor implicated in child undernutrition. The major household expenditure among all castes was food with 75.4, 67.2, 73.2, and 41.7 per cent of ST, SC, OBC, and FC households, respectively, reporting this to be the case (Table 5.25). There is a significant difference in the major household expenditure according to caste. A significantly higher number of ST, SC, and OBC households compared to FC households cited food as their primary expense. Since FC households were generally wealthier, they were able to attend private clinics and hospitals and send their children to private schools. This is reflected in the data which showed that 33.3 and 25.0 per cent of FC households reported medicine and education as their major expenditure (Table 5.25). As Table 5.26 shows, the proportion of weekly household income spent on food was roughly the same among all groups. A logarithmic equation was the best choice to model the relationship between household income and food expenditure (Table 5.27 and Figure 5.4). Figure 5.4 shows that at around 3,000 Rs. (household income), food expenditure is similar for three castes, yet lower for OBC. There is no obvious explanation for this pattern.

Table 5.26. Proportion of weekly household income spent on food by caste

	N	Mean	Standard deviation
ST	63	0.52	0.24
SC	70	0.50	0.22
OBC	71	0.51	0.34
FC	96	0.53	0.29

$F = 0.1$, $df = 3$, $p = .9$.

Table 5.27. Choice of curve for relationship between household income and food expenditure (combined sample: $N = 298$)

	r^2	F	p
Linear	0.18	67.0	<.001
Logarithmic	0.25	98.2	<.001
Quadratic	0.23	43.7	<.001
Cubic	0.23	30.2	<.001

As Table 5.28 shows, there is a significant difference in the number of meals eaten per day according to caste. A greater percentage of ST households eat two or fewer meals per day on average. The expressed desires for food suggest that most people want more rice, meat, and vegetables (Table 5.29). This did not vary according to caste. Given an adequate income, households would aspire to a diet balanced both quantitatively and qualitatively. Thus, the constraint on healthy eating is income, not knowledge.

These findings are similar to a study done by Save the Children UK which looked at the minimum cost of a healthy diet.[15] Save the Children UK undertook this research to examine whether poor communities are able to feed their children adequately with the quantity and quality of dietary intake necessary for healthy growth. In particular, they attempted to determine the minimum cost and affordability of a diet for the household by taking into account seasonal and local variations in availability and price of food. The four study locations were Bangladesh, Myanmar, Ethiopia, and Tanzania. The report found that an adequate diet remains unaffordable for large proportions of the populations in all four study communities. Using these findings, the report concludes that poverty is a significant cause of endemic undernutrition and that strategies to address undernutrition might address economic constraints that limit access to food.

Table 5.28. Meals per day by caste

	N	2 or less (%)	3 (%)
ST	63	28.6	71.4
SC	70	14.3	85.7
OBC	71	8.5	91.5
FC	96	5.2	94.8

$\chi^2 = 20.1$, $df = 3$, $p < .001$.

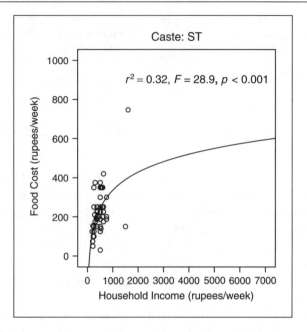

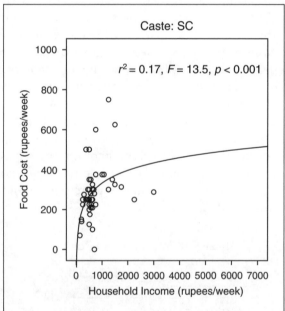

Figure 5.4. Relationship between household income and food expenditure by caste

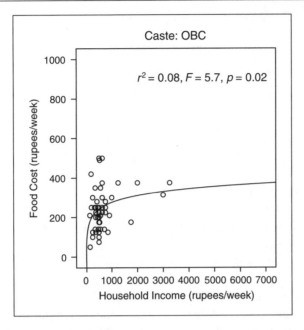

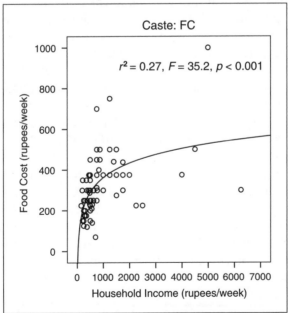

Figure 5.4. (*Continued*)

Table 5.29. Expressed desires for food by caste

	N	Animal products (%)	Rice, pulses, wheat (%)	Vegetables, fruits (%)
ST	59	39.0	39.0	22.0
SC	66	37.9	47.0	15.2
OBC	56	32.1	51.8	16.1
FC	91	35.2	35.2	29.7

$\chi^2 = 8.0$, $df = 6$, $p = .2$.

Engendering Nutrition

However, increasing household purchasing power is not enough. Conventional development theory and practice assume that if men's wages are increasing, all of the household members will be better off. However, studies in South Asia have shown that improvements in welfare depend not only on the levels of income but also on who earns it, since men and women spend differently.[16] Women spend a high proportion of their income on food and health care for children while men use their wages for personal expenditure. In India, women relative to men are less likely to spend their earnings on themselves. Women's incomes are indeed more strongly associated with improvements in children's health and nutritional status.

Joan Mencher's study in Tamil Nadu and Kerala substantiates this claim by comparing earnings versus contributions to household maintenance between women and men.[17] Throughout Tamil Nadu, the amount women contribute (contribution/earning) varies from 95 to 99 per cent compared to men who give 62 to 91 per cent. While the ratio of women's to men's earnings varies from 0.45 to 0.71, the ratio of women's to men's contribution varies from 0.57 to 1.94. In some instances in Tamil Nadu, women must even contribute to their husbands' personal expenses such as betel leaf chewing or smoking in addition to household maintenance. One woman told me, 'Men play cards all day then demand money from the women and beat them.' Studies in South Asia by Barbara Miller and Joel Gittelsohn show that additional female income results in superior nutritional outcomes for women and men, while additional male income only benefits the men.[18] Duncan Thomas shows that the probability that a child will survive in Brazil is 20 times higher when the income is controlled by the women rather than the men of the household.[19]

While several economic explanations have been given for the positive effect of women's income,[20] my observations suggest that this might be a direct consequence of assigned gender roles based on cultural and societal norms in Tamil society. In India, among the many cultural definitions of the female, one is her association with the inside, the home, and courtyard where she must care for her family, while in contrast, men belong outside, in the fields and bazaar where livelihoods are earned and economic and political power are wielded.[21] In Tamil Nadu, a 'good woman' is constructed as someone who sacrifices her own interests for her family and children. When she is not working, she must spend most of her time caring for her children and maintaining the household. Women are seen as on the inside, not full members of public life.

A man, in contrast, must spend his earnings on role-maintaining activities and appearances in social settings, such as sitting in teashops, drinking alcohol, smoking, and wearing nice clothes. He must be 'in society', earning money, and paying tax. Men are not necessarily negatively inclined towards their children. Rather, this behaviour is in line with their perceived 'nature'. As one Tamil man stated, 'It is part of being a man',[22] or as another one justified, 'It's always been this way'.

Women are indeed the key to child nutrition. However, they face structural constraints in everyday life, and these have direct effects on the outcomes of nutritional schemes such as TINP. I turn now to TINP to examine the project from a gendered perspective. Earlier in this book, I have discussed how women are conceived of as being 'ignorant'. Barbara Harriss-White notes, 'Food behaviour among rural Tamil people has been described as "untoward", good nutrition thwarted by "formidable cultural variables", such that "behavioural technologists" are needed to develop (targeted) nutrition education.'[23] Reflecting on the stereotypes in development, Jean-Pierre Olivier de Sardan notes that 'superstitions, customs, mentalities are repeatedly and routinely called upon to account for the "backwardness" of peasant populations, their inertia or their resistance to development operations'.[24] Culture is viewed as a barrier to progress. In addition, there is the conflation of superstition, backwardness, immorality, and criminality.[25] As one health worker said to a mother, 'You are doing wrong (*tappu*). You are not giving what you should give to the child and yet you are saying that you are not doing anything wrong.'

From my fieldwork in India, women often mentioned lack of time, money, or control over household expenditure to explain why their child was not healthy. For example, when a woman had stopped breastfeeding before the World Health Organization recommended 12 month period, it was usually because she had limited time, insufficient milk, or because she was sick. Many of the *Dalit* and tribal women must work in the fields all day and upon returning felt that since they had been separated for more than eight hours, their breasts were engorged and the milk was sour.[26] Out of fear of being chided for not breastfeeding if they asked for formula, they would hide this fact from the health workers by giving the baby sugar water, or cow, or water buffalo milk. These substitutes increase the risk of infection and are even more detrimental to child health than formula. The health worker was more concerned with the value of breastfeeding itself in poor communities rather than looking at the social conditions which force poor women into labour that does not provide them the time or space for breastfeeding.[27]

In addition, it has been shown that in most developing countries that men are the decision-makers in the household. For example, Manesha's husband is an agricultural worker and she does not know how much money he makes a month. She estimates it is 2,000 Rs. but she does not know because he does not give her any money. Although he does not drink or smoke, he spends his money on *paan* (betel leaf chew). Despite their dominance within the household, men are absent in many Bank documents, which I term the 'missing men' phenomenon, or if we construct men as fathers, the 'missing fathers' phenomenon. In these health education efforts, men are not included. In addition, mothers-in-law wield enormous power. The story of Rhena illustrates this. Rhena has three girl children and one of them (age 4 years) was visibly undernourished. Her husband is a tailor and although he makes a good income, Rhena complained that he gives all his money to his mother who lives with them. Then her mother-in-law gives her the exact amount of money to buy the basic necessities for the household.

Women must bring their child into *anganwadi*. Only in rare instances does a man bring his child in because the programme is promoted as a 'women and child' intervention. Thus, women must go to work and earn money in the public sphere as well as take full responsibility for the health of their children. As shown in the data on occupations, it is predominantly lower-caste women who work. While it has been argued that 'work strengthens a woman's position. The woman who works can command respect in her home and can raise her voice in any decision',[28] evidence exists that working women have less time for childcare. Ghosh et al. examine the effect of maternal factors (mother's age, number of live births, birth interval, and mother's work status) and sex of the infant on the duration and bout frequency of breastfeeding in a 27-month longitudinal study of 140 Bangladeshi mothers.[29] The authors discovered that housewives consistently showed greater breastfeeding duration and bout frequency than women in paid employment. Maternal work status was the main factor associated with the duration and frequency of breastfeeding. Similarly, M. Sivakami examined the linkage between mothers' work and child health in Tamil Nadu and found that working women spend on average 1.7 hours less than non-working women on childcare.[30] The duration of breastfeeding is also shorter. In addition, children of working women were at a significantly greater risk of morbidity even when socio-economic factors were controlled for. Thus, while employment might reduce gender inequality, it increases the burden on women for childcare through reducing the limited resource of time.

Lower-caste women, who are on average less well-off, must use their already constrained time to go to *anganwadi*. Remarking on this adverse impact of development on women, Irene Tinker notes,

Overburdening of women refers to the increasingly common instances where women remain fully responsible for the home even while they must earn an income outside the home but are not given any public management functions of decisive importance.[31]

The continual emphasis placed on changing the caring practices of mothers can be viewed as part of a framework of blame: essentially a mother is admonished by health workers if her child is undernourished because she did not do something correctly. Biha who works as an agricultural labourer apologized for not being able to take better care of her children: 'I am sorry for working but I have no choice. I have to leave my children alone.' Since undernutrition is seen as preventable, women must bear the burden of the responsibility for the illness.[32] Women not only face a double bind of having to do both public and domestic labour, but also face another burden in that they are blamed for not having certain attributes, such as knowledge or patience, to care properly for their children. While I only partly agree with Lisbeth Sachs, who argues that all preventive thinking is founded on perceptions of responsibility and blame,[33] in the case of TINP the woman is classified as either a 'good mother' or a 'bad mother' based on the moral judgement of the health worker. Instead of punishing mothers, development interventions should be protecting them.

TINP was designed to target women and children because in Tamil Nadu women are perceived as being responsible for childcare. As a doctor in Chennai remarked, 'Only by working within the cultural context of the sacrifice of women to their husbands and children can you achieve better nutritional status for pregnant and lactating women.'[34] Thus, TINP is viewed as being a 'culturally appropriate' project since its aim is to change practices which are perceived as deleterious without changing the social structure that leads to the practices in the first place.

While this might seem a valid strategy, it neglects the fact that gender roles are constructed and malleable. A programme such as TINP reinforces the power structures within Tamil society by justifying the avoidance of childcare by men. It validates the attitude of men that they are not responsible for children. If a man brought his child in, it would be abnormal since it is a 'women and child' programme. Ann Whitehead argues that it is the routine assignment of women and men to certain tasks that become intimately connected with what it means to be a man or a woman in a specific context.[35] As Naila Kabeer expresses,

The gender division of labour becomes a social structure because this allocation poses a constraint on further practice...the prior divisions of labour become sedimented through practice so that they take on the significance of social rules.[36]

TINP allocates the task of childcare only to women. Perhaps, as Tinker has argued, this reflects that the Western stereotype of appropriate gender roles and occupations have been exported with aid programmes.[37] In the 1970s, at the time TINP was created, in Western countries women were still predominantly responsible for the household.

Similar to my findings, based on research conducted on nutrition in Tamil Nadu, Barbara Harriss-White makes the compelling argument that the two major obstacles to improving child nutrition are men's control of the household budget and the high frequency of intense alcohol consumption.[38] The effect of alcohol consumption on child nutrition will now be discussed.

Alcohol Consumption

In the early 1990s, Barbara Harriss-White noted that alcohol is an 'aspect of nutrition not conventionally accepted by nutritionists as comprising their territory'.[39] Despite the passage of over 15 years, this statement still holds true. For nutritionists, alcohol is usually discussed in the context of obesity and risk factors for chronic disease. For health economists, alcoholic beverages are treated as an ordinary commodity[40] which ignores the serious health and social problems related to alcohol consumption. A search for primary or secondary literature on alcohol and child under-nutrition in India revealed the dearth of knowledge on this area. This can be partially explained by the difficulty in obtaining accurate data on alcohol consumption at the individual and household level. Harriss-White's 1991 book on child undernutrition in India, her 2004 article on nutrition policy, Bonu et al.'s 2004 article on household tobacco and alcohol use, and Jejeebhoy's (1998) article on wife beating and child death are the only literature that could be located pertaining to this topic.

There are three main types of alcohol in Tamil Nadu: India-Made Foreign Liquor, country liquor, and illicit liquor. Foreign liquor is expensive so most of the SC, ST, and OBC households that consume alcohol drink either country liquor or illicit liquor. Country liquor in Tamil Nadu is predominantly palm liquor or *toddy* as well as *arrack* (from paddy or wheat). *Toddy* is made by fermenting the sap of a coconut palm. It is white and sweet with a characteristic flavour. It has an alcohol content of between 4 and 6 per cent.[41] *Arrack* is produced by distilling fermented molasses, raw brown sugar, palm wine, rice or palm sugar. It has an alcohol content ranging from 20 to 40 per cent.

As Table 5.30 shows, there is no significant difference in the percentage of men who drink, according to caste. Given the taboo nature of alcohol consumption, it is estimated that the actual rates are higher than reported. Of the study group, 74 women chose not to answer this question. In ST, SC, OBC, and FC households, respectively, 44, 20, 37, and 26 per cent of weekly household income was spent on alcohol. There is no association between household income and alcohol expenditure for any of the castes

Table 5.30. Percentage of men who drink by caste

	N	%
ST	63	31.7
SC	44	29.5
OBC	53	28.3
FC	66	21.2

$x^2 = 1.9$, $df = 3$, $p = .6$.

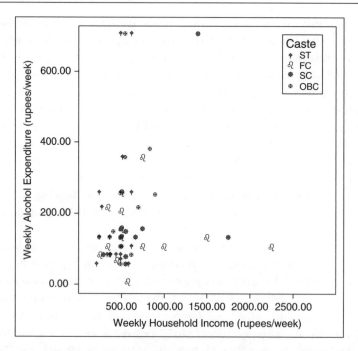

Figure 5.5. Weekly household income vs. weekly alcohol expenditure

(Figure 5.5 and Table 5.31). In several cases, where alcohol expenditure exceeded weekly income, households borrowed from moneylenders, mortgaged assets or received supplementary money from relatives. These households are accruing severe debt. It is likely that alcoholism is an issue for some households. In one situation, a woman reported her husband had a liver problem due to excessive drinking.

Drinking and alcohol consumption are rarely discussed in Tamil society, although acknowledged as an inevitable part of a man's life. The communities of the present study have a minority of heavy drinkers

Table 5.31. Weekly household income vs. weekly alcohol expenditure

	N	r^2	p
ST	20	0.10	.17
SC	13	0.08	.36
OBC	15	0.23	.07
FC	14	0.01	.77
Total	62	0.10	.10

with a majority of abstainers, rather than having a low level of overall drinking. As a well-known Indian activist Swami Agnivesh recently said, 'In rural India people either don't drink or are alcoholics, there is no in-betweens.'[42] My study also shows that there is no association between household income and severity of alcohol consumption.[43]

Alcohol affects child nutrition through two major pathways. In the face of severe resource constraints, alcohol is a major leakage of income. If this income could be redirected towards food and health services, a structural constraint, namely lack of purchasing power, on households would be slightly lifted. In addition to the money spent on alcohol, drinkers usually have lower wages (because of missed work and lowered efficiency on the job), increased medical expenses for illnesses and accidents, and decreased eligibility for loans.[44]

Alcohol use is also a major determinant of domestic violence which exacerbates gender inequality within the household. Vijayendra Rao's analysis shows that the greater the proportion of the family's expenditures on alcohol, the higher the probability that the wife will be beaten.[45] Biologically, alcohol alters brain receptors and neurotransmitters that can result in more aggressive behaviour and reduced fear and anxiety of the social, physical, and legal consequences of one's actions.[46] Based on my conversations with Tamil women during fieldwork, alcohol-related aggressive behaviour is almost always directed towards women who are further rendered powerless and weak.

It has been suggested that when women are treated as equals and partic-ipate in household decisions they are better able to care for their family.[47] Many women feel that domestic violence and the exacerbation of poverty associated with it have made alcohol abuse the single most important problem for women in India.[48] The following quotes taken from my interviews with *Dalit* women illustrate the magnitude of the issue.

During the monsoons, I was in Mumbai with my family. My house was flooded and a rat was eating my toe. My neighbour's husband was upset at his wife for going out alone . . . I think he was drinking . . . so he drenched her in kerosene then went looking for the matches to light her on fire. She had three boys so one took the matches and ran away and hid with them.

I have three girls. My husband beats me every night for not having boys. But this is my plight. All men do this.

No, I don't allow alcohol in my house but I worry about my married children. I have two daughters.

My husband does not drink. I made sure of this before marrying him.

I am ashamed about my husband especially in the community. He drinks twice a day but I can't stop him.

My husband used to beat me every night, so much until I could not even stand up. When my parents and brother came to restrain him, he ran away with my son [four-years old] and I have not seen him since. It has been three weeks. I called the police but they said that since he's the father, he has claim over the child as well. The only way to get the police to listen is through bribes. I don't know what to do.

My husband spent all his money on alcohol. He was sick. He went to detox in Chennai. I haven't seen him.

He is despicable and I wish that he would die! He has made my life miserable and even now he beats me up. He returns home drunk and creates a lot of commotion at night. Our children are grown up, and even though they are aware of what is happening, this doesn't stop him. I wish he would never return home. It hardly matters whether he lives or dies. He collects tiger prawn seedlings, and he spends all his earnings on drinks. He doesn't contribute anything towards running the household.[49]

A Hindustan Times article notes,

The threat that alcoholism poses to the likes of the rural poor can hardly be exaggerated. Money that should go to food, medicine and education is siphoned away to purchase alcohol ... Alcoholics regularly borrow money from village moneylenders at exorbitant rates of interest and end up mortgaging their lands and other assets.[50]

It has been suggested that a major reason why men drink is due to a general feeling of hopelessness and poverty. As one health worker told me 'People drink because of a lack of entertainment, harsh lives and societal conditioning.' Men drink to forget their problems.[51] In addition, the active encouragement by the state government to consume liquor results in easy availability of alcohol.

Alcohol sales proceeds have been estimated to account for as much as 45 per cent of the total revenue collection in India.[52] This money goes largely to the state government. In Tamil Nadu, the tax on alcohol results in an estimated 9.5 per cent of total revenue.[53] Given this situation, and the fact that the production and sale of alcohol is a state, not a federal, responsibility, the government has two contradictory roles in regards to alcohol. While the Ministry of Welfare is primarily responsible for preventing alcohol consumption, the Ministry of Finance depends financially on maintaining it. The tension between these two ministries is dampened by the medicalization of excessive alcohol consumption by the state which takes it out of the political arena and into the medical sphere. For alcoholism to be addressed effectively, it needs to be framed as a social problem, not a medical one. In addition, the state needs to take an active role in making this a priority.

The linkage between alcohol consumption and child nutrition outcomes has not been sufficiently incorporated into nutrition schemes. When I pressed a World Bank associate in New Delhi about this, he said, 'That's just a southern phenomenon. That doesn't happen here.' As noted in the previous section, TINP has limited effectiveness in poor communities because changing the behaviour of women has little impact in the face of these structural constraints. Within the nutrition community, there needs to be an increased awareness of and discussion on the close links between undernutrition and alcohol consumption and an incorporation of the role men should play in child welfare.

Conclusions

As the findings in this chapter demonstrate, inadequate knowledge and childcare practices are less implicated in child malnutrition rates in the communities of this study than the underlying determinants of inadequate purchasing power and gender inequality. In this situation, focusing on changing individual behaviour through growth monitoring and nutrition counselling are not effective for the reduction of child undernutrition in south India. Unless policymakers address structural determinants, major obstacles remain to battling hunger. Circumstance, not choice, seems to produce child hunger. In the following chapter, these findings will be linked to the wider issue of what works in reducing rates of child undernutrition.

Notes

1. World Bank (2006), p. 204.
2. This is a fictitious name.
3. Kapadia (1995), p. 252.
4. *Source*: National Family Health Survey (NFHS-2).
5. Guruswamy and Abraham (2006).
6. Levinson (1972).
7. In TINP, nutrition teaching is focused on food quality and quantity (e.g. vegetables have vitamins).
8. Nichter and Nichter (1996), pp. 39–40.

9. van Hollen (2003), p. 179.
10. Ibid. p. 175.
11. Griffiths, Dicken, and Favin (1996), p. 23.
12. Kumar (2007).
13. Manandhar et al. (2004).
14. This has also been discussed by Harriss (1981), p. 63.
15. Save the Children UK (2007).
16. Fapohunda (1988), Dwyer and Bruce (1988), and Senauer (1990).
17. Mencher (1988).
18. Miller (1992) and Gittelsohn (1991).
19. Thomas (1990).
20. Hopkins et al. (1994).
21. See Bennett (1992).
22. Mencher (1988).
23. Harriss (1991), p. 87.
24. Olivier de Sardan (2005), p. 76.
25. See van Hollen (2003), p. 187.
26. See van Hollen (2003).
27. Ibid.
28. Ibrahim (1985), p. 296.
29. Ghosh et al. (2006).
30. Sivakami (1997).
31. Tinker (1976).
32. Marantz (1990), p. 1186.
33. Sachs (1996).
34. van Hollen (2003), p. 176.
35. Whitehead (1991), cited in Kabeer (1994), p. 59.
36. Kabeer (1994), pp. 58–9.
37. Tinker (1976), p. 33.
38. Harriss (1991), p. 40.
39. Harriss (1991), p. 51.
40. Room et al. (2005), p. 527.
41. WHO (2004), p. 4.
42. Rao (1997), p. 1172.
43. See Mahal (2000), p. 3964.
44. Saxena (1999), p. 51.
45. Rao (1997), p. 1177.
46. Room et al. (2005), p. 521.
47. Hall et al. (2001).
48. Assunta (2001).
49. Last quote from Chowdhury et al. (2006), p. 729.
50. Hindustan Times (1999).
51. See Chowdhury et al. (2006), Rao (1997), and Harriss (1991).

52. Soumya (2001), data from http://excise.dehgovt.nic.in. Currently, all the states that had implemented total prohibition have repealed it, with the exception of Gujarat. Andhra Pradesh and Haryana were two states that overturned prohibition in the 1990s due to the necessity of state revenues. A nationwide survey in 1990 discovered 'that almost all states are unwilling to do away with their lucrative excise revenue from liquor trade, and hence are averse to introducing prohibition laws' (Hindustan Times 1990).
53. Government of Tamil Nadu (2005), Table 37.2.

6

What Works?

Let's accept that reality is very, very far from what we think, in a research environment, is the best thing to do. But then I think we have to be extremely responsible, as a nutrition community, about taking these kinds of debates into environments where it will be interpreted as being, you nutritionists do not know what you're doing or what you should be doing, and, therefore, rather than some resources for nutrition, there will be no resources for nutrition.

World Bank Staff Member

Given the shortcomings of the nutrition education approach, what works in addressing undernutrition? This is not an easy question to tackle, and any attempt at an answer is necessarily complex and intricate. This chapter explores this question tying my own findings into the debates in the development community. The debates largely revolve around the structure/agency axis. In addition, the institutional puzzle remains, why has the Bank nutrition team continually promoted the TINP model despite doubts as to its effectiveness? The second half of this chapter attempts to go 'inside' the Bank to examine the institutional drivers affecting nutrition policy.

Choice Versus Circumstance

There are currently two prevailing viewpoints in the nutrition community regarding how nutrition programmes should be designed. The first, which is promoted by the World Bank nutrition team, frames undernutrition as a result of detrimental caring practices by mothers and can be viewed as the choice or agency argument. In this approach, women are 'agents of change'. A 2006 Bank nutrition report states, 'Poor caring practices

156

are the biggest worldwide causes of protein–energy malnutrition.'[1] It is argued that if mothers are educated on healthy childcare practices, undernutrition rates will subsequently drop. The Bank *Nutrition Toolkit* notes, '[I]mprovements in child nutrition so often depend on changing feeding and care-giving behaviours in the home.'[2]

Based on this representation of nutrition, a behavioural change intervention is promoted which is executed using tools such as growth monitoring and promotion, supplementary feeding, and intensive nutrition counselling. These three are educational tools aimed at modifying detrimental childcare practices in developing countries. This intervention has become the World Bank's approach to a stand-alone nutrition project used in India (TINP) as well as in many other countries.

Limited evidence supports the idea that solely changing care practices will have a direct impact on child nutritional status. A prominent article is that of Ruel et al. who argue that good caregiving practices can compensate for the negative effects of poverty and low maternal education on children's height-for-age z-scores, which are an indicator of growth and thus child nutritional status.[3] Exclusive breastfeeding is the caring practice that is often pointed to as having a significant impact on child nutritional status.[4] In situations of extreme deprivation, breastfeeding is an affordable method for ensuring the nutritional status of the growing child[5] although temporal constraints often limit the ability of a woman to breastfeed regularly.

Proponents of the detrimental caring practices perspective use positive deviance to argue that even in conditions of deprivation, households can adopt strategies to improve the nutritional status of their children. Positive deviance refers to children who grow much better than the median of their community. It is used to identify children who 'grow and develop well in impoverished environments where most children are victims of malnutrition and chronic illness'.[6] While the existence of positive deviance is not contested, the explanation for the better growth is. Proposed explanations are that positive deviant households have better childcare practices, or perhaps better access to financial resources through extended family, saving or loan schemes, or maybe more 'social capital' (e.g. access to community leaders).

The second perspective focuses on structural determinants and frames undernutrition as a product of poverty. This can be viewed as the circumstance or structure argument. While poor caring practices are identified as an immediate cause of growth faltering, this is attributed to the obstacles that women face rather than as an indication of women's lack of knowledge. Undernutrition is viewed as a result of inadequate purchasing power, gender discrimination, and infectious disease, which manifest themselves biologically in the form of an undernourished child.

Extensive literature supports this viewpoint.[7] Most recently, the UN Task Force on Hunger pointed to inadequate purchasing power as the primary cause of hunger in the world today.[8] From his research in West Bengal in the 1950s, Derrick Jelliffe argues that poverty is the main factor causing undernutrition. He notes, 'In almost all cases poverty or economic inability to purchase costly protein foods, such as animal milk, was the prime etiologic factor, often associated with repeated attacks of enteritis and intestinal parasitism.'[9] Specifically for Tamil Nadu and TINP, Shekar et al. outline the characteristics of households whose children have poor growth. They have lower maternal wealth, greater incidence of diarrhoea, less regular consumption of pulses, and a higher consumption of cheaper rice substitutes.[10] Similarly, C. Gopalan notes that the poorer child growth commonly observed in impoverished communities is due to social factors, primarily caloric deprivation, and infection, rather than ethnic differences.[11] He compares the growth of children in both developed and developing countries and notes that children with moderate to high socio-economic status are larger than their counterparts with low socio-economic status.[12]

Based on this framework for nutrition, the intervention promoted consists of societal interventions such as income redistribution in the form of cash transfer schemes. This intervention strategy is, of course, harder to implement for political reasons. Interventions using this framework normally focus on social protection and welfare programmes rather than nutrition programmes per se, thus taking an integrated approach to the multifaceted causes of undernutrition.

Agency Approach: Growth Monitoring and Promotion

A cornerstone of the agency approach is growth monitoring and promotion. In 1982, UNICEF announced the GOBI initiative (growth monitoring, oral rehydration, breastfeeding, immunization) as the new child survival strategy, thus providing strong support for the inclusion of growth monitoring in nutrition interventions. Growth monitoring forms a crucial part of TINP and of the general World Bank approach to nutrition interventions. It has three main purposes: as a communication tool, as an educational strategy for intensive nutrition counselling, and as a screening device to target supplementary feeding. Despite the backing of both the World Bank and UNICEF, growth monitoring has been the subject of controversy relating to whether it is operationally effective as well as to whether its fundamental rationale is sound. Table 6.1 shows the extensive data collected on the positive and negative operational aspects of growth monitoring. The table also illustrates the numerous problems encountered by mothers when involved in a project which includes growth monitoring.

Since David Morley derived growth monitoring in the 1960s, controversy has surrounded the effectiveness of this strategy in developing countries, especially in areas where most of the population is illiterate. It is often used as a diagnostic tool, rather than as intended as a preventive tool. Thus, in the 1990s, the Bank changed its terminology to refer to growth monitoring as growth promotion which refers to the process of 'weighing a child, graphing the weight, assessing the growth, and providing counselling and motivation for other actions to improve growth'.[13] Although the rhetoric has attempted to overcome the previous obstacles to growth monitoring, many problems on-the-ground still remain. For example, Morley recently stated that he is dismayed by its effectiveness in practice:

In West Africa in the '60s I developed the 'home based' weighing chart with the 'calendar system' to record the child's age that is in wide use … For many years I have realised that growth monitoring was not working. I am now appalled at the large sums which … are being spent on it. I have gone through a learning curve on which I suggest growth monitoring has failed.[14]

Morley puts forth two main reasons for its failure. The first is the problem of calculating the age in months of a child for the purposes of plotting their size on a weight or height-for-age chart. The second involves the complexity of understanding and making decisions from a growth chart. Other reasons include the high cost of growth monitoring, and the logistics of screening large numbers of children.[15]

Growth monitoring is also used as a data collection exercise to assess whether projects are achieving their nutritional objectives. In a traditional community-based nutrition project, workers report growth data to their supervisors and the data from a country/region is statistically analysed to determine whether the project has resulted in positive weight gain in beneficiaries. This data is used in both midterm and final evaluations which are jointly written by the government and the World Bank.[16]

159

Table 6.1. Positive and negative operational aspects of growth monitoring[a]

	Studies reporting problems
Negative aspects for mothers	
Little discussion about feeding	Stinson and Sayer (1991), Pearson (1995), Coulibaly et al. (2002), Gerein and Ross (1991)
Little advice/knowledge about signs of illness	Stinson and Sayer (1991)
No use of weight charts for education of mothers	Stinson and Sayer (1991), Pearson (1995), Gerein and Ross (1991), Ruel (1995), Reid (1984)
See growth chart as immunization card of access to health services	Lefevre et al. (2002), Roberfroid et al. (2005), Msefula (1993)
Long waiting times and overcrowded	Coulibaly et al. (2002), Gerein and Ross (1991)
Too expensive	Coulibaly et al. (2002)
Counseling time less than two minutes	Stinson and Sayer (1991), Pearson (1995), Gerein and Ross (1991), Msefula (1993)
Majority of mothers not told child's nutritional status	Stinson and Sayer (1991), Pearson (1995), Gerein and Ross (1991)
Inappropriate advice/lack of individualized advice	Stinson and Sayer (1991), Pearson (1995), Coulibaly et al. (2002), Msefula (1993)
Majority of mothers unable to interpret growth charts	Stinson and Sayer (1991), Pearson (1995), Coulibaly et al. (2002), Save the Children UK (2003)
Mothers not recognizing significance of static weight	Ruel et al. (1990)
Majority of mothers had no opportunity to ask questions	Stinson and Sayer (1991)
Health education sessions unhelpful	Stinson and Sayer (1991), Pearson (1995), Msefula (1993)
Procedures not clearly explained	Stinson and Sayer (1991)
Mothers lack time to implement advice	Pearson (1995), Roy et al. (1993)
Mothers' workload a problem	Pearson (1995), George et al. (1993), Gerein and Ross (1991)
Food insecurity a problem	Pearson (1995), Gerein and Ross (1991), Roberfroid et al. (2005)
Food suggested too expensive or unavailable	Pearson (1995), Msefula (1993)
Family apathy stops them from following advice	George et al. (1993)
Issues stopped mothers coming	Pearson (1995), Coulibaly et al. (2002)
Positive aspects for mothers	
Majority of mothers told nutritional status of child	Stinson and Sayer (1991), Pearson (1995)
Majority of mothers could interpret growth chart	Pearson (1995), Senanayake et al. (1997), Musaiger and Abdulkhalek (2001)

[a] Adapted from Brown (2005), p. 46.

The Bank's country departments prepare the Implementation Completion Report.

The evaluative process is also problematic. Nancy Gerein concludes that growth monitoring has been largely ineffective since children are weighed only for the sake of collecting weights and determining grade of malnutrition.[17] Health workers routinely collect massive amounts of data, usually not fully understanding why they do it or what the information should be used for. The monitoring of growth often distracts health workers from the welfare of children since they are more concerned with collecting data than consulting with mothers and children. The data is also often of extremely poor quality. Birth weights can be rounded up or health workers increase the weights of children, especially since they often work under performance-based incentives.

Growth Monitoring as a Communication Strategy

The first main objective of growth monitoring is to inform mothers about the nutritional status of their child.[18] This strategy assumes that mothers are unable to identify malnutrition in their children by themselves. A Director of an NGO in Chennai commented, 'These mothers have no realisation that their children suffer.' The rationale of growth monitoring is that charting the growth of children will make malnutrition visible to mothers so that they are motivated to better care for their children. The World Bank *Nutrition Toolkit* states:

The vast majority of parents are deeply concerned for their children's welfare. Despite this concern, motivating better nutrition practices and other preventive health actions has proven difficult, often because parents don't perceive the problem or see the results of their actions. One of the few ways to make the need for and the impact of preventive actions visible to the family and those who can assist in the community or health sector is through charting monthly changes in children's weights.[19]

This assumption is challenged by the critics of growth monitoring who argue that mothers are able to correctly identify their child's health status without assistance. For example, Roy et al. assessed mothers' perceptions about malnutrition and their ability to identify malnutrition in their own children. The authors discovered that 60 per cent of mothers correctly identified better nutritional status (weight-for-age >75% of NCHS median) and 67 per cent of mothers correctly identified malnutrition (weight-for-age <75% of NCHS median) in their children. In addition, 95 per cent of women were aware of how to improve their child's nutritional status through either having better food (31%), treatment of illnesses (22%), or both (42%).[20] Tonglet et al. found similar evidence showing that mothers' assessment of their child's growth was remarkably accurate.[21] In addition, Gerein and Roberfroid et al. suggest that children only attend a session of growth monitoring because their mothers have already identified a health problem with the child such as decreased appetite or recurrent diarrhoeal disease.[22]

The implementation of growth monitoring as a communication tool in community-based nutrition programmes has several shortcomings. The most apparent is that growth charts are complicated for mothers and health workers to understand. David Morley recently noted,

I hope you will emphasise why growth monitoring has failed. As you will see in the papers I am sending I am adamant that this is due to the complexities of understanding and making decisions from a line graph. It took me more than 20 years to appreciate this...In the 1980s when teaching in the LSH&TM [London School of Hygiene and Tropical Medicine] on the DTM&H [Diploma in Tropical Medicine and Hygiene] course for post-graduate doctors around 15% could not complete a weight chart and probably a much higher proportion could not interpret changes in it...A friend of mine, now head of department in the London Institute of Education found, that it took a full term to achieve an understanding of the graphic representation of number, when teaching at secondary school level.[23]

The difficulty in using growth charts results in a situation where both health workers and mothers are unable to interpret what they show. Gopalan, reflecting on *anganwadis* in Tamil Nadu, notes that although all nutrition workers had been trained in growth monitoring, only 46.3 per cent were found competent with respect to weighing, 30.2 per cent with respect to age assessment, 36.9 per cent with respect to plotting weights, and 32.2 per cent with respect to administration.[24]

Roberfroid et al. describe how District Medical Officers frequently report that parents fail to understand the growth chart.[25] A sample of officers discussing growth monitoring is provided below.

Because, in our country, they are illiterate. They do not understand too much what is written on it, it is not too much their concern.

They [health agents] also think that it is not that important that mothers understand, because the understanding point is quite low, you see.

But I am wondering if she really understands. Because it is simply, but sometimes nurses also have difficulties to fill in the growth chart.

Similarly, the Save the Children UK study on the Bangladesh Integrated Nutrition Project found that only 7 per cent of women in the project area were able to correctly interpret a growth chart.[26]

There is one article on TINP which is titled, 'Growth Monitoring Can and Does Work!' which is based on an epidemiological study of 42 villages in Madurai district, Tamil Nadu.[27] The authors argue that growth monitoring is a means to achieve community involvement in child health. From this line of thought, they argue that growth monitoring is working successfully as a communication tool. The evidence given for community involvement is that 'mothers are aware of the fact that their children are weighed and records are kept at the center'.[28] I argue that although women know that their children are weighed, this does not imply that they understand the reasons why their children are weighed, or what the growth charts are for. As a senior researcher at the Nutrition Foundation of India told me, 'Yes, all children are weighed, but this is not growth monitoring.' Growth monitoring is a process involving teaching mothers about a child's nutritional status leading to a conversation between the nutrition worker and mother regarding strategies to improve childcare. In the absence of such a negotiation, weighing is simply an action taken to fulfil the worker's requirements.

My study has shown that most women in all caste groups reported that their child was weighed. When pressed as to why their child was weighed, most women did not know. Rather, weighing was often mentioned as an obstacle to go through before children could receive food and health services. For this reason, David Nabarro and Paul Chinnock have called weighing a 'meaningless ritual'.[29] In terms of understanding of growth charts, under 10 per cent of women in all caste groups could give the correct explanation for what a growth chart shows, and around half claimed never to have seen a growth chart before or could not recognize what it was. Furthermore, there is no relationship between a woman's education level and recognition of a growth chart, indicating the complexity of implementing growth monitoring in almost any community. Thus, there is a major gap between action and interpretation: mothers go to *angan-wadis* to have their children weighed, yet the purpose of the process is not explained to them so that they can understand its importance. While growth charts might be appropriate in a clinic setting, their usefulness as a communication tool in a community-based nutrition intervention, such as TINP, is limited.

Growth Monitoring as an Educational Tool

The second objective of growth monitoring is as an educational tool. Growth monitoring is used as a launching point to embark on intensive nutrition counselling with women to teach them how to make better use of their resources. In support of this viewpoint, there is evidence from Uganda, Jamaica, and Thailand that nutrition education significantly reduced the prevalence and severity of malnutrition.[30] However, nutrition education typically results in an improvement in mothers' knowledge[31] but not in practices or nutritional status.[32] This section will first discuss the rationale of intensive nutrition counselling then turn to its implementation in Tamil Nadu.

Growth monitoring is used as an educational tool to teach mothers how to improve their child's health through showing them their child's growth on the chart (using the indicator weight-for-age).[33] The initial use of growth monitoring is to identify mothers in need of intensive nutrition counselling, because their child's growth is faltering. Following this, the nutrition worker has a 'nutrition negotiation'[34] with the mother discussing strategies to improve caring practices. It is designed to facilitate the adoption of a few specific practices to improve the nutrition and health status of her child. The communication consists of teachings on colostrum and breastfeeding, the timely introduction of complementary foods, the home management of diarrhoea, the importance of immunization, and hygiene.

Growth monitoring thus is an avenue into intensive nutrition counselling which the Bank argues will reduce rates of undernutrition. When speaking with a UN agency staff member who works closely with the World Bank in India about his perception of the primary cause of undernutrition in India he said, 'Indians are filthy.' I asked him if he meant poverty. He said, 'No, I mean culturally filthy. I've worked in Indonesia, West Africa, many other places, and here [in India] hygiene is the problem—there are huge rates of diarrhoeal diseases.' The 2006 Bank report on nutrition argues that the principal cause of undernutrition is inadequate knowledge about the benefits of exclusive breastfeeding and complementary feeding practices.[35] It argues that women cannot tell when their child is becoming malnourished and furthermore that good nutrition is not intuitive, since there are high levels of ignorance about food choice.[36] Thus, interventions should focus on improving maternal knowledge through counselling.[37]

However, this framework has been criticized for promoting interventions, such as growth monitoring, that are likely to increase the work burden on an already overwhelmed mother. George et al. conducted a community intervention trial in 12 villages in Tamil Nadu to investigate the benefits of growth monitoring. The authors argue,

Almost all mothers desire to provide better care but are overwhelmed by their workload and are often discouraged by the apathy of other family members towards the well-being of their children. In these villages mothers felt helpless on many occasions because of frequent verbal abuse, and not uncommonly, physical violence, alcoholism, and/or promiscuity of their husbands.[38]

Studies by several other academics have shown that mothers are chided for not attending clinics/sessions regularly, treated unsympathetically by health workers, have the information they give ignored, and are even blamed for their child's poor nutritional status.[39]

Growth monitoring as an educational tool has been difficult to implement effectively due to a number of factors. This is apparent in TINP. The first problem is that nutrition workers do not have enough time to discuss caring practices with women. A worker must weigh and chart each child, prepare supplementary food, and fill out a number of records. The vast collection of records is particularly remarkable. Each worker must maintain 30 data registers from which 15 detailed quantitative monthly reports and key indicators are prepared. A survey of 61 nutrition workers revealed that they spend on average from one to three hours daily (out of six total) completing the registers and an additional two days per month preparing the monthly reports.[40] As Meera Shekar and Michael Latham note, 'The major weakness of TINP . . . is the abundance and duplication of records that consume much of the worker's time.'[41]

For the educational component of TINP, films, filmstrips, slides, posters, flip books, flash cards, and pamphlets have been developed. An evaluation of the communications component of TINP shows that 48 per cent of beneficiary households had never seen any of these materials.[42] Alan Berg noted that more emphasis is usually placed on producing many different materials than on actually speaking to women about health and nutrition.[43] However, the written materials are not useful to women who are illiterate.

Berg's reflections are similar to my findings on the effectiveness of health education received during TINP sessions. A high percentage of women in all caste groups could not explain what they had learned at *anganwadi*. Semi-structured interviews revealed two explanations for why women in all caste groups could not explain what they had learned there. The first is that the priority of many of the women is to take advantage of the supplementary food and immunizations provided by the *anganwadi* as opposed to discussing health lessons with the nutrition worker. As a result, women did not make the connection between weighing and nutrition counselling although they did understand that weighing was required for their children to obtain food. The second reason is that the health messages are viewed as impractical; this is especially so for the tribal community. For example, a tribal woman was told that she should breastfeed her child. However, she noted that she was unable to do so during the day because she was a daily labourer. A District Medical Officer reflecting on the limited applicability of nutrition advice stated,

But they know it, they know that the child does not eat very well because it is the same meal every day. What are you going to propose? You are not going to propose anything because she won't have the capacity to apply it. This is a problem. Thus, I think that they are right not to come to [*anganwadi*] to be repeated the same thing again and again.[44]

As a result of these two factors, growth monitoring as an educational tool has not been effective in practice. In addition, the effectiveness of education is ultimately dependent on structural and environmental factors such as poverty, gender inequality, and seasonality.[45] For example, Mascie-Taylor et al. examined the cost effectiveness of four different regimes in reducing the prevalence and intensity of infection of *Ascaris lumbricoides, Trichuris trichiura,* and hookworm over an 18-month period in children aged 2–8 years living in rural Bangladesh.[46] Two of the regimes only involved chemotherapy while the other two included regular health education. The authors discovered that the two regimens involving health education were the least effective. As mentioned in the previous chapter, perhaps a more effective educational intervention could be through focusing on women's groups, which provide a morally neutral setting where health messages can be shared concurrently with economic and social empowerment activities.

Growth Monitoring as a Screening Device

The third main objective of growth monitoring is to identify children that qualify for supplementary feeding. This section will first discuss the assumption that supplementary feeding will improve child nutritional status, then outline the various aspects of its implementation in Tamil Nadu.

There is currently a debate in public nutrition policy circles over whether supplementary feeding is effective in improving child growth and pregnancy outcomes.[47] While the Bank nutrition team has promoted this view,[48] several development practitioners have questioned the rationale behind this. One stated,

It is misinformed to say that supplementary feeding during pregnancy has been 'shown to be effective...in numerous studies'...I find the reporting of the evidence on maternal food supplementation absolutely misleading...In particular, the evidence on the impact of maternal food supplementation on birth weight is limited to one study, conducted in a different continent, that was only effective in one season of the year. A recent WHO review of the evidence on this topic was very cautious, and even the author of the African study concedes that there is little reason to promote the intervention widely at this point...Furthermore, contrary to what is stated [in the World Bank report], there is no review anywhere in the document of the evidence on the impact of supplementary feeding on child growth. If there had been, it would have noted that the impact of supplementary feeding on child growth is limited to children who are wasted, with stunting wholly refractory to reversal through supplementary feeding. It has been repeatedly observed that one of the most egregious wastes of resources...is the insistence on feeding up stunted children.

The effect of caloric supplementation on growth of undernourished children is mixed,[49] as the quote suggests. Gopalan et al. carried out an investigation into this in India in 1973. They supplemented a total of 415 children between the ages of 1 and 5 years and belonging to the low-income groups.[50] The food supplement consisted of wheat flour (23 g), sugar (35 g), and edible oil (10 g) and provided 310 kcal and 3 g protein. As Table 6.2 shows, the growth of undernourished children improved strikingly with supplementation.

However, the authors caution against immediately focusing on food supplementation as a nutrition intervention. They note, 'It is not suggested that "empty calories" should be provided to these children to

Table 6.2. Gain in height and weight of children, supplemented vs. unsupplemented

Age in years	Increment in height (cm)			Increment in weight (kg)		
	Supplemented	Unsupplemented	p	Supplemented	Unsupplemented	p
1–2	9.3 (25)	6.5 (9)	<.001	2.35	1.74	<.03
2–3	9.5 (50)	7.8 (26)	<.001	2.34	1.71	<.001
3–4	9.1 (65)	7.4 (33)	<.001	2.04	1.58	<.01
4–5	8.4 (71)	7.3 (15)	<.014	1.86	1.38	<.02

make up the calorie deficit.'[51] Rather, they argue that their study shows that more importance should be put on raising purchasing power at the household level so that sufficient food can be acquired rather than on distributing 'elaborately processed "protein-rich formulations" which are unnecessary and expensive'.[52]

Although the Bank nutrition team promotes an approach including supplementary feeding, it has been acknowledged that for the Bangladesh Integrated Nutrition Project, supplementary feeding has not improved child growth, or weight gain in pregnant women, or birth weight.[53] The explanations given for this are:

mistargeting (errors of exclusion), sharing of food, substitution for other foods, inadequate ration size or incomplete participation, palatability issues, biological partitioning, inadequate feeding practices before, during and after illness, infection itself, restrictions in women's mobility, and high work and time demands on women.[54]

Several of these issues are apparent in the TINP project. TINP is not targeted towards children whose growth is faltering. Rather, all children who attend *anganwadi* receive the supplement. This was evident both in observations at *anganwadi* as well as during interviews with women. There are several possible explanations to account for this. One problem has been that the reading and plotting of weights is frequently inaccurate.[55] This relates to the difficulty in using and understanding growth charts. A survey of 322 health personnel in over 50 countries who had used growth charts for at least four years found significant difficulties with their use. A total of 78 per cent respondents had difficulty determining the month of birth, 49 per cent had difficulty plotting the weight, 47 per cent had difficulty understanding the use of the 'at risk' section of the chart, 43 per cent had difficulty interpreting the weight curve, and 30 per cent had difficulty weighing the child correctly.[56] As Gopalan has noted,

[W]orkers are 'weighed down' by (all their time and energy taken up with the mechanics of feeding, and with the job of just carrying out an elaborate) time-consuming selection process to identify 'beneficiaries' for feeding at the centres.[57]

Because of these difficulties, it is easier for the nutrition worker not to use growth monitoring to target food and just give rations to all children present that day.

A second explanation is that in the context of deprivation, albeit with slight variations in extent between households, it is difficult to withhold food from children whose growth is considered satisfactory, yet who are still hungry. As discussed earlier, anthropometry and self-expressions of hunger do not always relate.[58] One nutrition worker remarked that it was emotionally difficult not to give a *laddoo* to a child asking for food and expressing pangs of hunger.

Another issue apparent in the TINP project is that supplementary food turns into replacement food for children. Women attend *anganwadi* in the morning before work. Instead of giving the child their usual breakfast, they receive *laddoo*. The substitution, rather than addition, of caloric intake dampens the nutritional effect of the supplement. Although the supplement was specifically designed not to include rice so as to be perceived by women as a snack and not a meal, in practice, the *laddoo* is often used to replace breakfast.

The final issue pertains to the palatability of the supplement and the symbolism that food holds. As Richard Burghart notes, health educators promote the idea of food for health over food for taste.[59] The children who attend *anganwadi* are always given a *laddoo*. While it is eaten because the children are hungry and it is free, when I discussed *laddoos* with older children, they complained that it was the same taste everyday and that it did not taste good. The children expressed a desire to have more variety. This was recognized by an Indian Planning Commission advisor who noted that one of the problems with TINP is that children lose interest with the food and want variety and taste.

In addition, the *laddoo* is simply a powder mixed with water and made into a ball. This supplement does not fulfil the needs and wishes of individuals who desire food for its symbolic and social meanings.[60] Food represents religion, community, and belief. It reveals familial relations, feelings, and emotions. During fieldwork in south India, a young woman remarked, 'You ask me what hunger is? Hunger is the fear of not filling my belly or my children's belly.' During our conversation, she emphasized the insecurity of not knowing whether she could feed her children that day. This statement reflects the concern that women have for the welfare of their children. Their notion of poverty and hunger is intricately bound up with their children's happiness and health. In addition, often in grain shops in India, low-quality grain normally eaten by animals is given at subsidized prices to the poor, despite the fact that they do not want to eat this food.[61] This can also be viewed in the recent media campaign by the Tamil Nadu government to encourage women to eat *ragi* instead of rice.[62] The government argues that women's self-sacrifice for the family is part of the cultural ethic. Women do not normally eat much rice in the household because it is the highly valued food. *Ragi* is as nutritious as rice, but it is associated with low social status. Thus, if women were to eat *ragi*, then they would not feel as if they were depriving men.

Ellen Messer notes that food selection is governed, at a basic biological level, by a number of sensory characteristics such as taste/smell, texture, colour, sound, and physiologically perceived characteristics such as 'fillingness' and 'burn'.[63] In terms of food symbolism, she discusses binary aspects of food such as hot/cold, wet/dry, male/female, heavy/light, yin/yang, clean/poison, ripe/unripe, and other humoural categories. Although sensory and symbolic meanings are inherent in dietary selection, Messer argues that the overriding consideration in dietary choice seems to be economic, in the sense that monetary factors determine whether an individual can satisfy his or her choices. Messer's conclusion is that food and diet, and I would argue nutrition, are social aspects of a community, transcending their physical state and assuming a sensory and symbolic importance.

Similarly, Stanley Ulijaszek and Simon Strickland present three tenets of a holistic approach to nutrition: humans do not eat everything that is potentially nutritious, food choice cannot be explained in simple biological terms, and finally, although many factors determine food preference and choice, the basis lies in culture.[64] This dietary pattern influences nutritional status. The key issue that emerges from their work is that it is impossible to promote nutritional change without first understanding the food meanings, practices, and beliefs, and the factors that might constrain them, within a particular group. Diet, food, and health are intertwined with local concerns ranging from religion to agricultural.

Arjun Appadurai's concept of gastro-politics is a useful framework to examine the social and political aspects of food.[65] Appadurai defines gastro-politics as the conflict or competition over specific cultural or economic resources as it emerges in social transactions around food. He notes that in Tamil Nadu, food is used as an idiom to express social ideas on sharing, redistribution, and power. Using the three arenas of the household, the marriage feast, and the temple, he notes that food can serve diametrically opposed semiotic functions, either homogenizing participating actors or heterogenizing them. He argues that gastro-politics is critically defined in the household arena by the tension between intimacy and distance, in the marriage feast by the tension between inequality and rank, and in the temple by the tension between solidarity and segmentation.

Different concepts of the body entail different definitions of what it takes to sustain it and what constitutes 'real food'.[66] Hunger can also be indicated by a lack of a dietary need that fulfils a cultural or social role, for example, a lack of milk or meat.[67] Although the diet might be sufficient according to caloric requirements, the individual might indicate that they are not satisfied with their food choice. For example, when I asked Aparna about her diet, specifically about milk, she noted that many days they went hungry because milk was too expensive. 'Do we have milk regularly? We have milk on the days we can afford it. But it is very expensive. Other days we just get by.' In addition, in Tamil Nadu, rice is valued as a source of life and is fundamental to any culturally relevant definition of meal. In Ayurvedic philosophy, the human body assimilates the qualities inherent in food and the body is viewed as a system which refines food into energy.[68] Food is seen to undergo a seven-stage transformation process. First, it is ingested, collected in the stomach, and heated by a digestive fire into style. The style is transported to the liver where it is heated and transmuted into blood. This blood is turned into flesh, flesh into fat, fat into bone, bone into marrow, and finally marrow into *dhatu* which gives physical vitality, mental energy, and strength of character. The six tastes of food (sweet, sour, salty, pungent, bitter, astringent) are used to maintain a humoural balance among style, phlegm (*kapha*), bile (*pita*), and *dhatu*. Thus, the connection between food and the body provides a rationale whereby individuals work out their diet within political-economic constraints.

The symbolism of food became apparent in this study during interviews when asking what food women liked their children to receive. Women in all caste groups predominantly stated vegetables, rice, *dal*, and egg which are summed up in the phrase *nalla chappada* (good food). In addition, two patterns emerge when examining women's expressed desires for food. First, meat and fish were often mentioned as too expensive but something women would like to eat. In 1952, Srinivas described how lower castes aspire to be more Brahmin, a form of Sanskritization, through emulating the Brahmin practice of vegetarianism.[69] Tamil Brahmins usually do not eat meat, fish, or other foods that are perceived as impure. In this way, caste differences could be naturalized through dietary means. The higher castes could justify their superior position by arguing that lower castes eat crude things (e.g. beef); thus they are by virtue what they eat.[70] When lower castes emulate Brahmin dietary practices, Srinivas argued that they are attempting to improve their social position. However, my data reflects that lower castes are not aspiring to this dietary standard. Rather, they would like to have a diet similar to wealthier high-caste Shudra (Telugu Naidu) households who are able to consume more animal products. Perhaps this reflects the increasing societal importance of class over caste.

The second pattern was the expressed desire for dietary diversity and fatty foods. Women cited fruits, sweets, and spicy food as important to them, indicating that taste is as important to them as the need to fill their stomachs. In addition, women want to eat *nai* (melted butter), cream, dairy, eggs, sweets, the foods that the upper class eat because they are expensive. Eating these foods and serving them at social functions demonstrates the high social status of the family, the wealth of the family, and being a good host. Food is the medium through which relationships are expressed. One woman complained, 'All I have is rice, roti, dal, we're not rich people.' Greens are considered the 'poor man's food'.

Although supplementary feeding helps to temporarily eliminate hunger, it might not be the most suitable intervention to bridge the household caloric gap. Supplementary feeding is expensive in both money, occupying roughly 50 per cent of TINP's budget and time, since nutrition workers must prepare the food and give it to the children. The multi-dimensional (monetary, cultural, symbolic, temporal) aspects of feeding should be addressed when examining interventions that aim to increase children's caloric intake. Growth monitoring is not an effective tool in these Tamil Nadu communities. As a Bank consultant noted,

I mean, for twenty years there have been meetings about growth monitoring, and we've all had very serious doubts about the benefits of growth monitoring, as practiced in 90% of countries, and yet we go to a meeting in Antwerp last year, where 60 people out of 80 believe that growth monitoring is not what should be the centre of most programmes because it's not working, and yet year after year it goes on. I think we need to discuss that.

The failure of growth monitoring reflects a larger problem which is that nutrition interventions in isolation from social welfare interventions do not work. Hunger is very much about the circumstances in which individuals and households live.

Alternative Strategies to Address Undernutrition

Given the shortcomings of TINP and the nutrition education approach, what are possible strategies to address undernutrition? Given the findings outlined above, it is apparent that there needs to be increased attention by the nutrition community to power structures that constrain individual agency. As Amartya Sen and the UN Task Force on Hunger note, purchasing power at the household level must be increased. This can be achieved through several strategies: economic growth (macroscale), improved water and sanitary infrastructure (macro and microscale), and conditional cash transfers (microscale). It should be noted that all three areas are part of the World Bank's broader activities, but take place primarily outside the Health, Nutrition, and Population sector.

The first alternative, which is supported by most macroeconomists, is that economic growth and improved material standard of living will have a greater impact on child nutrition rates than any direct intervention. Dr. Ramachandran of the Nutrition Foundation of India told me that when comparing states in India, there is a clear relationship between increased GDP and reduced rates of child undernutrition. In addition, she noted that maternal literacy and gender equality, such as in Kerala, have reduced infant mortality rates to those comparable to the Western world. She noted that 50 years ago, Kerala had worse rates of undernutrition than Tamil Nadu. Kerala's communist government adopted a holistic approach to development emphasizing women's education and literacy, land redistribution, and secure employment, while Tamil Nadu focused on interventions like TINP and the midday meal scheme. Kerala also benefited from high levels of remittances from Gulf migrant workers since 1973. While Kerala's rates are the lowest in India (28.5% underweight), Tamil Nadu's child malnutrition rates are estimated at 48.2 per cent, placing the state near the all-India average of 53.4 per cent.[71]

Economic growth appears to be a necessary condition for poverty reduction and undernutrition. However, economic growth has only a marginal effect on poverty reduction and undernutrition in conditions of high inequality or where the growth primarily benefits richer households. This is apparent when examining child undernutrition rates since India's 1993 economic liberalization. While the economic growth rate has been on average 8–9 per cent per annum since it began, the 2005–06 National Family Health Survey data reveals the lack of significant reduction in child wasting and stunting. As a UN senior staff member stated, 'It is actually quite remarkable that the growth has not had more of an impact—one would expect growth to have a much greater effect.' Proposed hypotheses for the lack of impact are that the growth is occurring in certain urban centres (e.g. Bangalore) among the educated middle class, not in villages where the heart of the undernutrition problem is located. Thus, economic growth has limited effect unless specifically targeted at the poor.[72]

An additional limitation of economic growth is that poverty reduction at the household level, in certain situations, has only a marginal effect on child undernutrition. This has been captured by the construct 'caloric-income elasticity (CIE)' which is the responsiveness of individual caloric intake to household income, and the associated issue of responsiveness of health, and anthropometrics, to extra calories so obtained. This has been an issue of great debate as CIE estimates have ranged from 0.7 to 0.8 in the 1970s, to 0.1–0.2 in the 1980s, to 0.35–.0.45 in the 1990s. The lower the CIE, the more risk that household poverty reduction, while having long-term effects, will be too slow to avoid serious undernutrition and permanent damage for many children. Part of the explanation for this is that any increases in purchasing power which raises a household out of poverty occurs through the head of the household (predominantly male) who does not spend his income to improve the welfare of the children.[73]

Other than economic growth, improved water and sanitation infrastructure has an enormous impact on child nutritional status, yet is not traditionally associated with nutrition projects. Improving infrastructure in these two areas affects child nutrition through two pathways: a reduction in disease and a reduction for mothers in water-collection activities leaving more time for childcare.[74] Water-borne diseases are a major cause of childhood illness. For example, Minamoto et al. investigated the effect of contaminated water on acute childhood malnutrition through carrying out a survey of 761 children in 2 discrete rural areas of Bangladesh.[75] The authors discovered that children living in households with contaminated water were significantly more wasted than children living in non-contaminated households (mean difference = −0.361, $p < .001$). The difference remained highly significant even when taking into account differences in socio-economic status and prevalence of geo-helminths.

As the above study shows, at the individual level, health status is as important as dietary intake in the manifestation of undernutrition. Stanley Ulijaszek and Simon Strickland provide examples which show that seasonality of disease has as much impact on nutritional status as seasonal availability of food supplies.[76] The small body size found in countries like India is an outcome of both undernutrition and infectious disease that exist in a synergistic relationship.[77]

Infection exacerbates undernutrition. In many developing countries, including India, many children experience lower efficiency in nutrition absorption and utilization by the body due to the endemic frequency of infectious gastrointestinal episodes leading to diarrhoea, as well as upper and lower respiratory infections. Intestinal dysfunction can cause up to 9 per cent reduced absorption of nutrients. Mouth lesions and anorexia also result in reduced food intake.[78] Diarrhoea results in lower intake of food because of the loss of appetite and the withholding of food by caregivers.[79] It is, in fact, the most important non-dietary cause of growth faltering in growth children in developing countries.[80] Children and infants in developing countries spend 15–20 per cent of their time suffering from morbidity, and since infections result in increased energy needs for fever and tissue repair, most of the body's resources are devoted to basic maintenance.[81] The energy spent fighting infections comes at a cost to body weight; 1 per cent of body weight is lost daily during episodes of diarrhoea and fevers.[82]

Similarly, undernutrition increases susceptibility to infection by reducing the capacity to fight disease. About half of all child deaths occur because of caloric deprivation, which prevents children's immune systems from effectively resisting even common childhood ailments. These diseases include diarrhoea, measles, malaria, and respiratory infection which, in total, account for one-third of the deaths of children under age 5 globally.[83] Even mildly underweight children are twice as likely to die prematurely as children who have normal weight.[84] Thus, improving water and sanitation can have a significant impact on child undernutrition rates through a reduction in childhood illness.

While promoting pro-poor economic growth and infrastructure development might well be effective avenues, both of these strategies are slow. Economic growth is estimated to take many years to affect the poorest people in developing countries. For example, an analysis by the Bank nutrition team shows that at realistic levels of sustained per capita GDP (3% for India), and using an elasticity figure (change in malnutrition rates relative to per capita income growth) of −0.5, it would take until 2035 for India to achieve the nutrition Millennium Development Goal (MDG).[85] A World Bank staff member remarked, 'We assumed that if incomes increased they might increase for many, many years without actually denting this huge, severe undernutrition problem...So that was our assumption.'

Given the long-term nature of economic growth and improved infrastructure, short-term interventions in the form of conditional and unconditional cash transfers have been implemented to increase the purchasing power of households, thus enhancing food security. The most well-known conditional cash transfer programme is Mexico's PROGRESA (Programa de Educación, Salud y Alimentación) which has been renamed Oportunidades.[86] PROGRESA's objectives are to improve the health and nutritional status of all members of poor households, especially mothers and children, as well as to improve school enrolment, attendance, and educational performance. PROGRESA supports families living in extreme poverty through both supply (provision of services) and demand (increase capability of households to obtain services) side interventions in education, health, and nutrition. Cash transfers are disbursed conditional on the household engaging in a set of behaviours designed to improve health and nutrition. The size of the cash transfer is large, at US$13 per household per month in 1999 which is on average one-third of the household income of the beneficiary family. The transfer is received every two months through an electronic card given to the mother.

Transfers are conditional on the families fulfilling certain requirements. First, every family member has to receive preventive health services. Carers of children aged less than 60 months are required to take the child to the clinic every two months for growth monitoring, immunizations and health education. Each month, children aged 4–24 months and pregnant and lactating women are given 30 nutritional supplements containing 100 per cent of recommended daily micronutrient requirement and 20 per cent of recommended energy requirement. All adult household members (including men) have to participate in regular meetings at which health, hygiene, and nutrition issues and best practices are discussed with nurses and physicians. Targeting is first done geographically then at the household level. Households do not have to apply, but are informed that they are eligible, using door-to-door methods.

The PROGESA evaluation shows a significant increase in nutrition monitoring and immunization rates. Infants under 3 years of age participating in the programme increased their growth monitoring visits between 30 and 60 per cent and beneficiaries aged 0–5 had a 12 per cent lower incidence of illness compared to non-PROGRESA children. The data also suggest that PROGRESA has had a significant impact on increasing child growth. Children aged 12–36 months grew, on average, 1 cm more than the control group children over a 12-month period. The population prevalence of stunting has been reduced by nearly 10 per cent.

Food consumption levels have also increased. Households receiving PROGRESA benefits in treatment localities obtained approximately 7 per cent more calories than did comparable households in control localities. The increase in household consumption was driven by higher expenditures on fruits, vegetables, and animal products.

The primary characteristic of PROGRESA is that it provides households with a large and regular source of income. Since such transfers are made to women, they improve their status both within the community and the household. In addition, as noted earlier, women are more likely to spend their income on food and health care for children than are men. PROGRESA's targeting is transparent and fair. Similar to TINP, coverage is high: 76 per cent of households in the selected areas were targeted for cash transfers and of these 97 per cent took up the programme. The final aspect is that for PROGRESA, the Government of Mexico funded 100 per cent of the programme and controlled its development from the beginning. There was no donor or foreign influence on the project. The project was really owned by the government.[87]

Another distinguishing feature of PROGRESA is that all members of the household are required to attend health education classes. Men are also targeted and made responsible for the health of their household. This sort of framework has been termed by Irene Tinker 'responsible paternity' which she defines as the awareness of men of their role in the care and education of their children.[88] Nutrition projects must take into consideration the fact that men are household decision-makers in much of the world and ensure that they are targeted, as much if not more so than women, to take responsibility for the members of their household. If projects aim to reshape, rather than reproduce, gender roles, then perhaps gender inequality and the burden of women can be slightly reduced.

The significant effect of PROGRESA on child nutritional status is not unique for a cash transfer scheme. A similar programme in Nicaragua, Red de Protección Social (RPS) resulted in a significant decline in underweight children from 15.3 to 10.4 per cent and prevalence of stunting from 41.9 to 37.1 per cent over two years. In Brazil, the Bolsa Alimentação (BA) increased beneficiary household food expenditure by 9 per cent. In Colombia's Programa Familias en Acción (PFA), food consumption increased in beneficiary households by 19 and 9 per cent in rural and urban households, respectively. There was a significant increase in consumption of protein-rich foods, cereals, fats and oils, and fruits and vegetables. In addition, heights increased on average 0.44 cm for children aged 0–12 months over a one-year period. Finally, in Zambia, the Kalomo District Social Cash Transfer Scheme decreased the prevalence of underweight children aged 0–5 years from 41 to 33 per cent over 12 months.

Thus, cash transfer schemes have the potential to improve children's diet and nutritional status through increasing purchasing power at the household level. While I am not claiming that they are the 'silver bullet' and agree that further research is necessary before conclusions, the reported positive outcomes of these schemes far exceed those reported from stand-alone nutrition projects such as TINP and the Bangladesh project. However, as of June 2006, there has been no attempt by the World Bank to introduce conditional transfers into the South Asia region.[89]

Conditional cash transfer programmes such as in Honduras and Colombia have been supported financially by the Social Protection sector of the Bank. The Health, Nutrition, and Population sector, although acknowledging that conditional cash transfer schemes effectively reduce rates of undernutrition in certain situations, argue that they are too expensive, costing on average US$70–77 per child enrolled. A 2006 World Bank nutrition report points out that community-based programmes, such as TINP, are much cheaper, costing only US$11–18 per child.[90] Despite this cost differential, the Social Protection sector within the Bank has been rapidly growing.

Going 'Inside the Bank': The Institutional Drivers

Given the promise of the alternatives described in the previous section, the question remains why the TINP model has been promoted despite the lack of substantive evidence that the approach is effective. This section goes 'inside' the Bank to examine three institutional drivers that could explain this. As David Mosse and David Lewis have noted, it is not possible to study technologies of power without an analysis of the political rationality underpinning them.[91] The World Bank was created to be a rational institution in that policy should be guided by organizational factors in the service of given fundamental values and principles. Although there are strong ideological and political constraining factors, staff show considerable ingenuity in negotiating them and moulding them to their own purposes. A recurring theme within this section is the diversity of opinion within the Bank concerning how nutrition should be addressed, which manifests itself as internal disagreement and conflict.

Within the Bank, the nutrition team feel that they are mainstreaming nutrition and pro-poor policies into the broad development agenda, thus ensuring that the Bank's mission includes a broad definition of development. As noted in Chapter 4, they feel that the macroeconomists prefer to make loans for large infrastructure projects that have a high, measurable return on the investment in a short time frame because this ensures that the loan is paid off quickly and countries do not default. These projects include highways, dams, and bridges which contribute to a country's GDP and economic growth. Nutrition programmes are viewed by macroeconomists as a distraction from the weighty infrastructure projects.

Stand-alone schemes such as TINP are judged too expensive since the increase in GDP is miniscule in relation to the vast amount of staff time and lending resources these projects occupy. In this situation, the nutritionists feel one of their jobs within the Bank is to counter the viewpoint of the macroeconomist and to ensure that a holistic approach to development is incorporated into the Bank. When actors, such as Save the Children UK, evaluate their work, Bank nutritionists feel that this criticism simply fuels the economist argument that the Bank should not lend for nutrition and instead focus exclusively on large infrastructure projects. They do not see criticism as being productive. This frustrates Bank staff advocating nutrition-related lending and partially explains the reluctance by staff to talk to external researchers.

The scepticism of macroeconomists also derives from the mainstream view within the Bank that undernutrition has multiple causes. It is seen as an intractable problem that has no easy or simple answers. Thus, there is widespread disbelief towards anyone who claims to have a silver bullet, such as growth monitoring.

Bank nutrition staff regard themselves as the best in their field and feel that they produce high-quality research with the vast resources that are available to them. Most of the Bank nutrition staff interviewed were aware of the gender dimensions of nutrition in India and the shortcomings of TINP. One staff member remarked that the one-word explanation for high malnutrition rates in India is gender, and then discussed the oppressed status of women in India compared to Sub-Saharan Africa. When nutrition policy is unsuitable, the problem is not due to ignorance or obstinacy. Bank staff working on nutrition must engage in, what David Mosse has called, 'an inter-disciplinary game' in which nutritionists are less powerful than economists which results in a situation where they must make compromises to ensure the survival of lending for nutrition. The situation for Bank nutritionists is that either it is the TINP model, or nothing.

As mentioned earlier, in the 1980s when the Bank started lending in this new area, the proponents of TINP were a tiny group of enthusiasts who felt themselves under siege and having to fight the whole organization in order to try to obtain a larger programme of lending for nutrition. Obvious setbacks in pre-TINP nutrition projects meant that the future of nutrition lending came to be seen as dependent on showing that Tamil Nadu was a 'success'. Given that TINP was and continues to be the standard-bearer for the nutrition team, it has been vital for their goal of giving nutrition a higher profile in Bank lending activities to show that at least one project has been successful. In light of this pressure, perhaps it is not surprising that the official evaluation was skewed in a positive direction and that claims of success have been overstated.

Given this situation, the translation of nutrition into economic terms and the creation of a success story can be viewed as a triumph of ingenuity and good will. Money that would have instead been allocated to loans for infrastructure projects has been acquired to help the undernourished. Thus, the first explanation for the promotion of the TINP model is that given grave doubts within the Bank regarding whether nutrition lending is effective, and the pressure from economists to show measurable results in a short time-frame, the TINP model has been portrayed as a success as the future of nutrition lending depends on the upholding of this story.

The second pressure is at the organizational level. As I have described in Chapter 5, nutrition is a complex phenomenon involving a number of disparate issues such as water and sanitation, agriculture, economic growth, welfare, and tribal resettlement. Since the Bank has staff working on each of these areas in India, the nutrition team struggles to find a distinct identity for itself. In the past five years, the Social Protection sector of the Bank, which runs parallel to the Health, Nutrition, and

Population sector in the Human Development Network, has made loans to enable governments to implement conditional cash transfer schemes. It appears that these have an impact on undernutrition. There is tension between the Social Protection sector and the Health, Nutrition, and Population sector as their activities overlap, and project design and framework contradict each other. In the Health, Nutrition, and Population sector, behavioural change is seen as the key to project design. In contrast, the Social Protection sector argues that increasing purchasing power at the household level is necessary. This encroachment by the Social Protection sector has restricted the nutrition team in the Health, Nutrition, and Population sector as staff are further constrained in what constitutes their domain. What the Social Protection sector and other sectors do not address are the issues of behavioural change and nutrition education. This is the domain of the nutrition team, and they must promote the priority of these issues in order to remain important and stay alive as an entity, especially given the recurring discussions by the Executive Board on restructuring and downsizing the Bank. Nutrition is defined as a problem of caring behaviour because this definition emphasizes the need for a nutrition team.

The final force influencing nutrition policy within the Bank is at the individual level. In 1992, the Wapenhan's Report noted that staff were under extreme pressure to disburse loans. Interviews with borrowers for the report revealed that Bank staff were more driven by the necessity to lend than to ensure successful project implementation. This pressure continues today.

The Matrix Programme Cycle for a Health, Nutrition, and Population sector project is estimated to last 10 months from project conception to approval. The first step is a Project Concept Note which takes about a month to complete. The second step is the Preparation Mission which lasts roughly a month. During this process, a mission of development partners, led by the World Bank, works with authorities in the borrower government and local organizations for the preparation of the tentative project. Once the Project Preparation mission has returned, the aide-memoire is circulated. It contains the main issues discussed and agreements reached during the mission. The memo first reflects on the agreed principles and agreed actions for cooperation and project preparation between the borrower country and the World Bank mission. It outlines the next mission (pre-appraisal) and the next steps. Due to the tight timeline to which the Mission team must adhere, good use is made of existing policy papers. A draft Project Preparation Mission Aide-Memoire prepared for Bangladesh states,

> Given the fact that (1) the support for HNPSP [HNP Sector Programme] needs to be approved by the World Bank and DP [Development Partners] by December 2004, and (2) a HNP Strategic Investment Plan for the period 2005–2010 (or further) is in an early stage of development, the timeline for project preparation (see Annex 1) is constrained. However, project approval by the Executive Board of the World Bank could be achieved by December 2004, if good use is made of existing policy papers—including the Conceptual Framework and Policy Options paper come to mind—and PIP 2003–2006. Government and DPs have developed numerous papers dealing with sub-sectoral or multi-sectoral HNP issues. Bangladesh is also developing a National Strategy for Economic Growth and Poverty Reduction (PRSP). Therefore, the development of a 6-year Strategic Investment Plan 2005–2010 (SIP) for the HNP sector should heavily rely on these documents. The SIP would only need to be detailed only for the first few years of the program, both in terms of interventions and in financial plans.

Three months later, after a number of reports have been completed (e.g. Strategic Investment Plan, Environmental Assessment, Social Assessment, Land Assessment), the Pre-Appraisal mission is sent to the borrower country.[92] The mission usually lasts 12–14 days. The timetable might look like:[93]

Day 1: Thursday

09:00–10:30 World Bank Health Team Pre-Appraisal Mission Introduction

11:00–12:30 Discussion on the Mission Agenda with Joint Chief of Planning of the Ministry of Health and Family Welfare of borrower country

14:00–17:30 Health, Nutrition, and Population Consortium Meeting Mission Introduction

Day 2, Day 3: Friday, Saturday

Day 4: Sunday

09:00–17:00 Meeting with all mission members to discuss the organization and conducting of the mission, mission tasks, and roles and responsibilities, discussion of four groups involved in mission (Organizational Issues, Service Delivery, Human Resources, and HNP financing and financial management), logistic issues

17:30–18:30 Update on progress of mission with World Bank country office

Day 5: Monday

09:00–16:00 Presentation by the Ministry of Health and Family Welfare of borrower country on how it wants to be supported financially by donors to all mission members, presentation of Strategic Investment Plan, project versus budget support

17:30–18:30 Update on progress of mission with mission team

Day 6: Tuesday

14:30–16:30 Meeting with Ministry of Health and Family Welfare and Planning Commission of borrower country to discuss action plan for reforms and Bank technical assistance

17:30–18:30 Update on progress of mission with mission team. Initiate discussion on joint financing and implementation arrangements among donors, budget support, etc.

Day 7: Wednesday

14:30–16:30 Discussion session with senior officials in borrower country Ministries (Finance, Education, Agriculture, etc.) to determine ownership of respective multisectoral elements. Complete a poverty reduction strategy paper (PRSP)

17:30–18:30 Update on progress of mission with mission team

Day 8: Thursday

14:30–16:00 Meeting with professional associations

16:00–17:30 Presentation by co-leaders of four appraisal groups

17:30–18:30 Update on progress of mission with mission team

Day 9, 10: Friday, Saturday

Day 11: Sunday

16:00–17:30 Meeting with Academics

17:30–18:30 Review of mission progress, presentation on field findings by mission members and recommendations, discuss draft aide-memoire

Day 12: Monday

09:00–12:00 Complete draft aide-memoire

13:00–16:00 Discussion on draft aide-memoir with HNP Consortium

17:30–18:30 End of the day mission meeting to finalize draft aide-memoire

Day 13: Tuesday

15:00–18:00 Discussion with civil society members

Day 14: Wednesday

10:00–12:00 Pre-wrap up meeting with Joint Chief in Ministry of Health and Family Welfare to share draft of aide-memoire

Day 15: Thursday

10:00–12:00 Wrap-up meeting with borrower country to finalize aide-memoire

13:00–14:00 Post–wrap-up meeting of mission team to finalize aide-memoire

Once the Pre-Appraisal Aide-Memoire from the mission has been completed, a Quality Enhancement Review (QER) is conducted. The purpose of the review is to provide technical assistance to staff and managers working on a project. It is not to assess staff but rather to help the team improve the quality of the design or implementation of a particular project. This is achieved through closely examining project documentation, interviewing the task team leader and other team members and country and sector directors, as well as relevant operational staff familiar with the project. It is a tripartite partnership among the region (e.g. South Asia), the sector (e.g. Health, Nutrition, and Population), and the Quality Assurance Group (QAG) of the Bank.

The time between the Pre-Appraisal Mission and the Project Appraisal is usually two to three months. Once the Project Appraisal occurs, a revised Project Implementation Plan is sent for review to the borrower country. Another month is spent negotiating the terms of the loan and project before approval.

One staff member stressed to me that the purpose of the Bank's mission is not to create a 'Bank' project. He said, 'So, whatever, at the end, is done or not done, these things are due to the government.' This was contested by an individual who works for a development partner of the Bank. She stated,

What we seem to be seeing . . . is the reliance on people coming in from outside into the country for very short periods of time, engaging in very rapid consultation processes and writing design documents often outside the country leads to a situation where it's very difficult for national stakeholders to actually challenge the approaches which are being put forward. Blueprint approaches.

During interviews with Bank staff, I received mixed messages about the flexibility in the policy process for the borrower country to make changes. One staff member said, 'We had a very flexible design [in Tamil Nadu] with capacity to learn from experience. Every mission we set the stage for the project to evolve.' Another staff member disagreed, 'Well, TINP was meticulously planned. [The mission leader] didn't let the client design the programme but wanted to rigidly decide the role of the team. For example, me and a friend wanted to make a recommendation for the project yet [the mission leader] didn't let us say anything.' A World Bank associate in Delhi also remarked, 'The Bank does take India's money then tells them what to do.' A former Bank–India interlocutor noted that the process has changed over time. He noted, 'Thirty years ago, the central government was able to hold its stand more because of central government power but recently there has been more dealing with states directly. States are anxious to get the money so they are less likely to use collective power to negotiate better conditionality.'

The timetable presented above also reflects the enormous amount of work given to each individual staff member. One reason that Bank staff are reluctant to do interviews is that they are just too busy. They are required to produce an enormous amount, travel often, all in an environment in which every interview, every journalist or researcher, could potentially result in a public affairs debacle. The workload on staff has been steadily increasing over the past half century. In 1981, a Bank staff member remarked,

Every few years there is a new factor that we must take into account, but we are not given more time or staff to accommodate it. This makes me think that the Bank's senior management is responding to outside pressures by delegating the hard choices to us. I don't have any clear understanding of whether we are supposed to pay lip service to, say, the environment or the role of women in development, or to take them seriously. Even worse, I don't know to what extent the Bank wants me to take any one of these things seriously when they conflict with one another. I can make up my own mind on this, but am I supposed to?[94]

Designing a project is a long and arduous process and staff simply do not have time to put together a whole new project template. In fact, if a project takes too long or costs too much, it is seen as a failure on the part of the staff. One staff member recounted the difficulties with how the Bank 'thinks'. In his words, 'The Bank likes to think big, because otherwise it is not worth the time of staff if they're not going to move lots of money.' In addition, he noted that the Bank is forced actively to 'sell' projects to governments.

Spending too long on local complexities is considered as creating a problem and hampering the real work of the loan point-person. Staff already have project documents that can be exported to every country so they rely on these. As Ngaire Woods notes,

Junior officials are regularly sent to far-away places to analyze rather alien and difficult solutions. As mentioned above, a clear blueprint of models and policies provide the Fund and Bank staff with a well-structured starting point from which to define the problem, map out the stakes, prescribe the solution, evaluate the chances of success, and assess the implications of their prescription. Obviously, the simpler and clearer the model the more usefully it fulfils these functions.[95]

Due to limited time and resources, staff rely on a blueprint despite acknowledging that the blueprint is flawed. Reflecting on the Bangladesh Integrated Nutrition Project in 2005, a former nutritionist at the Bank noted,

I think, firstly, that it's clear from the ICR, the Implementation and Completion Report of BINP, discussions within the Bank that there's no doubt that with hindsight we all agree that moving forward with NNP too quickly was a mistake. The Bank has said so publicly, has written it down. There is no doubt about that. That there were very strong political reasons for doing that is also a reality, and I think understanding some of that, and acknowledging some of that, and how do we as technical people respond to those kinds of realities I think is something we all need to deal with.

Defending the continuation of a nutrition project in spite of negative evaluations, a Bank staff member noted,

And I would also say that stopping implementation of projects, if there is the concern that great harm will be done if one goes forward—let's say we're building a dam and there are very serious design questions—that certainly is an appropriate remedy. If the concern is that we're not being as effective as we ought to be, that's a different threshold where I would say the remedy might not necessarily be to impose a moratorium.

Thus the way the TINP model is justified by the nutrition advocates in the Bank is that first, it is better than nothing, second, that the project is better than large, infrastructure schemes, and third, it is not doing any harm.

Arguably, this type of pressure at the individual level is due to the combination of the bureaucratic nature of the Bank with small spaces for entrepreneurship. As Ngaire Woods has noted, bureaucracies create the appearance of being apolitical, impersonal, technocratic, and neutral.[96] The individuals within these bureaucracies perceive of their work as following 'the rules' of the institution, so they are just doing 'the job' and following 'rationally established norms'. Michael Barnett and Martha Finnemore argue that it is precisely this presentation that makes bureaucracies so powerful.[97] Drawing on Max Weber's research, they identify several features which characterize a bureaucracy.[98] These are apparent in the Bank. First, bureaucracies have a distinct, internal culture and are established as rational actors to accomplish certain goals and promote particular values. In order to gain legitimacy in their environment, bureaucracies create social knowledge and promote a particular perspective of the world. This results in 'ritualized behaviour' where responses to the environment result in a standard action (e.g. negative evaluations by consultants become internal documents). Bureaucracies classify and compartmentalize the world in order to organize external influences into those that are able to be managed by the institution's rules, rituals, and beliefs. Bureaucracies often tailor their missions to address external influences so that they fit the 'existing, well-known and comfortable rulebook'.[99]

Bureaucracies must also work in numerous contexts at once using the same universal rules and categories. Thus, bureaucrats 'flatten' diversity. This is apparent in the World Bank's use of a blueprint to address undernutrition in countries which vary in history, political situation, size, wealth, and ethnic composition. The *Nutrition Toolkit* homogenizes the world and assumes undernutrition can be solved using the same 12 tools regardless of local circumstances: 'The template is necessary because it guides staff working in countries all over the world, permitting them to act with the full backing of their institution and to put agreements in place with a minimum of time and resources.'[100] The question lingers whether an institution like the Bank could operate without a blueprint approach given the time and resources it would take to design micro-scale social sector projects specifically for local communities across the world and without appearing as if Bank staff are attempting to social engineer societies to resemble the US and Western European countries.

The straightforward model of a bureaucrat explains behaviour in terms of career advancement. Hans Gerth and Wright Mills note that promotions are given to those who follow the rules although they might be 'lacking in heroism, human spontaneity, and inventiveness'.[101] They discuss how new approaches within a bureaucracy are frowned upon since they are perceived as a threat to the professional integrity of the staff. Within the Bank, the main criterion to be promoted is the production of 'punctual, technically tight work'. This is not necessarily brilliant work, but must be efficient and display managerial promise.[102] A Bank official notes, 'The ethos of the Bank is that no one challenges his supervisor, there is no room for boat rocking.'[103] Loyalty is valued over best practices. A survey of the Bank in 2002 revealed that only 51 per cent of staff believed promotions were made on an objective basis.[104] If a staff member diverges in their methods from the institution, this disagreement is ultimately resolved at headquarters in Washington, DC quite possibly with a managing director: 'This prevents staff "going native".'[105] It has been noted that, 'any new consideration can be viewed as mitigating the cold calculus of economic viability'.[106] An anthropologist who works at the Bank told me, 'Pragmatism is rewarded over passion.' The Bank prides itself on technical prowess and as being a leader in the development arena. Thus, every project should use a well-proven strategy to address a solvable problem and achieve a measurable goal. This attitude discourages innovation and unusual approaches, and resistance to innovation is apparent in many organizations, not only the World Bank.

In addition, as Ngaire Woods notes, staff face a strong career incentive to stick to the blueprint; 'If all staff speak with one voice and prescribe the same things, then it is the institution as a whole that must bear the brunt of any criticism',[107] not the individual. There is no incentive for staff to try something new since the Bank will not take responsibility for a novel approach.[108] Thus, many staff are reluctant to work in an unfamiliar field especially if there are no career benefits arising from this.[109] Staff are concerned with protecting their jobs, thus they are likely to stay with the existing structures if they offer some sort of security. Reflecting on this, Sebastan Mallaby states, 'If you are a Pakistani or Nigerian water specialist with twenty years' experience at the Bank, losing your job means losing both your income and your US visa, and uprooting your baseball-playing kids from the culture they grew up in.'[110]

Thus, given all the incentives at the individual level, Bank nutrition staff stick with the TINP model that has been portrayed as successful. They can then use this model to lobby for greater attention to nutrition. The decisions about what the Bank does in any country is the result of contesting opinions about whether and in what proportions the Bank should lend for nutrition, health, water and sanitation, social protection, roads, and so on. At this stage, the outcome is not determined by rules and norms, but by the power of persuasion of the proponents of different viewpoints and the evidence that they can use to support it. The story of TINP's success serves as an advocacy tool for the proponents of stand-alone nutrition projects within the Bank.

Given the three institutional drivers described above, the Bank nutrition staff have continued to rely on the TINP model. Individuals are faced with a number of structural, organizational and personal factors that influence their room to manoeuvre with nutrition policy. Thus, while staff are aware of how a better project might be designed, there are constraints that limit their ability to change the Bank's nutrition approach. Powerful incentives and limitations, as well as clever negotiating of the system by certain individuals, define how staff work and approach development issues.

Conclusion

This chapter has attempted to address the straightforward question of what works in effectively addressing hunger. The answer is complex and intricate as undernutrition ties into the fundamental structure and organization of communities. The first step towards designing policy is to recognize that undernutrition is the result of political, economic, and social forces which are challenging to address in a stand-alone scheme, especially one rooted in growth monitoring and nutrition education. The next step, as the previous section has discussed, is for the Bank to recognize certain institutional drivers leading to the promotion of an approach to nutrition which is questionable. Structures, both in poor communities as well as in the Bank, significantly affect the agency of the individuals living and working within them.

Notes

1. World Bank (2006), p. 204.
2. Griffiths, Dicken, and Favin (1996), p. 22.
3. Ruel et al. (1999).
4. See Adair, Popkin, and Guilkey (1993), Dugdale (1982), Jelliffe (1972), Raphael (1979), and Chetley (1986).
5. Das et al. (1982).
6. Shekar (1990), p. 162.
7. Pinstrup-Anderson and Jaramillo (1991), Lipton and Longhurst (1989), p. 109, Osmani (1992b), Martorell, Mendoza, and Castillo (1988), Nabarro et al. (1988), and Leatherman (2005).
8. UN Millennium Project (2005), p. 73.

9. Jelliffe (1957), p. 130.
10. Shekar et al. (1992), p. 710.
11. Gopalan (1985, 1988).
12. Gopalan (1992), where socio-economic status is determined by education, occupation, and income.
13. Griffiths, Dicken, and Favin (1996), p. ix.
14. Morley (2003).
15. Jelliffe and Jelliffe (1989), p. 303.
16. Heaver (2006), p. 14.
17. Gerein (1988).
18. Rohde (2005), p. 203.
19. Griffiths, Dicken, and Favin (1996), p. 1.
20. Roy et al. (1993).
21. Tonglet et al. (1999).
22. Gerein (1988), Roberfroid et al. (2005).
23. Morley (1999, 2003).
24. Gopalan (1985).
25. Roberfroid et al. (2005), p. 210.
26. Save the Children UK (2003), p. 20.
27. Shekar and Latham (1992).
28. Ibid. p. 10.
29. Nabarro and Chinnock (1988), p. 946.
30. McDowell and Hoorweg (1975), Gwatkin et al. (1980), and Hornick (1985).
31. Mascie-Taylor et al. (2003).
32. Hoorweg and Njemeijer (1980).
33. Cerquiera and Olson (1995), p. 67.
34. Project language.
35. World Bank (2006), p. 29.
36. Ibid. p. 32.
37. Ibid. p. 60.
38. George et al. (1993), p. 351.
39. Blaise et al. (2002), Latham (2002), Lefevre et al. (2002), and Save the Children UK (2003).
40. Shekar (1991).
41. Shekar and Latham (1992), p. 11.
42. Chidambaram (1989), cited in Cerquiera and Olson (1995), p. 76.
43. Berg (1985), cited in Cerquiera and Olson (1995), p. 76.
44. Roberfroid et al. (2005), p. 210.
45. Mark and Mimi Nichter have done an excellent job of examining traditional health beliefs and shown how many health messages are useless, even counterproductive. Nichter and Nichter (1996).
46. Mascie-Taylor et al. (1999).
47. See White (2005) and Levinson and Rohde (2005).

48. Pelletier, Shekar, and Du (2005), p. 37.
49. Martorell et al. (1994) and Mascie-Taylor et al. (forthcoming).
50. Gopalan et al. (1973).
51. Ibid. p. 565.
52. Ibid. p. 566, see Ulijaszek and Strickland (1993), ch. 8.
53. Pelletier, Shekar, and Du (2005).
54. Ibid. p. 37.
55. See Gopalan and Chatterjee (1985).
56. O'Brien (1978).
57. Gopalan (1984).
58. There has been a move towards self-reported nutritional need. In this formulation, hunger is defined by the food insecure themselves. Importance is given to whether the poor have access to the food they would like to eat as well as the level of insecurity the individual feels regarding the possibility of hunger in the future. Although some may feel that nutritional needs cannot be operationally incorporated into nutrition projects, certain successful attempts have shown that it is possible to document the subjective dimensions of hunger. For example, the Indian National Sample Survey has emphasized individual perception, including questions on the lack of choice as well as the acquisition of food in socially unacceptable ways. This qualitative data complemented the quantitative data collected in the survey.
59. Burghart (1990), see Prabhu (2001), p. 232.
60. See Harriss-White and Hoffenberg (1994) and Mintz and Bois (2002).
61. Mooij (2000) and Sen (2005).
62. van Hollen (2003), p. 176.
63. Messer (1984a).
64. Ulijaszek and Strickland (1993).
65. Appadurai (1981).
66. See Simoons (1991, 1994).
67. See DeGarine (1972), Holmberg (1950), Jochim (1981), Lee (1969), Messer (1984a, 1984b, 1989), Ogbu (1973), Richards (1939), and Pagezy (1982).
68. This paragraph from Burghart (1990).
69. Srinivas (1952), p. 32.
70. See Mayer (1996).
71. Source: National Family Health Survey (NFHS-2).
72. See Ravallion (1990).
73. Ibid.
74. Burger and Esrey (1995).
75. Minamoto et al. (2005).
76. Ulijaszek and Strickland (1993), p. 127.
77. Ibid. p. 127, Tomkins (1988).
78. Harriss (1990) and Wilson (2001).
79. Ulijaszek and Strickland (1993), p. 127.

80. Ibid. p. 124.
81. Harriss (1990) and Wilson (2001).
82. Sukhatme (1982).
83. Conway (1997), p. 3.
84. von Braun (1995).
85. World Bank (2005), p. 29. This information is just used to emphasize the argument that certain individuals have made against relying only on economic growth. Between 1990 and 2015 the MDG is to halve the proportion of people who suffer from hunger.
86. This case study is taken from Sridhar and Duffield (2006).
87. In 1995, two Mexican social scientists, Santiago Levy and Jose Gomez de Leon, created PROGRESA. Levy, an economist, currently serves as director general of the Mexican Institute of Social Insurance. He was undersecretary in Mexico's Finance Ministry in 1995, when President Zedillo put him in charge of a team that would draft a plan to address poverty. PROGRESA was the resulting programme. Gomez de Leon is a demographer who headed Mexico's National Commission on Population and was PROGRESA's first national coordinator. Levy and Gomez de Leon launched a pilot project funded by the federal government in three cities in the southern state of Campeche using the database of beneficiaries of two existing subsidized milk and tortilla programmes. The pilot was a success and PROGRESA was launched in 1997.
88. Tinker (1976).
89. Heaver (2006), p. 9.
90. World Bank (2006), p. 132.
91. Mosse and Lewis (2006), p. 9.
92. A former Bank–India interlocutor remarked on the Bank missions that he was involved with:

    These external organizations spend more on overhead costs, like transportation, hotels, food, rather than on the actual help people are getting. It's frustrating so I didn't want to work on the family planning project. You know, there's a saying 'Everyone can only eat three meals a day, sleep in one bed.'

93. Based on a real internal Bank timetable for nutrition project.
94. Ascher (1983), p. 430.
95. Woods (2006), p. 55.
96. See Herzfeld (1993).
97. Barnett and Finnemore (1999), p. 708.
98. Ibid. p. 718, Weber (1947, 1978).
99. Beetham (1985), p. 76.
100. Woods (2006), p. 63.
101. Geerth and Mills (1978), p. 216.
102. Ascher (1983), pp. 426–7.
103. Sherk (1994), cited in Woods (2006), p. 62.

104. Mallaby (2005), p. 378.
105. Woods (2006), pp. 55–6.
106. Ascher (1983), p. 429.
107. Woods (2006), p. 63.
108. Ibid. p. 63.
109. Heaver (2006), p. 19.
110. Mallaby (2005), p. 378.

7

The Way Forward

> [The] model of structural violence is a vivid reminder that most vio-
> lence acts are not deviant. They are defined as moral in the service
> of conventional norms and material interests. As ethnographers we
> can best contribute by rendering visible these erased and unexpected
> linkages between violence, suffering, and power.
>
> Phillippe Bourgois and Nancy Scheper-Hughes[1]

This concluding chapter reflects on the way forward. It focuses on the
theoretical and empirical findings that have emerged from the research.
After discussing the wider theoretical issues raised by the case study
of the World Bank, it turns to policy implications. That is, it attempts
to shed light on strategies for removing obstacles to effectively address
hunger in India. This chapter concludes by returning to the choice versus
circumstance debate.

Tracing Global–Local Linkages

This book has argued that there is a mismatch between how malnutrition
is defined, measured, and evaluated by the Bank, and how it is lived
and experienced in affected communities. In addition to its empirical
contribution, the objective of this research is to put forward an innovative
theoretical framework for the study of links between international organizations and local communities, tracing the ways in which power creates
webs and relations between actors, institutions, and discourses over time
and space.[2]

My research is an attempt at 'studying-through' by tracing the ways
in which nutrition policy within the Bank—its discourse, prescriptions,
and programmes—affects the beneficiaries of Bank projects in developing

countries. My field is not a discrete, local community but a social, political space articulated through relations of power and systems of governance. I have attempted to trace 'policy connections between different organizational and everyday worlds, on issues where actors in different sites do not know each other or share a moral universe'.[3]

As Cris Shore and Susan Wright have recognized, globalization has resulted in an interdependent world in which understanding the plight of poor people requires an understanding of the way institutions such as banks, governments, multinational companies, and geopolitics operate.[4] This research needs to take place at multiple levels, starting at the designers of the policy (e.g. World Bank, WHO), and moving to the front-line implementers of the policy (e.g. community workers) and finally to the beneficiaries themselves (e.g. women and children in poor communities). All three categories of actors exist in a dynamic relationship. As policies move from the top level down and back up again, they are renegotiated and reinterpreted at each level based on the actor's beliefs, motivations, and circumstances.

The Designers of Nutrition Policy: The World Bank

Regarding the first level, there is a growing ethnographic literature on how the World Bank approaches 'development' and the consequences of that framework on local communities. Two approaches have been previously used by anthropologists to study the Bank: critical discourse analysis and being a participant-insider. This book has attempted to use a combination of ethnographic interviews and critical discourse analysis to understand nutrition operations within the Bank. It has endeavoured to understand the world view of Bank staff while also maintaining a clear research relationship. This has been an uncomfortable position. Using traditional anthropological methods to study-up is problematic because of issues of anonymity, informed consent, and access. However, within these limitations, this book has striven to do justice to the Bank staff members and to recognize the constraints under which they operate.

During the 1970s when the World Bank started making loans for health-related projects, undernutrition was defined by the nutrition team as 'the pathological condition brought about by inadequacy of one or more of the essential nutrients that the body cannot make but that are necessary for survival, for growth and reproduction, and for the capacity to work, learn, and function in society'.[5] This definition frames malnutrition as a disease located within the body with an organic basis in biochemistry and physiology. The cure advocated by the Bank for the disease of hunger is educating to women through the tools of growth monitoring and short-term supplementary feeding.

Once nutrition is packaged as a 'curable' problem, the Bank inserts the construct into a human capital framework. In nutrition projects, the worth of project beneficiaries is based on their contribution to the economic growth and GDP of the borrower country. The Bank frames health as an asset, a form of capital that should be invested in so that a country can increase its national output. This aspect of productivity is emphasized as the sole characteristic upon which resource allocation and loan decisions can be made. The Bank does not use human rights language in project documents since it is considered political and thus not permissible according to its economic mandate. The Bank must make loan decisions based on sound, economic analysis that can only be used to justify involvement in a nutrition project. The worth of an individual is determined by his or her contribution to the economy.

The human capital framework for nutrition within the Bank is a reflection of the dominance of economics in public health projects. This constitutes the economic gaze. Even within the Bank's Health, Nutrition, and Population sector, operations and activities are dominated by economic paradigms and frameworks. Only by presenting undernutrition as an issue of lost productivity and packaging it as an element of human capital were Bank nutritionists able to convince managers to make stand-alone nutrition loans.

Economists run the 'development apparatus' of the Bank. Within the Bank, the discipline of economics is hegemonic, the only way of examining problems, of defining their essential features, and suggesting solutions. The strength of economic knowledge is seen to lie in its ability to manage the details of a local issue, reduce the complexity, and extract indicators and specific policy goals.[6] Local knowledge is considered messy, complicated, political, and incomprehensible to the institution. Thus, an economic approach reduces problems, such as nutrition, to their core elements so that the experts can digest them and prescribe solutions.

The nutrition approach of the Bank is based on a combination of biomedical and health economic models. As a Bank health economist in New Delhi said, 'We use the medical model but bring in the cost aspects.' However, this approach is not only based on expert analysis and knowledge. Rather, it is a reflection of the political pressures and institutional constraints operating within the Bank along with self-justifying altruism. Technical expertise is ultimately moulded by political, institutional, and bureaucratic incentives. The structure and organization of the Bank ultimately shape the way it defines its problems and promotes solutions: 'Each institution fashions its policies to fit the resources available.'[7] The morally righteous belief, a key element in groupthink, in the 'mission' to eradicate world hunger provides Bank staff insularity from feedback.

The Bank frames nutrition using biomedical and economic inputs because it ultimately has to construct a problem that its own instruments can address. The Bank is in the lending business. It makes time-bound, repayable loans. Any Bank actions have to fit within the overall Bank goal of lending for growth. Thus, loans have to be made for profit-creating projects that have measurable economic returns. To address undernutrition, the Bank has to ensure that it is defined as a 'curable' problem (a disease) that when addressed will have an impact on GDP and economic growth (human capital). The prevailing policy is shaped by 'economic analysis, institutional constraints and bureaucratic organization'.[8]

The Renegotiation by Implementers and Beneficiaries

While the biomedical approach to undernutrition might be suitable in a clinic setting, it is problematic when exported to stand-alone community nutrition projects such as TINP. TINP defines undernutrition as a medical disease resulting from women's lack of knowledge on proper childcare practices. The disease can be visually detected in the child through the use of growth monitoring and promotion. Community workers determine if the child is 'sick' (i.e. undernourished) and in need of treatment through the use of growth monitoring. The 'cures' promoted for this disease are educational tools: growth monitoring to show a mother her child's growth is faltering, supplementary feeding for 90 days to teach mothers that small amounts of additional food can 'cure' their child, and nutrition counselling on hygiene, food quality, and quantity.

However, as fieldwork in Tamil Nadu revealed, these educational tools are not effective at addressing undernutrition in India. Growth monitoring is not working as a communication strategy to inform mothers about the nutritional status of their children. Most women in all caste communities reported that their child was weighed, yet the majority could not recognize a growth chart or correctly explain what it showed.

The front-line workers believe that growth monitoring occurs for data collection purposes. Thus, while children are weighed, the purpose of the process is not explained to women so that they can understand the educational importance of growth monitoring. Women, who are the beneficiaries of the project, mention weighing as an obstacle to go through, a 'meaningless ritual'[9] before children can receive food and health services.

In the course of fieldwork, several issues became apparent with the use of supplementary feeding as a 'cure' for undernutrition. First, supplementary feeding is not targeted towards children whose growth is faltering. Rather, all children who attended *anganwadi* received the supplement. This is not necessarily negative. There are several possible explanations for the lack of targeting. At the level of the front-line community worker, one problem has been that the reading and plotting of weights is frequently inaccurate. Because of the difficulty in weighing a child, plotting the weight, and interpreting the growth chart, it is easier for the worker to give rations to all children present that day. In addition, in the context of deprivation, albeit with slight variations in extent between households, it is difficult to withhold food from children whose growth is considered satisfactory, yet who still express feelings of hunger.

In terms of the beneficiaries, the supplementary food turns into replacement food for children, which is a problem found in other stand-alone nutrition projects. Women attend *anganwadi* in the morning before work. Instead of giving the child the usual breakfast, the child receives the supplement. In addition, while women appreciated that TINP included supplementary food, the majority of women in all caste groups preferred for their children to receive 'healthy foods' such as vegetables, dairy products, and eggs rather than the *laddoo*. While the *laddoo* is eaten because the children are hungry and it is free, when discussing the supplement with older children, they complained that it did not taste good and expressed a desire to have more variety.

Intensive nutrition counselling has also been difficult to implement in Tamil Nadu due to a number of factors. A high rate of women in all caste groups could not report what they had learned in *anganwadi*, indicating that neither educational level nor income level has improved the receptivity to the nutrition worker's teachings in these communities. At the level of the front-line community worker, the problem is that workers do not have enough time to discuss caring practices with women. There also tends to be more emphasis placed on producing different educational materials than on actually speaking to women about health and nutrition.

However, the written materials are not useful to women who are illiterate.

In terms of the beneficiaries, many women prefer to take advantage of the supplementary food and health services provided by the *anganwadi* as opposed to discussing health lessons. In their opinion, the health messages are impractical. While health education is important, its effectiveness is ultimately dependent on structural and environmental factors such as gender inequality and purchasing power that constrain individual agency.

Despite the problems with individual nutrition counselling, there is a high level of knowledge in all four caste communities on proper caring practices, as defined by the WHO. Over 80 per cent of women in all caste groups had received three antenatal check-ups as well as iron tablets during pregnancy. Over 90 per cent of women in all caste groups reported that it was important to take rest during pregnancy, although fewer actually did so. The structural constraints of lack of time and money were the primary reasons given for not taking rest. In addition, most women in all four groups ate more during pregnancy, were aware of colostrum, and knew about the recommended breastfeeding duration.

The main places where caring practices are being learned, other than kinship networks and *anganwadi*, are through television and women's groups. The primary beneficial aspect of TINP at the local level is the creation of women's groups by community workers. These groups give women the space to share educational lessons along with social and economic empowerment activities. However, this facet of the project has not been identified by the Bank as the key feature of TINP. The Bank focuses on growth monitoring as the crucial component along with health counselling and supplementary feeding.

In these communities, inadequate knowledge and ignorance are not the factors implicated in high rates of child undernutrition. Rather, inadequate purchasing power and alcohol consumption by males can be viewed as responsible. The major household expenditure in all four castes was food, with a significantly higher number of tribal households compared to high-caste Shudra households reporting food as their primary expense. In addition, there is a significant difference in the number of meals eaten per day according to caste, with a higher percentage of tribal households eating two or fewer. The expressed desires for food suggest that most people want more rice, meat, and vegetables indicating that given an adequate income, households would aspire to a diet balanced both quantitatively and qualitatively. In addition, 44, 30, 37, and 25 per cent of weekly household income in the tribal, *Dalit*, low-caste Shudra, and high-caste Shudra households, respectively, was spent on alcohol. Alcohol affects child nutrition through two pathways. Economically, it is a major income leak. Socially, it exacerbates gender inequality within the household and reduces the ability of women to care for their children. Inadequate knowledge and childcare practices are less implicated in child malnutrition rates in the communities of this study than inadequate purchasing power and gender inequality. In this situation, the TINP tools of growth monitoring and nutrition counselling are not effective for the reduction of child undernutrition in Tamil Nadu, while the creation of women's groups has been a beneficial aspect.

Choice Versus Circumstance

The choice versus circumstance framework used throughout this book is useful to understanding not only undernutrition in India but also the policy process within the Bank. This book is not arguing that agency is absent in either of these cases. Certain individuals are remarkably entrepreneurial and skilful at manipulating the system to pursue their agenda. Rather it is calling for increased emphasis by researchers and policymakers on the structures within with individuals make decisions.

In India, as discussed in the previous section, inadequate purchasing power and gender inequality are the fundamental drivers of undernutrition. At the community level, undernutrition is not a disease. While medicalizing malnutrition by defining it as a disease can be a useful way of treating symptoms, this act depoliticizes a social condition and neglects the underlying conditions of inequality. It avoids uncomfortable issues such as redistribution. In this way, biomedicine can disguise disadvantage as a disease. Child undernutrition should be viewed as the individual biological manifestation of social, economic, and political forces and the interplay of gender, caste, class, household, and community dynamics. It is a complex phenomenon that cannot be cured or eradicated like a disease. It cannot be addressed in a short time frame.

Nutrition is a condition that reflects the well-being of a community as a whole. Arguably, undernutrition is a much better indicator of poverty at the individual and community level than economic indicators. Undernutrition should be viewed as the embodiment of structural inequality such as poverty, gender discrimination, or caste prejudice. It is both a biological and social event. Instead of focusing on the individual level, research should examine the processes through which social forces come to be embodied as biological events.

Thus, when designing interventions to address undernutrition in India, the circumstances of the poor must be taken into account. The TINP case study can be viewed as illustrating the difficulty in conceptualizing and making operational a 'nutrition scheme' which overemphasizes the agency of women and neglects the harsh circumstances within which they live.

In terms of the World Bank policy process, the nutrition staff should be credited with putting nutrition on the Bank agenda. The designers of TINP made a major contribution to nutritional planning by integrating a number of tools to address undernutrition. It is much easier a task to critically examine a project than to create one. However, the growing concern over the validity of the TINP model should be taken into consideration by the Bank. As described above, several components of TINP are not effective in practice. The Bank is not offering grants. It is offering loans. As one academic reflecting on this scenario stated, 'This seems to me a gross waste of money...if we know these things don't work and we're spending a lot of money.'

This 'faith-based blindness' is a result of the Bank's reliance on a template, which guides staff working all over the world.[10] The benefit of a template is that it permits the Bank to stand-above local knowledge, to claim universally applicable expertise, and to show that it treats all borrowers the same. In addition, 'most bureaucracies fall back on existing habits and solutions to deal with problems, tailoring solutions or advice to match the available resources. What they do is not just a product of how good the economics is.'[11]

An analysis of the political rationality underpinning the Bank blueprint reveals three institutional drivers that result in the promotion of the TINP approach. First, given grave doubts within the Bank regarding whether nutrition lending is effective, and the pressure from economists to show measurable results in a short time-frame, the TINP model has been portrayed as a success as the future of nutrition lending depends on the preservation of this story. Second, undernutrition is defined as a problem of detrimental childcare practices because this definition emphasizes the need for stand-alone nutrition loans. Third, staff within the Bank are faced with a number of incentives to stick with a template both at the organizational and individual level. Thus, staff work within certain ideological and political circumstances that affect the decisions they make.

201

To return to the initial question driving this research, why have strategies to address undernutrition in India failed so badly? This book has argued that insufficient attention has been paid to circumstances both in the World Bank and in impoverished communities.

What is the way forward? In terms of the policy process, the case of TINP illustrates what seems to happen when a small group of specialists push forward an idea and generate enthusiasm for it despite the lack of a substantive evidence base, in this particular case, the push for growth monitoring and nutrition education as the 'silver bullets' to address undernutrition. As the TINP approach moves out of the mainstream and into the margins, new ideas will be brought forward that reflect what is 'fashionable' in development circles, not necessarily what is evidence-based. What seems to occur is 'policy-based' evidence-making.

In 2008, undernutrition has become central again to the Bank. Current Bank President Robert Zoellick stated that he would use the 2008 World Economic Forum in Davos to 'draw attention to hunger and malnutrition, the forgotten Millennium Development Goal'.[12] The Bank's return to this topic is mainly a result of the launch of the *Lancet* child nutrition series which the Bank co-authored and co-financed. Despite a clear move in rhetoric away from the TINP approach (in contrast to the 2006 nutrition report), the new strategies again seem to neglect the realities on the ground of undernutrition in poor communities. Despite the push by former Bank President Wolfensohn to integrate social development concerns into the Bank and to incorporate systematic assessment of the social context in all World Bank activities, there is still a startling lack of attention to the needs and concerns of local communities, the social realities of village life, and a heavy reliance on biomedical and economic approaches that address undernutrition in a technocratic manner. Thus, a clear first step for the Bank is to examine how its existing frameworks, organization, and incentive structure could be changed to better integrate the needs of its beneficiaries in India and elsewhere in the world. Without systematic attention to local concerns, projects are doomed to failure.

At the community level, more emphasis should be put on hunger-reduction strategies that can not only increase household purchasing power but also improve the position of women, e.g. schemes such as cash transfers and the creation of women's groups. Attention should be paid to the circumstances within which households and individuals make choices. As we move into the twenty-first century, action must be taken to successfully address the underlying determinants of undernutrition for the millions of poor and hungry who deserve and have a right to a life free from hunger, disease, and suffering.

Notes

1. Bourgois and Scheper-Hughes (2004), p. 318.
2. Reinhold (1994), p. 477.
3. Shore and Wright (1997*b*), p. 14.
4. Shore and Wright (1996), p. 475.
5. Berg (1987), p. 4.
6. Woods (2006).
7. Ibid. p. 46.
8. Ibid. p. 56.
9. Nabarro and Chinnock (1988), p. 946.
10. Woods (2006), pp. 63–4.
11. Ibid. p. 2.
12. World Bank (2008).

Bibliography

Abbasi, K. (1999*a*). 'The World Bank and World Health: Focus on South Asia-II: India and Pakistan', *British Medical Journal*, 318: 1132–5.

—— (1999*b*). 'The World Bank and World Health: Under Fire', *British Medical Journal*, 318: 1003–6.

—— (1999*c*). 'The World Bank and World Health: Changing Sides', *British Medical Journal*, 318: 865–9.

Adair, L., B. Popkin, et al. (1993). 'The Duration of Breastfeeding: How Is It Affected by Biological, Sociodemographic, Health Sector, and Food Industry Factors', *Demography*, 30(1): 63–80.

Appadurai, A. (1981). 'Gastro-Politics in Hindu South Asia', *American Ethnologist*, 8(3): 494–511.

Arnold, D. (1988). *Famine: Social Crisis and Historical Change*. Oxford: Blackwell Publishers.

Ascher, W. (1983). 'New Development Approaches and the Adaptability of International Agencies: The Case of the World Bank', *International Organization*, 37(3): 415–39.

Assunta, M. (2001). 'Impact of Alcohol Consumption on Asia', *The Globe Special Issue*, 4: 4–8.

Ayres, R. (1983). *Banking on the Poor: The World Bank and World Poverty*. Cambridge: MIT Press.

Balachander, J. (1989). Tamil Nadu Integrated Nutrition Project, India. *Managing Successful Nutrition Programmes—Nutrition Policy Discussion Paper No. 8*. J. Jennings, S. Gillespie, J. Mason, M. Lotfi, and T. Scialfa. Geneva, United Nations Administrative Committee on Coordination, Subcommittee on Nutrition.

Banik, N., S. Nayar, et al. (1972). 'The Effect of Nutrition on Growth of Pre-School Children in Different Communities in Delhi', *Indian Journal of Pediatrics*, 9(8): 460–6.

Barnett, M. and M. Finnemore (1999). 'The Politics, Power and Pathologies of International Organizations', *International Organization*, 53(4): 699–732.

Bavadam, L. (2005). 'Irreversible Violation of the Right to Live', *Frontline* 22(19).

Beaton, G., et al. (1997). 'Errors in Interpretation of Dietary Assessments', *American Journal of Clinical Nutrition* 65(4 Supp): 1100S–07S.

Beetham, D. (1985). *Max Weber and the Theory of Modern Politics*. New York: Polity Press.

Behrman, J. (1995). 'Household Behavior, Preschool Child Nutrition, and the Role of Information', in P. Pinstrup-Andersen, D. Pelletier, and H. Alderman (eds.), *Child Growth and Nutrition in Developing Countries*. Ithaca: Cornell University Press, pp. 32–52.

——and A. Deolalikar (1987). 'Will Developing Country Nutrition Improve with Income? A Case Study for Rural South India', *Journal of Political Economy*, 95(3): 492–507.

Bender, D. and D. Millward (2005). 'Protein Metabolism and Requirements', in C. Geissler and H. Powers (eds.), *Human Nutrition*. London: Elsevier Press, pp. 143–64.

Bennett, L. (1992). *Women, Poverty, and Productivity in India*. Washington, DC: World Bank.

Berg, A. (1973). *The Nutrition Factor: Its Role in National Development*. Washington, DC: Brookings Institute.

——(1981). *Malnourished People: A Policy View*. Washington, DC: World Bank.

——(1987). *Malnutrition: What Can be Done?: Lessons from World Bank Experience*. Washington, DC: World Bank.

Béteille, A. (1996). *Caste, Class and Power: Changing Patterns of Stratification in a Tanjore Village*. Oxford: Oxford University Press.

Bhatia, B. M. (1970). *India's Food Problem and Policy Since Independence*. Bombay: Samaiya Publications.

Blaise, P., G. Kegels, et al. (2002). 'Child-Centred Care in African Health Care Systems: Why Is There so Little of It? And What Can be Done?', in P. Kolsteren, T. Hoeree, and E. A. Perez-Cueto (eds.), *Promoting Growth and Development of Under Fives: Proceedings of the International Colloquium, Antwerp*. Antwerp: ITG Press, pp. 116–32.

Boseley, S. (2003). World Bank Poverty Drive a Failure, Says Report. *The Guardian*, July 3. http://www.guardian.co.uk/international/story/0,3604,989847,00.html.

Bourgois, P. and N. Scheper-Hughes (2004). 'Comment on Farmer's "An Anthropology of Structural Violence"', *Current Anthropology*, 45(3): 317–18.

Brass, P. (1994). *The Politics of India Since Independence*. Cambridge: Cambridge University Press.

Briefel, R., et al. (1997). 'Dietary Method Research in the Third National Health and Nutrition Examination Survey: Underreporting of Energy Intake', *American Journal of Clinical Nutrition* 65(4Supp): 1203S-1209S.

Brink, E. W., I. Khan, et al. (1976). 'Nutrition Status of Children in Nepal, 1975', *Bulletin of the World Health Organisation*, 54(3): 311–18.

——W. Perera, et al. (1978). 'Sri Lanka Nutritional Status Survey, 1975', *International Journal of Epidemiology*, 7(1): 41–7.

Brown, R. (2005). *Should Growth Monitoring be Abolished: A Review of History, Concepts, Practice & Future Challenges*. M.Sc thesis. London: Institute of Child Health, University College.

Burger, S. and S. Esrey (1995). 'Water and Sanitation: Health and Nutrition Benefits for Children', in P. Pinstrup-Anderson, D. Pelletier, and H. Alderman (eds.), *Child Growth and Nutrition in Developing Countries*. Ithaca: Cornell University Press, pp. 153–75.

Burghart, R. (1990). 'The Cultural Context of Diet, Disease and the Body', in G. Harrison and J. Waterlow (eds.), *Diet and Disease: In Traditional and Developing Countries*. Cambridge: Cambridge University Press, pp. 307–25.

Buse, K. and C. Gwin (1998). 'The World Bank and Global Cooperation in Health: The Case of Bangladesh', *Lancet*, 351(9103): 665–9.

——and G. Walt (2000). 'Role Conflict? The World Bank and the World's Health', *Social Science and Medicine*, 50(2): 177–9.

Cambrosio, A. and P. Keating (1992). 'A Matter of FACS—Constituting Novel Entities in Immunology', *Medical Anthropology Quarterly*, 6(4): 362–84.

Cantor Associates, et al. (1974). Tamil Nadu Nutrition Study: An Operations-Oriented Study of Nutrition as an Integrated System in Tamil Nadu. Washington, DC, USAID.

Caufield, C. (1996). *Masters of Illusion: The World Bank and the Poverty of Nations*. London: MacMillan.

Cernea, M. (2004). Culture? At the World Bank? (Letter to a Friend). L. Arizpe, Paris.

Cerquiera, M. T. and C. Olson (1995). 'Nutrition Education in Developing Countries: An Examination of Recent Successful Projects', in P. Pinstrup-Anderson, D. Pelletier, and H. Alderman (eds.), *Child Growth and Nutrition in Developing Countries*. Ithaca: Cornell University Press, pp. 53–77.

Chapman, M. (1999). 'Social Anthropology and Business Studies: Some Considerations of Method', in D. Gellner and E. Hirsch (eds.), *Inside Organisations: Anthropologists at Work*. Oxford: Berg, pp. 19–33.

Chen, L., A. Chowdhury, et al. (1982). 'Anthropometric Assessment of Energy-Protein Malnutrition and Subsequent Risk of Mortality Among Preschool Aged Children', in P. V. Sukhatme (eds.), *Newer Concepts in Nutrition and Their Implications for Policy*. Pune: Maharashtra Association for the Cultivation of Science Research Institute.

Chetley, A. (1986). *The Politics of Baby Foods: Successful Challenges to International Marketing Strategies*. London: Palgrave Macmillan.

Chowdhury, A., J. Ramakrishna, et al. (2006). 'Cultural Context and Impact of Alcohol Use in the Sundarban Delta, West Bengal, India', *Social Science and Medicine*, 63(3): 722–31.

Clausen, A. (1982). *Global Interdependence in the 1980s, Address to the Yomiuri International Economic Society*. Tokyo: World Bank.

Conway, G. (1997). *The Doubly Green Revolution*. Ithaca: Cornell University Press.

Corbridge, S. (1997). 'Review Essay: The Merchants Drink our Blood: Peasant Politics and Farmers' Movements in Post-Green Revolution India', *Political Geography*, 16(5): 423–34.

Coulibaly, F., H. Delisle, et al. (2002). 'Evaluating the Quality of Growth Monitoring and Promotion Programmes in Cote D'Ivoire: Maternal Satisfaction and Normative Assessment', in P. Kolsteren, T. Hoeree, and E. A. Perez-Cueto (eds.), *Promoting Growth and Development of Under Fives: Proceedings of the International Colloquium, Antwerp*. Antwerp: ITG Press, pp. 260–73.

Crane, B. and J. Finkle (1981). 'Organizational Impediments to Development Assistance: The World Bank's Population Program', *World Politics*, 33(4): 516–53.

Csordas, T. (1994). 'Introduction', in T. Csordas (ed.), *Embodiment and Experience: The Existential Ground of Culture and Self*. Cambridge: Cambridge University Press, pp. 1–23.

Das, R. (2002). 'The Green Revolution and Poverty: A Theoretical and Empirical Examination of the Relation Between Technology and Society', *Geoforum*, 33(1): 55–72.

Das, D., J. Dhanoa, et al. (1982). 'Exclusive Breastfeeding for 6 Months—An Attainable Goal in Poor Communities', *Bulletin of the NFI*, 3: 2–5.

Das Gupta, M., M. Lokshin, et al. (2005). *Improving Child Nutrition Outcomes in India: Can the Integrated Child Development Services Program be More Effective?* Washington, DC: World Bank.

Dasgupta, P. and D. Raj (1990). 'Adapting to Undernourishment: The Biological Evidence and its Implications', in J. Drèze and A. Sen (eds.), *The Political Economy of Hunger: vol. I*. Oxford: Oxford University Press, pp. 191–246.

Davis, J. (2003). *The Theory of the Individual in Economics: Identity and Value*. London: Routledge.

—— and R. McMaster (2004). *The Individual in Mainstream Health Economics: A Case of Persona Non-Grata?* European Association for Evolutionary Political Economy Annual Conference, University of Crete, Rethymno.

de Beyer, J., A. Preker, et al. (2000). 'The Role of the World Bank in International Health: Renewed Commitment and Partnership', *Social Science and Medicine*, 50(2): 169–76.

DeGarine, I. (1972). 'The Social-Cultural Aspects of Nutrition', *Ecology, Food, and Nutrition*, 1: 143–63.

Delgado, H., A. Lechtig, et al. (1978). 'Nutrition, Lactation, and Postpartum Amenorrhea', *American Journal of Clinical Nutrition*, 31(2): 322–7.

Dickey, S. (1993). *Cinema and the Urban Poor in South India*. Cambridge: Cambridge University Press.

Douglas, M. (1986). *How Institutions Think (Frank W. Abrams Lectures)*. Syracuse: Syracuse University Press.

Douglas, M. (1996). *Natural Symbols: Explorations in Cosmology*. London: Routledge.

Drèze, J. and A. Goyal (2003). 'The Future of Mid-Day Meals', *Frontline* 20(16).

Dugdale, A. (1982). 'Infant Feeding—An Unfinished Debate', *Ecology of Food and Nutrition*, 12: 71–4.

Dumont, L. (1971). *Religion, Politics and History in India: Collected Papers in Indian Sociology*. Paris: Mouton.

Dyson, T. (2004). 'India's Population—The Past', in T. Dyson, R. Cassen, and L. Visaria (eds.), *Twenty-first Century India: Population, Economy, Human Development and the Environment*. Delhi: Oxford University Press.

Eisenberg, L. and A. Kleinman (eds.) (1980). *The Relevance of Social Science for Medicine*. Dordrecht: Reidel.

Elder, L. and L. Kiess (2004). *Nuts and Bolts. Nutrition Toolkit 2*. Washington, DC: World Bank.

FAO (2004). *The State of Food Insecurity in the World*. Rome: FAO.

FAO/WHO/UNU (1985). 'Energy and Protein Requirements'. Report of a Joint FAO/WHO/UNU Expert Consultation. Geneva: WHO.

Fapohunda, E. (1988). 'The Non-Pooling Household: A Challenge to Theory', in D. Dwyer and J. Bruce (eds.), *A Home Divided: Women and Income in the Third World*. Stanford: Stanford University Press, pp. 143–54.

Farmer, P. (1999). *Infections and Inequalities: The Modern Plagues*. Berkeley: University of California Press.

—— (2004). 'An Anthropology of Structural Violence', *Current Anthropology*, 45(3): 305–25.

Fassin, D. (1996). *L'Espace Politique de la Sante. Essai de Genealogie*. Paris: Presses.

Favin, M. and M. Griffiths (1999). *Using Communication to Improve Nutrition. Nutrition Toolkit 9*. Washington, DC: World Bank.

Finnemore, M. (1997). 'Redefining Development at the World Bank', in F. Cooper and R. Packard (eds.), *International Development and the Social Sciences: Essays on the History and Politics of Knowledge*. Berkeley: University of California Press, pp. 203–27.

Frankel, F. and M. Rao (eds.) (1989). *Dominance and State Power in Modern India, vol. I*. Oxford: Oxford University Press.

Fuller, C. and V. Benei (eds.) (2001). *The Everyday State and Society in Modern India*. London: Hurst.

Gavin, M. and D. Rodrik (1995). 'The World Bank in Historical Perspective', *American Economic Review Papers and Proceedings*, 85(2): 329–34.

Geerth, H. and C. W. Mills (1978). *From Max Weber: Essays in Sociology*. New York: Oxford University Press.

George, S., M. Latham, et al. (1993). 'Evaluation of Effectiveness of Good Growth Monitoring in South Indian Villages', *Lancet*, 342(8867): 348–51.

Gerein, N. (1988). 'Is Growth Monitoring Worthwhile?', *Health Policy and Planning*, 3(3): 181–94.

——and D. Ross (1991). 'Is Growth Monitoring Worthwhile? An Evaluation of its use in Three Child Health Programmes in Zaire', *Social Science and Medicine*, 32(6): 667–75.

Ghosh, S. (1981). *The Feeding and Care of Infants and Children*. New Delhi: Voluntary Health Association of India.

Ghosh, R., C. G. N. Mascie-Taylor, et al. (2006). 'Longitudinal Study of the Frequency and Duration of Breastfeeding in Rural Bangladeshi Women', *American Journal of Human Biology*, 18(5): 630–8.

Gibson, R. (2005). *Principles of Nutritional Assessment*. Oxford: Oxford University Press.

Gittelsohn, J. (1991). 'Opening the Box: Intra-Household Food Allocation in Rural Nepal', *Social Science and Medicine*, 33(10): 1141–54.

Godlee, F. (1997). 'WHO Reform and Global Health', *British Medical Journal*, 314(7091): 314.

Good, B. (1994). *Medicine, Rationality and Experience: An Anthropological Perspective*. Cambridge: Cambridge University Press.

Gopalan, C. (1984). 'Choosing "Beneficiaries" For Feeding Programmes', *Nutrition Foundation of India Bulletin*, October.

——(1985). 'Growth Monitoring: Intermediate Technology or Expensive Luxury?', *Lancet*, 2(8468): 1337–8.

——(1988). 'Stunting: Significance and Implication for Public Health', in J. Waterlow (ed.), *Linear Growth Retardation in Less Developed Countries*. New York: Raven Press, pp. 265–84.

——(1992). 'Undernutrition: Measurement and Implications', in R. Osmani (ed.), *Nutrition and Poverty*. Oxford: Oxford University Press, pp. 17–47.

——and M. Chatterjee (1985). *Use of Growth Charts for Planning Child Nutrition: A Review of Global Experience*. New Delhi: NFI.

——M. Swaminathan, et al. (1973). 'Effect of Calorie Supplementation on Growth of Undernourished Children', *American Journal of Clinical Nutrition*, 26(5): 563–6.

Gordon, D. (1988). 'Tenacious Assumptions in Western Medicine', in M. Lock and D. Gordon (eds.), *Biomedicine Examined*. Dordrecht: Kluwer, pp. 19–56.

Gorstein, J., K. Sullivan, et al. (1994). 'Issues in the Assessment of Nutritional Status using Anthropometry', *Bulletin of the World Health Organisation*, 72(2): 273–83.

Government of Tamil Nadu (2003). *Tamil Nadu Human Development Report*. New York: UNDP.

——(2005). Statistical Handbook 2005. Chennai, Department of Economics and Statistics, Government of Tamil Nadu.

Gregory, J., et al. (1990). *The Dietary and Nutritional Survey of British Adults*. London, the Stationary Office.

Griffiths, M., K. Dickin, et al. (1996). *Promoting the Growth of Children: What Works. Rationale and Guidance for Programs. Nutrition Toolkit 4*. Washington, DC: World Bank.

Gupta, A. (2001). 'Governing Population: The Integrated Child Development Services Program in India', in Hansen, T. B. and F. Stepputat (eds.), *States of Imagination: Ethnographic Explorations of the Postcolonial State*. Durham: Duke University Press, pp. 65–96.

Guruswamy, M. and R. Abraham (2006). *Redefining Poverty: A New Poverty Line for a New India*. New Delhi: Centre for Policy Alternatives.

Gwatkin, D., J. Wilcox, et al. (1980). 'The Policy Implications of Field Experiments in Primary Health and Nutrition Care', *Social Science and Medicine*, 14(2): 121–8.

Hall, A. et al. (2001). *When the Decision-Maker is a Woman: Does it Make a Difference for the Nutritional Status of Mothers and Children?* Dhaka: Helen Keller International.

Harriss, O. (1981). 'Households as Natural Units', in K. Young, C. Wolkowitz, and R. McCullagh (eds.), *Of Marriage and the Market: Women's Subordination in International Perspective*. London: CSE Books, pp. 136–55.

Harriss, B. (1986). 'Meals and Noon-Meals in South India: Food and Nutrition Policy in the Rural Food Economy of Tamil Nadu State'. East Anglia: School of Development Studies, University of East Anglia.

—— (1990). 'The Intrafamily Distribution of Hunger in South Asia', in J. Drèze and A. Sen (eds.), *The Political Economy of Hunger vol. I*. Oxford: Oxford University Press, pp. 224–86.

—— (1991). *Child Nutrition and Poverty in South India*. New Delhi: Concept.

Harriss-White, B. (2004). 'Nutrition and its Politics in Tamil Nadu', *South Asia Research*, 24(1): 51–71.

—— and R. Hoffenberg, (eds.), (1994). *Food: A Multidisciplinary Perspective*. Oxford: Blackwells.

Heaver, R. (2002). *India's Tamil Nadu Nutrition Program: Lessons and Issues in Management and Capacity Development*. Washington, DC: World Bank.

—— (2006). *Good Work—But Not Enough of it: A Review of the World Bank's Experience in Nutrition*. Washington, DC: World Bank.

Heerstrass, D., et al. (1998). 'Underreporting of Energy, Protein, and Potassium Intake in relation to Body Mass Index', *International Journal of Epidemiology* 27(2): 186–93.

Herzfeld, M. (1993). *The Social Production of Indifference*. Chicago: University of Chicago Press.

Holmberg, A. (1950). *Nomads of the Long Bow*. Washington, DC: Smithsonian Institute Press.

Hoorweg, J. and R. Njemeijer (1980). *The Nutrition Impact of the Pre-School Health Programme at Three Clinics in Central Province Kenya*. Leiden: African Studies Centre, University of Leiden.

Hopkins, J., C. Levin, et al. (1994). 'Women's Income and Household Expenditure Patterns: Gender or Flow? Evidence from Niger', *American Journal of Agricultural Economics*, 76(5): 1219–25.

Hornick, R. (1985). *Nutrition Education: A State of the Art Review*. Rome: FAO.

Horton, S. (1992). *Unit Costs, Cost-Effectiveness, and Financing of Nutrition Interventions*. Washington, DC: World Bank.

Hossain, S. M., A. Duffield, et al. (2005). 'An Evaluation of the Impact of a US$60 Million Nutrition Programme in Bangladesh', *Health Policy and Planning*, 20(1): 35–40.

Huffman, S. L., A. K. Chowdhury, et al. (1978). 'Postpartum Amenorrhea: How is it Affected by Maternal Nutritional Status?', *Science*, 200(4346): 1155–7.

Hufner, K. (2004). 'Expenditures of UN Specialized Agencies 1971–2003'. http://www.globalpolicy.org/finance/tables/expend2.htm.

Humphries, J. (1998). 'Towards a Family-Friendly Economics', *New Political Economy*, 3(2): 223–40.

Ibrahim, B. (1985). 'Cairo's Factory Women', in E. Fernea (ed.), *Women and the Family in the Middle East*. Austin: University of Texas Press, pp. 293–9.

Jack, W. (1999). *Principles of Health Economics for Developing Countries*. Washington, DC: World Bank Institute.

Jelliffe, D. (1957). 'Social Culture and Nutrition: Cultural Blocks and Protein Malnutrition in Early Childhood in West Bengal', *Pediatrics*, 20(1): 128–38.

—— (1972). 'Commerciogenic Malnutrition?', *Nutrition Reviews*, 30(9): 199–205.

—— and E. Jelliffe (1989). *Community Nutritional Assessment*. New York: Oxford University Press.

Jochim, M. (1981). *Strategies for Survival*. New York City: Academic Press.

Kabeer, N. (1994). *Reversed Realities: Gender Hierarchies in Development Thought*. London: Verso Press.

Kamath, S. (1992). 'Foreign Aid and India: Financing the Leviathan State', *CATO Policy Analysis*, 170: 1–26.

Kapadia, K. (1995). *Siva and her Sisters: Gender, Caste and Class in Rural South India*. Boulder: Westview Press.

Kapur, D., J. Lewis, et al. (1997). *The World Bank: Its First Half Century vol. I: History*. Washington, DC: Brookings Institution.

Karim, E. and C. G. N. Mascie-Taylor (1997). 'The Association Between Birthweight, Sociodemographic Variables and Maternal Anthropometry in an Urban Sample from Dhaka, Bangladesh', *Annals of Human Biology*, 24(5): 387–401.

King, F. and A. Burgess (1993). *Nutrition for Developing Countries*. 2nd edn. Oxford: Oxford University Press.

Kleinman, A. (1988). *Illness Narratives: Suffering, Healing and the Human Condition*. New York City: Perseus Books Group.

Krueger, A. (1998). 'Whither the World Bank and the IMF?', *Journal of Economic Literature*, 36(4): 1983–2020.

Kumar, V. (2007). 'Building the Social Capital of the Poor and Hungry'. Speaker Summary Notes. IFPRI 2020 Conference: Taking Action for the World's Poor and Hungry People, Beijing.

Kumar, B. G. and F. Stewart (1992). 'Tackling Malnutrition: What Can Targeted Nutritional Interventions Achieve?', in B. Harriss, S. Guhan, and R. Cassen (eds.), *Poverty in India*. Bombay: Oxford University Press, pp. 259–81.

Lasker, G. W. (1994). 'Place of Anthropometry in Human Biology', in S. Ulijaszek and C. G. N. Mascie-Taylor (eds.), *Anthropometry: The Individual and the Population*. Cambridge: Cambridge University Press, pp. 1–6.

Latham, M. (2002). 'Trends in Nutrition Policy and Programmes and How They Focus on Growth and Development', in P. Kolsteren, T. Hoeree, and E. A. Perez-Cueto (eds.), *Promoting Growth and Development of Under Fives: Proceedings of the International Colloquium, Antwerp*. Antwerp: ITG Press, pp. 233–48.

Latour, B. (1993). *We Have Never Been Modern*. Cambridge, MA: Harvard University Press.

Leatherman, T. (2005). 'Space of Vulnerability in Poverty and Health: Political-Ecology and Biocultural Analysis', *Ethos*, 33(1): 46–70.

Lee, R. (1969). 'Kung Bushmen Subsistence: An Input-Output Analysis', in A. Vayda (ed.), *Environment and Cultural Behavior*. Garden City: Natural History Press, pp. 47–76.

Lee, K., S. Collinson, et al. (1996). 'Who Should be Doing What in International Health: A Confusion of Mandates in the United Nations?', *British Medical Journal*, 312(7026): 302–7.

Lefevre, P., T. Hoeree, et al. (2002). 'Appropriation of the Growth Chart by Mothers of Under Fives in Bolivia', in P. Kolsteren, T. Hoeree, and E. A. Perez-Cueto (eds.), *Promoting Growth and Development of Under Fives: Proceedings of the International Colloquium, Antwerp*. Antwerp: ITG Press, pp. 97–103.

Levinson, J. (1972). *Economic Analysis of Malnutrition Among Young Children in Rural India*. PhD thesis. Division of Nutritional Sciences, Cornell University.

——B. Rogers, et al. (1999). *Monitoring and Evaluation: A Guidebook for Nutrition Project Managers in Developing Countries. Nutrition Toolkit 3*. Washington, DC: World Bank.

——and J. Rohde (2005). 'Responses to: "An Evaluation of the Impact of a US$60 Million Nutrition Programme in Bangladesh"', *Health Policy and Planning*, 20(6): 405–6.

Lipton, M. and R. Longhurst (1989). *New Seeds and Poor People*. London: Routledge.

Lock, M. (1988). 'Introduction', in M. Lock and D. Gordon (eds.), *Biomedicine Examined*. Dordrecht: Klower.

Luhrmann, T. (2000). *Of Two Minds: The Growing Disorder in American Psychiatry*. New York City: Knopf.

Lumsdaine, D. (1993). *Moral Vision in International Politics: The Foreign Aid Regime, 1949–1989*. Princeton: Princeton University Press.

Mahal, A. (2000). 'What Works in Alcohol Policy? Evidence from Rural India', *Economic and Political Weekly*, November 4: 3959–68.

Mallaby, S. (2005). *The World's Banker: A Story of Failed States, Financial Crises, and the Wealth and Poverty of Nations*. New York: Penguin Press.

Manandhar, D. S., D. Osrin, et al. (2004). 'Effect of a Participatory Intervention with Women's Groups on Birth Outcomes in Nepal: Cluster-randomised Controlled Trial', *Lancet*, 364(9438): 970–9.

Marantz, P. (1990). 'Blaming the Victim: The Negative Consequences of Preventive Medicine', *American Journal of Public Health*, 80(10): 1186.

Martin, E. (1987). *Woman in the Body: A Cultural Analysis of Reproduction*. Boston: Beacon Press.

Martorell, R., L. Khan, et al. (1994). 'Reversibility of Stunting: Epidemiological Findings in Children from Developing Countries', *European Journal of Clinical Nutrition*, 48(Suppl. 1): S45–57.

—— F. Mendoza, et al. (1988). 'Poverty and Stature in Children', in J. C. Waterlow (ed.), *Linear Growth Retardation in Less Developed Countries*. New York: Raven Press, pp. 57–73.

Mascie-Taylor, C. G. N. (1991). 'Biosocial Influences on Stature: A Review', *Journal of Biosocial Science*, 23(1): 113–28.

—— M. Alam, et al. (1999). 'A Study of the Cost Effectiveness of Selective Health Interventions for the Control of Intestinal Parasites in Rural Bangladesh', *Journal of Parasitology*, 85(1): 6–11.

—— R. Karim, et al. (2003). 'The Cost-effectiveness of Health Education in Improving Knowledge and Awareness About Intestinal Parasites in Rural Bangladesh', *Economics and Human Biology*, 1(3): 321–30.

——, S. Nahar, et al. (2006). 'Abstract: The Impact of Food Supplementation on Maternal Weight Gain and Infant Weight Gain: A Review of the Bangladesh Integrated Nutrition Program (BINP)', *Annals of Human Biology*, 5(6): 654–5.

Martorell, R. and T. Ho (1984). 'Malnutrition, Morbidity, and Mortality', *Population and Development Review* 10(Supp): 49–68.

Mason, E. and R. Asher (1973). *The World Bank Since Bretton Woods*. Washington, DC: Brookings Institution.

Maxwell, S. (1996). 'Food Security: A Post-Modern Perspective', *Food Policy*, 21(2): 155–70.

Mayer, A. (1996). 'Caste in an Indian Village: Change and Continuity', in C. Fuller (ed.), *Caste Today*. Delhi: Oxford University Press, pp. 32–64.

McDowell, I. and I. Hoorweg (1975). 'Social Environment and Out-Patient Recovery From Malnutrition', *Ecology, Food, and Nutrition*, 4: 91–101.

McNamara, R. (1977). Address to the Board of Governors, World Bank.

Measham, A. and M. Chatterjee (1999). *Wasting Away: The Crisis of Malnutrition in India*. Washington, DC: World Bank.

Mencher, J. (1988). 'Women's Work and Poverty: Women's Contributions to Household Maintenance in Two Regions of South India', in J. Bruce and D. Dwyer (eds.), *A Home Divided: Women and Income Control in the Third World*. Stanford: Stanford University Press, pp. 99–119.

Messer, E. (1984a). 'Anthropological Perspectives on Diet', *Annual Review of Anthropology*, 13: 205–49.

Messer, E. (1984*b*). 'Sociocultural Aspects of Nutrient Intake and Behavioral Responses to Nutrition', in J. Galler (ed.), *Nutrition and Behavior: Human Nutrition*. New York City: Plenum, pp. 417–71.

——(1997). 'Intra-Household Allocation of Food and Health Care: Current Findings and Understandings—Introduction', *Social Science and Medicine*, 44(11): 1675–84.

Miller, B. (1992). 'Gender Discrimination in Intra-Household Food Allocation in South Asia: Debates and Dilemmas', paper presented at the Meetings of the American Anthropological Association, San Francisco.

Minamoto, K., C. G. N. Mascie-Taylor, et al. (2005). 'Arsenic-Contaminated Water and Extent of Acute Childhood Malnutrition (wasting) in Rural Bangladesh', *Environmental Sciences*, 12(5): 283–92.

Mintz, S. and C. D. Bois (2002). 'The Anthropology of Food and Eating', *Annual Review of Anthropology*, 31: 99–119.

Mitra, A. (1973). 'The Nutrition Movement in India', in A. Berg, N. Scrimshaw, and D. Call (eds.), *Nutrition, National Development and Planning*. Cambridge, MA: MIT Press, pp. 357–65.

Mooij, J. (2000). *Food Policy and the Indian State*. Delhi: Oxford University Press.

Morley, D. (1999). Letter Concerning Growth Monitoring. A. Taylor, London.

——(2003). *Letter Regarding 'Thin on the Ground'*. M. McLachlan, London.

Morsy, S. (1996). 'Political Economy in Medical Anthropology', in F. Sargent and T. Johnson (eds.), *Medical Anthropology: Contemporary Theory and Method*. Westport: Praeger, pp. 21–40.

Mosse, D. (1999). 'Social Research in Rural Development Projects', in D. Gellner and E. Hirsch (eds.), *Inside Organisations: Anthropologists at Work*. Oxford: Berg, pp. 157–82.

——(2003). 'The Making and Marketing of Participatory Development', in P. Quarles van Ufford (ed.), *A Moral Critique of Development: In Search of Global Responsibilities*. London: Routledge, pp. 43–71.

——(2006). 'Anthropologists at the World Bank', paper presented at the Institute of Development Studies, Sussex.

——and D. Lewis (2006). 'Theoretical Approaches to Brokerage and Translation in Development', in D. Lewis and D. Mosse (eds.), *Development Brokers and Translators: Ethnography of Aid and Agencies*. Bloomfield: Kumarian, pp. 1–26.

Msefula, D. (1993). 'How Can Growth Monitoring and Special Care of Underweight Children Be Improved in Zambia?', *Tropical Doctor*, 23(3): 107–12.

Musaiger, A. and N. Abdulkhalek (2001). 'Maternal Comprehension of Home-Based Growth Charts in Bahrain', *Tropical Doctor*, 31(3): 161–5.

Musgrove, P. (2005). 'Ideas Versus Money: A Conversation with Jean-Louis Sarbib', *Health Affairs*, W5(341).

Myrdal, G. (1968). *Asian Drama: An Inquiry into the Poverty of Nations*. New York: Pantheon Books.

Nabarro, D. and P. Chinnock (1988). 'Growth Monitoring—Inappropriate Promotion of an Appropriate Technology', *Social Science and Medicine*, 26(9): 941–8.

——et al. (1988). 'The Importance of Infections and Environmental Factors as Possible Determinants of Growth Retardation in Children', in J. Waterlow (ed.), *Linear Growth Retardation in Less Developed Countries*. New York: Raven Press, pp. 165–83.

Narayanan, N. (1996). 'Food and Nutrition in Tamil Nadu: Public Policy Options in the Federal State', paper presented at South Asia Research Group, Hilary Term Workshop, Queen Elizabeth House, Oxford.

Navarro, V. (1984). 'A Critique of the Ideological and Political Positions of the Willy Brandt Report and the World Health Organisation Alma Ata Declaration', *Social Science and Medicine*, 18(6): 467–74.

NCHS (1977). *National Centre for Health Statistics Growth Charts*. Atlanta, Centers for Disease Control.

Nelson, P. (1995). *The World Bank and Non-Governmental Organizations: Limits of a Political Development*. London: MacMillan.

Nichter, M. and C. Kendall (1991). 'Beyond Child Survival: Anthropology and the International Health in the 1990s', *Medical Anthropology Quarterly*, 5(3): 195–203.

——and M. Nichter (1996). *Anthropology and International Health: Asian Case Studies*. London: Gordon and Breach.

O'Brien, B. (1978). *Communication of Innovation in Health Care*. London: London School of Hygiene and Tropical Medicine.

OED (1995). *Tamil Nadu and Child Nutrition: A New Assessment*. Washington, DC: World Bank.

Ogbu, J. (1973). 'Seasonal Hunger in Tropical Africa as a Cultural Phenomenon', *Africa*, 13: 317–32.

Olivier de Sardan, J.-P. (2005). *Anthropology and Development: Understanding Continuity and Social Change*. London: Zed Books.

Osmani, R. (1992a). 'Introduction', in R. Osmani (ed.), *Nutrition and Poverty*. Oxford: Oxford University Press.

——(1992b). 'On Some Controversies in the Measurement of Nutrition', in R. Osmani (ed.), *Nutrition and Poverty*. Oxford: Oxford University Press, pp. 121–64.

Pacey, A. and P. Payne (1985). *Agricultural Development and Nutrition*. Rome and New York: FAO/UNICEF.

Pagezy, H. (1982). 'Seasonal Hunger as Experienced by the Oto and the Twa of a Ntomba village in the Equatorial Forest', *Ecology, Food, and Nutrition*, 12: 139–53.

Palanithurai, G. (1991). *Role Perceptions of Legislators*. New Delhi: Konark.

Pandian, M. S. S. (1996). 'Towards National-Popular. Notes on Self-Respecters' Tamil', *Economic and Political Weekly*, December 21.

Pearson, R. (1995). *Thematic Evaluation of UNICEF Support to Growth Monitoring*. New York: UNICEF.

Pelletier, D., M. Rahn, et al. (2001). 'Low Birth Weight, Postnatal Growth Failure, and Mortality', in R. Martorell and F. Haschke (eds.), *Nutrition and Growth*. Philadelphia: Lippincott Willams & Wilkins.

——M. Shekar, et al. (2005). *In the Eye of the Beholder: A Review of the Bangladesh Integrated Nutrition Project*. Washington, DC: World Bank.

——and R. Shrimpton (1994). 'The Role of Information in the Planning, Management, and Evaluation of Community Nutrition Programmes', *Health Policy and Planning*, 9(2): 171–84.

Phillips, M. and T. Sanghvi (1996). *The Economic Analysis of Nutrition Projects: Guiding Principles and Examples. Nutrition Toolkit 3*. Washington, DC: World Bank.

Pinstrup-Anderson, P. and M. Jaramillo (1991). 'The Impact of Technological Change in Rice Production on Food Consumption and Nutrition', in P. Hazell and C. Ramasamy (eds.), *The Green Revolution Reconsidered*. Baltimore: John Hopkins University Press, pp. 85–104.

Poleman, T. (1973). 'Food and Population in Historical Perspective', in T. Poleman and D. Freebairn (eds.), *Food, Population and Employment: The Impact of the Green Revolution*. New York: Praeger Publishers.

Prabhu, K. S. (2001). *Economic Reform and Social Sector Development*. New Delhi: Sage.

Price, G., et al. (1997). 'Characteristics of the Low-Energy Reports in a Longitudinal National Dietary Survey', *British Journal of Nutrition* 77(6): 833–51.

Pryer, J., et al. (1997). 'Who are the "low energy reporters" in the Dietary and Nutritional Survey of British Adults?', *International Journal of Epidemiology* 26(1): 36S–45S.

Rajivan, A. K. (2001). 'Nutrition Security in Tamil Nadu', in S. M. Dev, P. Antony, V. Gayathri, and R. Mamgain (eds.), *Social and Economic Security in India*. New Delhi: Institute for Human Development.

Rao, V. (1997). 'Wife-Beating in Rural South India: A Qualitative and Econometric Analysis', *Social Science and Medicine*, 44(8): 1169–80.

Raphael, D. (ed.) (1979). *Breastfeeding and Food Policy in a Hungry World*. New York: Academic Press.

Ravallion, M. (1990). 'Income Effects on Undernutrition', *Economic Development and Cultural Change*, 38(3): 489–515.

Reinhold, S. (1994). *Local Conflict and Ideological Struggle: 'Positive Images' and Section 28*. D.Phil thesis, University of Sussex.

Reiser, S. (1993). 'Technology and the Use of Senses in 20th Century Medicine', in W. Bynom and R. Porter (eds.), *Medicine and the Five Senses*. Cambridge: Cambridge University Press.

Richards, A. (1939). *Land, Labour and Diet in Northern Rhodesia: An Economic Study of the Bemba Tribe*. London: Routledge.

Roberfroid, D., P. Lefevre, et al. (2005). 'Perceptions of Growth Monitoring and Promotion Among an International Panel of District Medical Officers', *Journal of Health, Population and Nutrition*, 23(3): 207–14.

Robertson, A. I. (1984). *People and the State: An Anthropology of Planned Development*. Cambridge: Cambridge University Press.

Rohde, J. (2005). 'Going for Growth', *Journal of Health, Population and Nutrition*, 23(3): 203–6.

Room, R., T. Babor, et al. (2005). 'Alcohol and Public Health', *The Lancet*, 365(9458): 519–30.

Roseberry, W. (1988). 'Political Economy', *Annual Review of Anthropology*, 17: 161–95.

Roy, S. K., M. Rahman, et al. (1993). 'Can Mothers Identify Malnutrition in Their Children?', *Health Policy and Planning*, 8(2): 143–9.

Ruel, M., C. Levin, et al. (1999). *Good Care Practices Can Mitigate the Negative Effects of Poverty and Low Maternal Schooling on Children's Nutritional Status: Evidence From Accra*. Washington, DC: IFPRI.

Sachs, L. (1996). 'Causality, Responsibility and Blame—Core Issues in the Cultural Construction and Subtext of Prevention', *Sociology of Health and Illness*, 18(5): 632–52.

Saraswathi, S. (1995). *Government, Politics and People*. New Delhi: Manak.

Sastri, K. A. N. (1964). *Culture and History of the Tamils*. Calcutta: Mukhopadhyay.

Save the Children UK (2003). Thin on the Ground: Questioning Evidence Behind the World Bank-Funded Community Nutrition Projects in Bangladesh, Ethiopia, and Uganda. London: Save the Children UK.

——(2007). *The Minimum Cost of a Healthy Diet: Findings From Piloting a New Methodology in Four Study Locations*. London: Save the Children UK.

Saxena, S. (1999). 'Country Profile on Alcohol in India', *Alcohol and Public Health in 8 Developing Countries*. Geneva: WHO.

Scarry, E. (1987). *The Body in Pain: The Making and Unmaking of the World*. Oxford: Oxford University Press.

Schaffer, B. (1984). 'Towards Responsibility: Public Policy in Concept and Practice', in E. J. Clay and B. Schaffer (eds.), *Room for Manoeuvre*. London: Heinemann, pp. 142–90.

——(1985). 'Policymakers Have Their Needs Too: Irish Itinerants and the Culture of Poverty', in G. Wood (ed.), *Labelling in Development Policy*. London: Sage.

Schechter, M. (1988). 'The Political Roles of Recent World Bank Presidents', in L. Finkelstein (ed.), *Politics in the United Nations System*. Durham: Duke University Press, pp. 350–84.

Scheper-Hughes, N. (1984). 'Infant Mortality and Infant Care: Cultural and Economic Constraints on Nurturing in Northeast Brazil', *Social Science and Medicine*, 19(5): 536–46.

Scheper-Hughes, N. (2006). 'The Primacy of the Ethical: Propositions for a Militant Anthropology', in H. Moore and T. Sanders (eds.), *Anthropology in Theory: Issues in Epistemology*. Oxford: Blackwell, pp. 506–11.

Seckler, D. (1982*a*). 'Small but Healthy: A Basic Hypothesis in the Theory, Measurement, and Policy of Malnutrition', in P. V. Sukhatme (ed.), *Newer Concepts in Nutrition and Their Implications for Policy*. Pune: Maharashtra Association for the Cultivation of Science Research Institute.

——(1982*b*). 'Malnutrition: An Intellectual Odyssey', in P. V. Sukhatme (ed.), *Newer Concepts in Nutrition and Their Implications for Policy*. Pune: Maharashtra Association for the Cultivation of Science Research Institute.

Selowsky, M. (1978). *Economic Dimensions of Malnutrition in Young Children*. Washington, DC: World Bank.

Sen, A. (1981). *Poverty and Famines*. Oxford: Clarendon Press.

——(1990). 'Gender and Cooperative Conflict', in I. Tinker (ed.), *Persisting Inequalities: Women and World Development*. Oxford: Oxford University Press.

Senanayake, M., M. Gunawardena, et al. (1997). 'Maternal Comprehension of Two Growth Monitoring Charts in Sri Lanka', *Archives of Disease in Childhood*, 76(4): 359–61.

Shekar, M. (1990). *Positive and Negative Deviance in Child Growth: A Study in the Context of the Tamil Nadu Integrated Nutrition Project*. PhD thesis. Division of Nutritional Sciences, Cornell University.

——(1991). 'The Tamil Nadu Integrated Nutrition Project: A Review of the Project with Special Emphasis on the Monitoring and Information System', Ithaca, Cornell Food and Nutrition Policy Program.

——, J.-P. Habicht, et al. (1992). 'Use of Positive–Negative Deviant Analysis to Improve Programme Targeting and Services: Example From the Tamil Nadu Integrated Nutrition Project', *International Journal of Epidemiology*, 21(4): 707–13.

——and M. Latham (1992). 'Growth Monitoring Can and Does Work! An Example From the Tamil Nadu Integrated Nutrition Project in Rural South India', *Indian Journal of Pediatrics*, 59(1): 5–15.

Shore, C. and S. Wright (1996). 'British Anthropology in Policy and Practice: A Review of Current Work', *Human Organization*, 55(4): 475–80.

——(1997). 'Anthropology of Policy', in C. Shore and S. Wright (eds.), *Anthropology of Policy: Critical Perspectives on Governance and Power*. London: Routledge.

Simoons, F. (1991). *Food in China: A Cultural and Historical Inquiry*. Boston: CRC.

——(1994). *Eat Not This Flesh: Food Avoidances from Prehistory to the Present*. Madison: University of Wisconsin Press.

Sindzingre, A. (2004). ' "Truth", "Efficiency", and Multilateral Institutions: A Political Economy of Development Economics', *New Political Economy*, 9(2): 233–49.

Singer, M. and H. Baer (1995). *Critical Medical Anthropology*. Amityville: Baywood.

Sinha, R. P. (1961). *Food in India*. Oxford: Oxford University Press.

Sivakami, M. (1997). 'Female Work Participation and Child Health: An Investigation in Rural Tamil Nadu, India', *Health Transition Review*, 7(1): 21–32.

Sivathambi, K. (1995). *Understanding the Dravidian Movement*. Madras: Kannappa.

Soumya, H. B. (2001). *Tipsy Liquor Policy*. New Delhi: Centre for Civil Society.

Sridhar, D. (2005). 'Political Economy of Child Hunger in Tamil Nadu, India', paper presented at First International Conference on Family, Work and Community, Manchester University, Manchester.

——(ed.) (2008). *Inside Organisations: South Asian Case Studies*. Delhi: Sage.

——and A. Duffield (2006). The Effect of Conditional Cash Transfers on Child Nutritional Status. Working Paper.

Srinivas, M. N. (1952). *Religion and Society Among the Coorgs of South India*. Delhi: Oxford University Press.

Srinivasan, T. N. (2000). 'Poverty and Undernutrition in South Asia', *Food Policy*, 25: 269–82.

Steinhoff, M., A. Hilder, et al. (1986). 'Prevalence of Malnutrition in Indian Preschool-Age Children: A Survey of Wasting and Stunting in Rural Tamil Nadu', *Bulletin of the World Health Organisation*, 64(3): 457–63.

Stewart, F. (1985). *Planning to Meet Basic Needs*. London: MacMillan.

Stini, W. (1988). 'Biocultural Strategies for Coping with Drought', *MASCA Research Papers in Science and Archaeology*, 5: 21–8.

Stinson, W. and P. Sayer (1991). Growth Monitoring and Promotion: A Review of Experience in Seven Countries. Washington, DC, PRICOR for USAID.

Subramanian, N. (1999). *Ethnicity and Populist Mobilization: Political Parties, Citizens and Democracy in South India*. Delhi: Oxford University Press.

Sukhatme, P. V. (1982). 'Poverty and Malnutrition', in P. V. Sukhatme (ed.), *Newer Concepts in Nutrition and Their Implications for Policy*. Pune: Maharashtra Association for the Cultivation of Science Research Institute.

Swaminathan, P., J. Jeyaranjan, et al. (2004). 'Tamil Nadu's Midday Meal Scheme: Where Assumed Benefits Score over Hard Data', *Economic and Political Weekly*, October 30.

Thomas, D. (1990). 'Intra-Household Resource Allocation: An Inferential Approach', *Journal of Human Resources*, 25(4): 635–64.

Thorat, S. and J. Lee (2005). 'Caste Discrimination and Food Security Programmes', *Economic and Political Weekly*, September 24.

Tinker, I. (1976). 'The Adverse Impact of Development on Women', in I. Tinker and M. Bramsen (eds.), *Women and World Development*. London: ODC, 22–34.

Tomkins, A. (1986). 'Protein-Energy Malnutrition and Risk of Infection', *Proceedings of the Nutrition Society* 45: 289–304.

——(1988). 'Risk of Morbidity in a Stunted Child', in J. Waterlow (ed.), *Linear Growth Retardation in Less Developed Countries*. New York: Raven Press, pp. 185–99.

——et al. (1989). 'Nutritional Status and Risk of Morbidity among Young Gambian Children Allowing for Social and Environmental Factors', *Transactions of the Royal Society of Tropical Medicine and Hygiene* 83: 283–87.

Tomkins, A. (1994). 'Growth Monitoring: Screening and Surveillance in Developing Countries', in S. Ulijaszek and C. G. N. Mascie-Taylor (eds.), *Anthropometry: The Individual and the Population*. Cambridge: Cambridge University Press.

Tonglet, R., E. Lembo, et al. (1999). 'How Useful are Anthropometric, Clinical and Dietary Measurements of Nutritional Status as Predictors of Morbidity of Young Children in Central Africa?', *Tropical Medicine and International Health*, 4(2): 120–30.

Turner, B. (1987). *Medical Power and Social Knowledge*. London: Sage.

—— (1992). *Regulating Bodies: Essays in Medical Sociology*. London: Routledge.

Ulijaszek, S. (1997). 'Anthropometric Measures', in B. Margetts and M. Nelson (eds.), *Design Concepts in Nutritional Epidemiology*. Oxford: Oxford University Press.

—— and S. S. Strickland (1993). *Nutritional Anthropology: Prospects and Perspectives*. London: Eldred Smith-Gordon.

UN Millennium Project (2005). *Halving Hunger: It Can be Done*. New York: Task Force on Hunger, UN.

US Treasury (1998). Treasury Assistant Secretary (International Affairs) Timothy F. Geithner Testimony Before the House Banking Subcommittee on General Oversight and Investigations. Washington, DC: US Treasury.

van Hollen, C. (2003). *Birth on the Threshold: Childbirth and Modernity in South India*. Berkeley: University of California Press.

Vella, V., et al. (1992). 'Biological Determinants of Child Mortality in South West Uganda', *Journal of Biosocial Science* 24: 103–12.

Venkatasubramanian, K. (2004). 'The Mid-Day Meal Scheme', *The Hindu Business Line*, June 14.

Venkitaramanan, S. (1973). 'Tamil Nadu', in A. Berg and R. Muscat (eds.), *The Nutrition Factor: Its Role in National Development*. Washington, DC: Brookings Institute.

Vijayaraghavan, K. (1997). India. The Tamil Nadu Nutrition Project. A Case Study of the Communication Component. *Nutrition Education for the Public: Discussion Papers of the FAO Expert Consultation*. Rome: FAO.

von Braun, J. (1995). 'Agricultural Commercialization: Impacts on Income and Nutrition and Implications for Policy', *Food Policy*, 20(3): 187–202.

Waldman, A. (2002). 'India's Poor Starve as Wheat Rots', *New York Times*, December 2.

Waterlow, J., et al. (1977). 'The Presentation and Use of Height and Weight Data for Comparing Nutritional Status of Groups of Children under the age of 10 years', *Bulletin of the World Health Organization* 55(4): 489–98.

White, H. (2005). 'Comment on Contributions Regarding the Impact of the Bangladesh Integrated Nutrition Project', *Health Policy and Planning*, 20(6): 408–11.

Whitehead, A. (1994). 'Symbolism, Gender Power and the Family', in B. Harriss-White and R. Hoffenberg (eds.), *Food: Multidisciplinary Perspectives*. London: Blackwell Publishers, pp. 116–29.

Wilson, D. (1973). 'Economic Analysis of Malnutrition', in A. Berg, N. Scrimshaw and D. Call (eds.), *Nutrition, National Development and Planning*. Cambridge: MIT Press, pp. 129–44.

Wilson, S. (2001). 'Body Stature as a Measure of Health and Mortality', in N. Smelser and P. Baltes (eds.), *International Encyclopedia of the Social & Behavioural Sciences*. New York: Elsevier/Pergamon.

Wood, J. (1984). *State Politics in Contemporary India: Crisis of Continuity?* Boulder: Westview Press.

Wood, G. (1985). 'Politics of Development Policy Labelling', in G. Wood (ed.), *Labelling in Development Policy*. London: Sage.

Woods, N. (2000). 'The Challenge of Good Governance for the IMF and the World Bank Themselves', *World Development*, 28(5): 823–41.

—— (2002). The International Monetary Fund and World Bank. *Routledge Encyclopedia of Politics*. London: Routledge.

—— (2003). 'The United States and the International Financial Institutions: Power and Influence Within the World Bank and the IMF', in R. Foot, N. MacFarlane, and M. Mastanduno (eds.), *US Hegemony and International Organizations*. Oxford: Oxford University Press.

—— (2006). *The Globalizers: The IMF, the World Bank, and Their Borrowers*. Ithaca: Cornell University Press.

World Bank (1993). *World Development Report 1993: Investing in Health*. New York: Oxford University Press.

—— (1994). *Enriching Lives: Overcoming Vitamin and Mineral Malnutrition in Developing Countries*. Washington, DC: World Bank.

—— (2000). *Human Resources*. Washington, DC: World Bank.

—— (2004). 'HNP New Commitments by FY and Region'. http://devdata. worldbank.org/hnpstats/HNPLending/HNPdollar.pdf.

—— (2005*a*). *Nutrition and Economic Sector Work* (draft). Washington, DC: World Bank.

—— (2005*b*). *South Asia Regional Bank Contacts*. Washington, DC: World Bank.

—— (2005*c*). *To Nourish a Nation: Investing in Nutrition with World Bank Assistance*. Washington, DC: World Bank.

—— (2006). *Mainstreaming Nutrition into Development*. Washington, DC: World Bank.

—— (2008). Nutrition: The Forgotten MDG. Available at: http://web.worldbank. org/WBSITE/EXTERNAL/NEWS/0,contentMDK:21627646~pagePK:34370~piPK: 34424~theSitePK:4607,00.html.

World Bank Human Development Network (1997). *Health, Nutrition and Population*. Washington, DC: World Bank.

Bibliography

Wyatt, A. (2004). 'The Turn Away From Cultural Mobilization in Contemporary Tamil Nadu', in J. Zavos, A. Wyatt and V. Hewitt (eds.), *The Politics of Cultural Mobilization in India*. Delhi: Oxford University Press.

Young, M. E. (1996). *Early Child Development: Investing in the Future*. Washington, DC: World Bank.

Zaidi, A. (2005). 'Food, for Education', *The Hindu Spotlight* 22.

Zhang, J., et al. (2000). 'Under-and Overreporting of Energy Intake using Urinary Cations as Biomarkers: Relation to Body Mass Index', *American Journal of Epidemiology* 152(5): 453–62.

Index

Bibliography

Abbasi, K. (1999a). 'The World Bank and World Health: Focus on South Asia—II: India and Pakistan', *British Medical Journal*, 318:1132–5.

——(1999b). 'The World Bank and World Health: Under Fire', *British Medical Journal*, 318:1003–6.

——(1999c). 'The World Bank and World Health: Changing Sides', *British Medical Journal*, 318: 865–9.

Almroth, S., Bidinger, et al. (1973). 'The Duration of Breastfeeding: How is it Affected by Biological, Sociodemographic, Health Sector, and Food Industry Factors', *Demography*, 36(1): 63–80.

Arokiasamy, P. (1981). 'Gastro-enteritis Mortality in South Asia', *American Demographic*, 9(3): 494–513.

Arnold, D. (1988). *Famine: Social Crisis and Historical Change*. Oxford: Blackwell Publishers.

Ascher, W. (1983). 'New Development Approaches and the Adaptability of International Agencies: The Case of the World Bank', *International Organization*, 37(3): 415–39.

Assunta, M. (2001). 'Impact of Alcohol Consumption on Asia', *The Globe, Special Issue*, 4, 4–8.

——(...). *Banking on the Poor: The World Bank and World Poverty*. Cambridge, MA: MIT Press.

Balachander, J. (1989). 'Tamil Nadu Integrated Nutrition Project, India. Managing Successful Nutrition Programmes—Nutrition Policy Discussion Paper No. 8', J. Jennings, S. Gillespie, J. Mason, M. Sheang, and T. Sciala, Geneva: United Nations Administrative Committee on Coordination, Subcommittee on Nutrition.

Banik, N. D., Nayar et al. (1972). 'The Effect of Nutrition on Growth of Pre-School Children in Different Communities in Delhi', *Indian Journal of Pediatrics*, 9(8): 460–6.

Barnett, M. and M. Finnemore (1999). 'The Politics, Power, and Pathologies of International Organizations', *International Organization*, 53(4): 699–732.

Barn Junet, I. (2005). 'Irreversible Violation of the Right to Live', *Panikar*, 23(4).